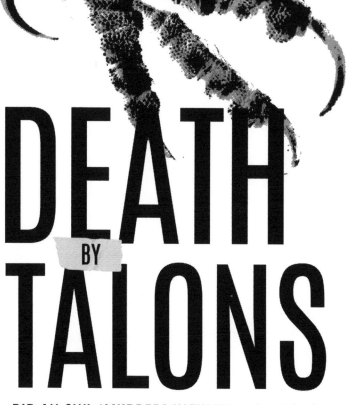

DEATH
BY
TALONS

DID AN OWL 'MURDER' KATHLEEN PETERSON?

TIDDY SMITH

WILDBLUE
PRESS

WildBluePress.com

DEATH BY TALONS published by:

WILDBLUE PRESS
P.O. Box 102440
Denver, Colorado 80250

Publisher Disclaimer: Any opinions, statements of fact or fiction, descriptions, dialogue, and citations found in this book were provided by the author, and are solely those of the author. The publisher makes no claim as to their veracity or accuracy, and assumes no liability for the content.

ISBN 978-1-957288-63-5 Trade Paperback
ISBN 978-1-957288-62-8 Mass Market Paperback
ISBN 978-1-957288-60-4 eBook
ISBN 978-1-957288-61-1 Hardback

Cover design © 2022 WildBlue Press. All rights reserved.

Cover Design by Tatiana Vila
www.viladesign.net

Interior Formatting by Elijah Toten
www.totencreative.com

DEATH BY TALONS

For Ingy, the long-suffering and all-forgiving

The owl of Minerva takes its flight only
when the shades of night are gathering
— Georg Wilhelm Friedrich Hegel

TABLE OF CONTENTS

*To view the color versions of the black and white images in this book, please visit **wbp.bz/DBTgallery***

ACKNOWLEDGMENTS

The information contained in this book has been gleaned from many minds. Most importantly, I wish to thank Larry and Brenda Pollard for several informative and lengthy discussions, without which this book would be a pale skeleton of its current state. The fact that Larry was willing to contribute to the book despite our disagreements on some of the details is a testament to his character. Brenda, Larry's bulldog, facilitated every exchange for her technophobic husband and suggested many important changes. Secondly, my wife Ingrid, perhaps understands the suffering that Brenda has had to endure over the last twenty years better than anyone else. Ingy has had to put up with years of neglect while the research for this book absorbed me entirely.

The WildBlue team (and it truly *is* a team) have been superb in every way. Jenn Waterman gave excellent editorial feedback and advice about rhetoric. Stephanie Lawson, the production manager, never left me hanging and was always helpful. And I am indebted to Steve Jackson and Mike Cordova for seeing the merit in this project.

Karen McLean aided in the development of several drafts, correcting my atrocious grammar, and suggesting stylistic amendments. Ramon Smith read through the manuscript faster than Phoebe Smith, but both encouraged me to keep on the fight. Diane Fanning assisted with schooling a budding author. Leya Booth at Genius Books also graciously provided (sometimes cutting) editorial feedback entirely free of charge! Dr. Janette Quennell was an essential source on all matters medical.

Kate Davis answered many questions, and Dr. Carla Dove also spent time, without reimbursement, attending to my emails. Aiden Fraser volunteered his time to procure certain documents in California. Brent Wolgamott, Kerry Sutton, and Pat Redig all provided useful information about their roles in this strange case. Carly Blake and Gregory Cooper, owl attack victims, were gracious enough to describe their experiences to me, while also sending several photographs. Veterinarians at the Bali Bird Park provided owl feathers and some expert opinions about common injuries from birds of prey.

The Records Department at Merced County Sheriff's Office, and Cassie Davis in particular, deserves thanks for sourcing documents relating to the fatal owl attack of Robert Schmidt in 1985.

The Durham Police Public Affairs Unit attempted to be helpful in providing contact details for several officers involved in this case, but soon distanced themselves from my project for reasons I can probably guess. Angie Shuff (née Powell) was a brave exception to the stonewalling I encountered from other agents who were on the scene that night. From one short interview, I gained great insight into some of the worries and concerns that occupied everyone searching 1810 Cedar Street between December 9 and 10.

Those who refused to be interviewed are so numerous that it would be a waste of ink to list their names. Many others were contacted who simply ignored my requests.

The staff at *Sama Dengan Kopi*, Kalibata City, provided all the essential caffeine. My son, Ramon, provided all the memes as well as every other intangible good.

INTRODUCTION

Let me be brief: an owl killed Kathleen Peterson. If that suffices, skip to the first chapter. If not, read on.

I came to the conclusion that an owl was probably responsible for Kathleen's death shortly after the world was first struck by Covid-19. In those early days, when lockdowns went on interminably and time was cheap, I had a moment to reappraise some of the evidence in the case against Michael Peterson. It began as a sort of macabre hobby. I had no idea where it would lead or how deep the rabbit hole would sink. I was lucky that material which had previously been unavailable was now open to public scrutiny. Most importantly, video of the entire trial had been released online by Court TV. It was the key to changing my own view. All quotations found in this book from the trial have been transcribed from the Court TV recordings.

I guess—once upon a time—I must have been pretty agnostic. Having first watched Jean-Xavier de Lestrade's *The Staircase* docuseries shortly after its initial release in 2004, it had been more than a decade since I had turned my attention to this true crime mystery. Back then, I was engrossed by the twists and turns in the story. All those years ago, my first impression of the case had been that Michael Peterson probably killed his wife. Hell, it was the only sensible conclusion. *What else could have happened?* A fall seemed inadequate to explain how Kathleen died. And if it wasn't a fall, then Michael did it.

But still, I was torn for purely emotional reasons. The family unit seemed strong and Michael seemed utterly sincere, even if a bit eccentric. However, putting my emotions to the side, it seemed that the balance of probabilities did not favor Michael at all. He was found guilty of Kathleen's murder, and probably rightly so, I thought.

In the years that followed, two events would drastically change my thinking about this case.

First of all, in 2003, Larry Pollard, a neighbor of the Petersons, began to publicize his so-called "owl theory." He conjectured that an owl had attacked Kathleen outside her house and that she later fainted in the stairwell. Michael was innocent because a bird was guilty! It was a crazy idea. Let me rephrase that: *batshit crazy*.

But crazy as it was, it became clear to me that the theory had some legs. I wondered how far those legs could truly run. I was impressed by the way in which Kathleen's injuries resembled the sorts of injuries one would expect from an owl attack. Ornithologists were largely unanimous on this point. I was also struck by the feather fragments found in Kathleen's hands. How *had* they gotten there? Had they really been left behind by a murderous bird of prey? As much as my interest was piqued by it, the theory was quite clearly improbable (who ever heard of a killer owl?) and still too many questions remained. I liked the theory, but I hardly called myself a believer.

Then, in 2019, I discussed the Peterson case with a stranger who revolutionized my perspective. I was defending the plausibility of the owl theory, even if I accepted that it lacked much evidence required to *prove* it. But this fellow was incredulous. He remarked that had an owl killed Kathleen, we should expect to find more than a couple of feather fragments in her hands. There should be feathers *everywhere*!

Everywhere…

This remark troubled me, for it was almost obviously true. If you think of a cat with a bird, the result is that feathers are strewn all over the place. Yet here was an alleged tussle between an *adult human being* and an owl, and all that remained were a couple of tiny feather fragments in her hands; not a single whole feather anywhere! Simply impossible. So where were all the feathers? In my mind, the equation was relatively simple: no feathers = no owl.

I decided to start again, to look at the total body of evidence afresh. I opened my eyes to the raw data. I tried, as hard as I could, to put any preconceived ideas to the side. I listened carefully to the testimony of investigators and experts. I analyzed the crime scene photographs and video at length. What I found, over a series of months, was shocking and perplexing. I spent many sleepless nights wondering if I was going mad. How had no one else spotted it? It can't really be like *this*!

So what had troubled me so badly?

I discovered a vast—overwhelming—body of evidence, much of which I can only conclude was suppressed by the prosecution, the defense, and the media alike. Hardly any of this evidence is well known, even among those internet sleuths who have spent many long hours investigating this strange case. Moreover, the evidence points unequivocally to an attack by a bird of prey. The evidence not only supports the case that a bird killed Kathleen but also supports the view that many actors conspired to keep this fact from the public eye. In re-examining the case, I had expected, at best, to find either support for or a refutation of Larry's owl theory. Instead, I unearthed a strange and troubling conspiracy. What I discovered indicated that officials had swept the obvious under the rug. It was the last thing I expected to find. And it was the very last thing I ever thought I would find myself believing.

Let me be clear. In writing this book, I have not been motivated by a desire to exonerate Michael Peterson. In fact, I have no real interest in the question of his guilt or innocence. This may surprise some readers, who assume that proponents of the bird-of-prey hypothesis are clutching at straws simply to save Michael's reputation. But I really couldn't care less. My motivation has always been to understand what happened that night. I wanted to understand the forensic evidence. The circumstances surrounding Kathleen's death remain mysterious in so many ways. And it is precisely the *circumstances* of her death that need to be explained.

It is easy to dream up sinister motives or to point to strange behavior. It is easy to point to lies or salacious personal histories. It is easy to draw inferences from a fog of speculation. But it is incredibly difficult to develop a theory that can account for all the evidence found at the scene. And in the case of Kathleen Peterson's death, the evidence is beyond bizarre. No current theory accounts for the evidence in a satisfying way. For that reason, you will find that this book is primarily a discussion of the evidence. It is not a deep discussion of the various personal dramas that enveloped the Peterson family in the midst of their misery. There are several other books already published which deal with those heart-wrenching stories far better, such as Diane Fanning's authoritative *Written in Blood,* and Aphrodite Jones' less reliable book, *A Perfect Husband.* Michael Peterson's own book, *After the Staircase,* is also available.

I cannot pretend to really know, warts and all, what occurred on that terrible night in December 2001. But there are several facts about which my confidence is high enough to call "certainty." They are as follows:

1. Kathleen Peterson was attacked by a *bird of prey*.
2. The attack continued *inside the house*.
3. Crucial evidence of this fact was *suppressed by investigators*.

Anything else that I might say in this book should be taken to be only informed conjecture.

In arriving at the above three conclusions, I have been left, for want of a more accurate term, angry. Those who perpetrated the cover-up remain free and without sanction. There has been no inquiry into their actions. Michael Peterson went to prison for murder. A retrial was called nearly a decade later. And after more than eight years inside, Michael finally accepted an Alford plea, a special legal agreement which would guarantee his release. In exchange for his freedom, he would admit that the evidence would probably be sufficient to convince a reasonable jury of his guilt. Eight years in prison will do that to a man. But the effect of the Alford plea effectively ends further legal processes which could indict those responsible for hiding/destroying the crucial evidence.

How was the cover-up executed? Largely by a combination of commission and omission. Crucial evidence which should have been examined was never collected. And much of the evidence that was examined, which pointed at a bird of prey, was deliberately ignored, destroyed, or obscured from view. Incredibly, a chipped talon, bird droppings, and hundreds of feathers were obscured from the view of the jury. Other evidence was deliberately withheld, altered, mislabeled, or destroyed. Had the defense had proper access to this evidence—and had the evidence been tested—it is very unlikely that Michael would have been imprisoned for killing his wife.

But he was.

And now, all that I can hope for is that the reader comes to see the evidence as it really stands. The evidence far from proves Michael's guilt. It proves something far more sinister. Unfortunately, even if this book demonstrates that the behavior of authorities was reprehensible, it can have no other effect. The trial is over. The verdicts are in. There is no hope for a retrial. We are now more than twenty years in the wake of Kathleen's death. The damage is done.

But the court of public opinion remains open. And here, some solace might be found. Even if the legal system failed severely in this case, the truth may yet come out. And the truth is simple to state: On December 9, 2001, a woman was killed by a bird. In the aftermath, a thousand lies and secrets were born in the city of Durham, North Carolina.

CHAPTER ONE: FIRST NIGHT

FIRST APPEARANCES

Outside the house, the bats flapped about in the black night. They came from the attic to hunt insects in the moonlight, but apart from that, things were very quiet and still. It was very late, nearly 3 a.m. It wasn't warm, nor terribly cold. It was mild for a winter's night in Durham, North Carolina. For weeks, a drought had been scorching the earth and a fire ban was in place. The date was December 9, 2001—the first day of Hanukkah. The terror attacks that had claimed three thousand lives, along with the innocence of the United States, were still at the forefront of the country's consciousness. The world was still shaking. Anxiety permeated every house. An invasion of Afghanistan was underway—dubbed Operation Enduring Freedom—and thousands of soldiers were being deployed. But for everyone else, the holiday season had arrived and the dawning promise of a new year was approaching. Better times lay ahead. Or so most families hoped.

Around the house, decorations had started appearing. A wreath with a red bow had been set on the front door. A pine tree had been brought inside and adorned with miniature bells and tinsel. On the bottom step of the ornate spiral staircase, oversized wooden nutcracker soldiers stood guard. In German tradition, nutcracker dolls are supposed to protect a home by frightening away evil spirits. On this night, the soldiers would fail their duty.

The house itself, 1810 Cedar Street, was more of a mansion. Indeed, it was the largest domestic property in all of Durham: ten thousand square feet, two stories, fourteen rooms, five bedrooms, as many bathrooms, four chimneys, two staircases (one a spiraled marvel, the other dark and narrow), an outdoor pool, extensive wooded grounds, and just a five-minute drive to Duke University. Duke, as it happens, was the alma mater of both occupants of this house, who were huddled together at the bottom of the stairs.

The Petersons were not having an ordinary night. Kathleen was dying. She was unconscious and soaked in blood. Michael was frantically dialing 911.

2:40 a.m.

911: Durham 911. Where is your emergency?
MICHAEL PETERSON: 1810 Cedar Street. Please!
911: What's wrong?
PETERSON: My wife had an accident. She's still breathing!
911: What kind of accident?
PETERSON: She fell down the stairs. She's still breathing! Please come!
911: Is she conscious?
PETERSON: What?
911: Is she conscious?
PETERSON: No, she's not conscious. Please!
911: How many stairs did she fall down?
PETERSON: What?
911: How many stairs did...
PETERSON: ...the back stairs!
911: How many stairs?
PETERSON: Oh... Uh!
911: Calm down, sir. Calm down.
PETERSON: Oh, 15, 20, I don't know. Please! Get somebody here, right away, please!

911: Okay, somebody's dispatching the ambulance while I'm asking you questions.

PETERSON: It's, ah… It's Forest Hills! Okay? Please! Please!

911: Okay, sir, somebody else is dispatching the ambulance. Is she awake now?

PETERSON: Ah… Uh… Uh…

911: Hello? Hello?

PETERSON: Uh… Uh…

911 operator Mary Allen jotted down a single word: "hysterical."

Muttering to himself and weeping, Michael put down the phone and held Kathleen's dying body in the dark. Her scalp was split open and she had lost a significant amount of blood. She was unconscious. The blood from her head flooded her hair, soaked her sweatshirt, and turned the hips of her white track pants a dark crimson. The blood was not restricted to Kathleen's body. Blood spray, smears, and spatter covered the walls of the stairwell. Bloodstains mottled the hardwood floor around her body. Blood was on Michael's white shorts. Blood drenched the towels, which had been placed under her head. Blood was clotted on the clumps of hair pulled out by the roots, found clasped in Kathleen's hands.

Earlier that evening, Kathleen had been drinking and she had also popped a Valium. A subsequent toxicology exam showed her blood alcohol to be somewhere close (.07 or 70mg/dl) to the 80mg/dl limit for legally driving in North Carolina. She had trace amounts of nicotine in her system. On top of that, there were traces of sedating muscle relaxants and antihistamines. It is easy to imagine that she was probably already drowsy when she—as Michael told the dispatcher—attempted to ascend the staircase before falling and cutting her head on the sharp, solid edges of the old oak stairs.

But despite the extent of her injuries, Kathleen was still alive. When Michael first called the operator, he stated that Kathleen was unconscious, but breathing; still breathing, but only just. Now, just six minutes later, he called the emergency line again. Things had deteriorated.

2:46 a.m.

911: Durham 911. Where is your emergency?
PETERSON: Where are they?! This is 1810 Cedar... She's *not* breathing! Please! Please! Would you hurry up!
911: Sir?
PETERSON: Can you hear me?
911: Sir? Sir, calm down. They're on their way. Can you tell me for sure she's not breathing? Sir? Hello? Hello?

Michael did not respond.
"Breathe," whispered Michael. "Breathe."
The phone cut out.
Two emergency paramedics, James Rose and Ron Paige, drove slowly along Cedar Street, struggling to find the Petersons' house. A Christmas wreath was hung over the front gate, partially obscuring the house number. The paramedics were lost.

After a few minutes of searching, they finally spotted the address. They parked, jumped from the ambulance, and ran quickly up the front path. As they rushed in, a dark shadow raced past them and was first to enter through the front door. The front door, it should be noted, was already wide open when they arrived. The shadow that raced ahead of the paramedics was Todd Peterson, Michael's son. His date for the night, an attractive young woman by the name of Christina Tomasetti, remained outside. She had just dropped off Todd and was waiting beside her maroon sports car.

Upon entering the open door, the paramedics looked to their left and immediately saw the body. Kathleen was sprawled across the hallway with her head resting on the bottom step of the dark and narrow staircase. She was not moving. They saw Michael kneeling there in the hall, crying over his wife. The paramedics hurried over and asked what had happened, but Michael was whimpering and unresponsive. Todd approached his shaking father and pulled him to one side. Todd saw his stepmother's body, motionless and silent.

He whispered to his father, "Dad, step away. Mom's dead. The paramedics are here."

Michael gave way to the emergency medical team.

"When did the fall happen?" one paramedic asked.

"I don't know," replied Michael. "I was just going outside to turn off the lights. I came back in and found her."

"Date of birth?"

"..."

"Any previous medical history?"

"..."

Michael stared back vacantly, in some kind of daze. He gave no information about when the accident happened. He could barely speak. He seemed unable to answer basic questions. Without any information, it seemed that whatever happened to Kathleen could have taken place hours ago. The paramedics checked Kathleen's vital signs. Todd was right. She was dead. Indeed, to the eyes of the paramedics, she had been dead for a long time. "Very dead" as paramedic Ron Paige put it. She was not breathing. There was no electrical activity in her heart. No measurable pulse. Her lips were blue. She was gone.

"Sorry. There's nothing we can do," James Rose told Todd Peterson.

Michael continued to cry as the paramedics began to remove the electrical monitors they had attached to Kathleen. They checked their equipment for blood. And then, abruptly, they put out a call to Durham police to investigate the scene. They couldn't shake some strange feeling. Something just seemed off.

Rose and Paige were the first outsiders to express doubts about Michael's claim that a fall killed Kathleen. In fifteen years, said Rose, he had never seen such a large volume of blood resulting from a fall. Crimson stains covered every surface. Not only that, but some of the blood appeared to be dry. It was dark and mottled. Stranger still, some of the bloody areas appeared to have been wiped. There was, Rose would later claim at Michael's trial, "dried blood on the steps, and also on the wall. It also looked like it had been wiped away... It had been smeared, instead of just blood droplets soaking down the wall."

Paige agreed with Rose that the blood was dry: "I've seen a lot of dry blood in my life, and it appeared to be dry." Rose and Paige arrived at that conclusion, despite the lighting being switched off in the hallway, where Kathleen's body was sprawled. Her body, and the blood that spilled from it, was dimly lit only by the ambient light of the adjoining kitchen. The stairwell itself was much darker. They could not have had a clear view.

With the benefit of hindsight, we can say that the sheer amount of blood was not necessarily the best reason to doubt that a fall had occurred. After all, perhaps Kathleen's fall had simply been particularly violent. Who knew how many steps her head had smacked against? And whether the blood was dry or wet says little about whether or not she fell. Perhaps Kathleen had been unconscious for hours after she first knocked her head. Perhaps she had been lying there unconscious and bleeding for quite some time, allowing much of the blood to coagulate before she was discovered by Michael.

But the amount of blood (and whether or not it was dry) was not the only evidence that seeded doubts in the minds of the paramedics. The real problem was that Michael had claimed that Kathleen fell down the stairs. Yet when paramedics entered the house through that open front door, they had seen the frame around it smeared in blood. Not just a smudged fingerprint or two—great big smears coated the frame and the lock. And this seemed impossible to explain. Sure, in principle, a fall down the stairs can wound a person terribly—extreme blood loss and death are not unheard of. But in principle, a fall down the stairs cannot wound a person so badly that they smear blood all over a door in a separate room. So why was there blood all over the front door?

With this evidence in mind, the paramedics were right to be suspicious: so much blood, some of it apparently dry, some apparently smeared or wiped away, and some discovered at a distance from the dead woman's body. Police investigators, who arrived at 3 a.m., came to share the suspicion of the frontline paramedics almost immediately. In the weeks and months that would follow, this suspicion would even come to be shared by members of Michael's immediate family.

By the end, this suspicion, this nagging doubt, ever growing and snowballing, would be enough for twelve members of a jury to unanimously find Michael guilty of murder nearly two years after Kathleen died. Twenty years after her death, it is more or less widely accepted that Kathleen was the victim of Michael's psychopathic, murderous rage. Despite appearances, and despite the family's claims to the opposite, most think this was no happy marriage.

So how did it happen? Did a loving husband really transform into a monstrous killer overnight? Or did Kathleen simply fall? It must be one or the other, so which is it? As this book will demonstrate, the answer is neither. The question itself is a sort of fallacy, a false dilemma. It was this false dilemma that ultimately sealed Michael's fate. At trial, the prosecution alleged "murder" and the defense pleaded "fall," and that was that. But what if that wasn't, in fact, that? What if it was neither a murder nor a fall? What if something else, something extraordinary, happened to Kathleen?

And something else did. The real story behind Kathleen's death, and Michael's subsequent imprisonment, is far stranger than fiction, more tragic than an accidental death, and far more sinister than a simple crime of passion. It is one of the most bizarre conspiracies in the history of American criminal justice. And it began the moment police arrived on the scene.

AFTER THE PARAMEDICS

It was only thirty seconds after the paramedics placed their first vital monitors on Kathleen that officers from the Durham County Fire Department walked through the door. The dispatcher had sent the fire and paramedic teams at the same time. In fact, their vehicles clumsily intersected as they both struggled to find parking outside the address. Upon entering the premises, the firemen held back while the paramedics worked on Kathleen. The police were dispatched shortly afterwards. The first police officers on the scene, Juanetta McDowell and Victor Figueroa, arrived just a few minutes after the fire and paramedic crews. By now, Michael was sitting on the couch in the open-plan kitchen lounge, bawling with his face in his hands.

The fire and police officers stood in the foyer, waiting for the paramedic team to wrap up. As they were watching the medical team work, Fire Captain Gary Paschall turned to the newly arrived police officers and whispered discreetly, "Look, until we determine whether this is a crime scene, we need to shut all this down."

Everything looked like a homicide. It was extremely doubtful that a fall had produced this much carnage. And if it was a homicide, the scene needed to be contained. The police needed to take charge. There were still too many questions.

Paschall's doubts were just like those of the paramedics. There was too *much* blood, too much *dry* blood, in too many *unusual* places. In fact, Paschall's colleague, Jayson Crank, found even more of Kathleen's blood where it shouldn't have been. He found heavy blood smears all over the back of the front door. And as he traced a line, he discovered a trail of blood droplets leading down the hallway between the staircase and the front door. If Kathleen fell down the stairs, she had taken quite a detour.

Blood wiped on the back of the front door.
Taken from the crime scene video.

Corporal Juanetta McDowell got on the radio. She requested immediate contact with the Criminal Investigations Division. Whatever happened to Kathleen, it had obviously been violent and, more specifically, *brutally* violent. McDowell requested the landline from Todd, who retrieved the cordless phone from one of the bottom steps, where it lay right beside Kathleen's head. Corporal McDowell phoned Sergeant Fran Borden at Criminal Investigations. Borden confirmed that an investigation would be set in motion. And so, only a few minutes after discovering the body, Michael was already locked in the sights of the Durham police. Even if not yet *officially* a suspect, *unofficially* his guilt had been very much presumed.

Twenty minutes passed. Michael moved outside to the patio, shivering and unresponsive. In order to check his father for shock, Todd had contacted a friend, a doctor by the name of Heather Whitson. Having now arrived at the home with her fiancé, Whitson was assessing Michael on the patio. It is unknown what her verdict was.

While Michael was being assessed for shock, Corporal McDowell came outside to check on him. As she walked out onto the patio, her eyes landed on something unusual. Behind Michael, a disturbed and upturned kettle had seemingly been tossed to the ground and sat beside a large spill of some kind of liquid. Beside the wet kettle, a small, soft, white toy was wedged beneath the French doors. To this day, it has been given no explanation.

Todd went back inside to bring back a can of soda for his confused and shaking father. As Todd was returning with the drink, the lead forensic technician, Dan George, strode into the house. George looked just how you would expect a cop to look: a round man with a short moustache. Pudgy and solidly built, he had everything except the donut in his hand. He had worked for IBM and General Motors before joining the force, initially as a 911 operator. Now he was in forensics, and his future in that career was looking bright. He was shortly followed by two younger police supervisors, Corporal Scott Kershaw and Sergeant Terry Wilkins. The three men were now the senior officers at the house. Together, George, Kershaw, and Wilkins had exactly the same thought as Fire Officer Paschall: *We need to shut all this down now*. The scene had become a circus and the risk of contamination was high.

The gravity of the situation was clear enough from the moment they saw Kathleen's body. They radioed for extra units. There was nearly a sense of anarchy among the uniforms. The situation was fast getting out of control. And it needed to be controlled. This was not just a possible homicide, after all, but a high-profile one. Michael was a bestselling author, essayist, and well-known candidate for the mayoralty of Durham. Kathleen was equally distinguished: a director of information services at the international telecommunications giant Nortel and an esteemed Durham socialite. The officers knew whose house they were in. The couple was famous in this community. This death would undoubtedly generate substantial media attention and the police were under no misapprehensions.

As they were calling for more units, Michael walked into the kitchen. His hands were covered in Kathleen's blood. He began to wash his hands and wrists. He wrung them together under a running faucet in the sink, in plain view of Kershaw and Wilkins.

"Stop that," said Wilkins. Michael complied.

With three senior investigators now in the home, and a steady stream of officers arriving, the chaos of the scene was beginning to be contained. First of all, access to Kathleen's body was restricted. Crime scene tape was arranged to prohibit access to the hallway, stairwell, and parts of the kitchen. The front door, smeared with blood, was cordoned off. And later, the entire length of the front path was secured as a location of interest. Access to all these areas was now prohibited, except at the discretion of the senior officers.

And as of that moment, the house belonged to the Durham police and their forensics team. It was 3:20 a.m. It had been forty minutes since Michael's first 911 call. Up to this point, only three people had come into close physical contact with Kathleen's corpse: Michael and the two paramedics. Michael had spent the entire time without his glasses on and, as of yet, no person had seen Kathleen's body under good lighting. How the scene of her death truly appeared was yet to be properly known. Several hours would have to pass before a proper visual inspection could be made.

For now, Kathleen lay alone and cold and (like everyone else) quite in the dark.

ACCESS DENIED

After the police secured the family home, Michael and Todd were herded into the library, along with Todd's date, Christina Tomasetti, and his friend Dr. Heather Whitson and her fiancé Ben Maynor. The library was positioned at the far end of the house, quite distant from the critical areas that had been cordoned off by police. Sergeant Wilkins tasked Officer James McVay to keep these five persons contained in the isolated room. They were to be prevented from leaving, and they were not to converse with each other. They were remanded to an impromptu cell. They were forbidden from watching the police.

In the face of what he perceived as police heavy-handedness, Todd began to argue. He disputed whether the police had any right to detain them in the library or to prohibit them from speaking to one another. Why had they been removed from observing the police activity? Was he, or, indeed, was his father, under arrest?

"Why are we being held here?"

"It's too cold for you to be out on the patio," argued McVay.

"If you are going to detain us like this, then are you charging us with something?"

"No."

"Then why are you holding us here? Why can't we leave? We need to speak with a lawyer."

"We need you to stay here for now. We can't have you contaminating the scene or influencing each other."

"Can you get the head officer? This is really ridiculous! My father needs a grief counselor too. Just look at him! We need all kinds of things."

McVay radioed Wilkins for help. Todd was being disruptive and was failing to follow orders. Wilkins suggested separating the men and the women. Do not, Wilkins repeated, allow any talking whatsoever: "One hundred percent no talking."

The women were taken to the living room, where they were placed on opposite couches and ordered to not speak by McVay. Both women reclined and rested. The officer then returned to the men, ordering them to remain silent. Michael paced, anxious and upset. Todd and Ben Maynor were still suspicious of, and rightly aggrieved by, the apparently unconstitutional police detention taking place. They whispered to each other every now and then.

"Hey! I said no talking, no communicating, nothing!"

The two young men continued to whisper intermittently, and so they were separated once again. Maynor was removed and set alone in the living room. And now Todd was positively irate. Everyone was being detained against their will, confined to areas of the house where they could not observe the actions of the police. No statements had yet been collected. Regular police protocol seemed to have been abandoned. Todd called his uncle, attorney Bill Peterson, for help.

Meanwhile, as the witnesses were being herded about and Todd continued to protest, Sergeant Fran Borden from Criminal Investigations was parking outside. He entered the back door of the house and surveyed the scene. Immediately, he saw the blood on the floor of the hallway and pooling around Kathleen's body. He talked with the other officers, trying to ascertain the state of the scene. He walked through the kitchen, looking for clues, when his eyes fell on something totally anomalous.

There, on the kitchen cabinets, lay spots of something red. Was it blood? He followed the small spots and found even more red flecks around the kitchen. On a beige leather couch, a meter or two from the kitchen counter, he found more red marks. It was enough for him, there and then, to all but rule out an accident. People may fall down stairs and bleed to death, but their blood does not end up all over the house.

He extended the police cordon to double its previous area and thereby designated the entire kitchen and open-plan lounge a no-go zone. He closed off a large portion of the downstairs area of the house.

After Borden did this, with a deliberate seriousness in his voice, he said to the supporting officers, "This is officially a crime scene."

The time was 3:50 a.m.

Back in the library, Todd pleaded with his father, "Dad, don't talk to the police without a lawyer. That's what Bill just told me. We need to get support."

Todd's insistence gave the police even more reason for suspicion. What innocent person, after all, needs a lawyer? But the reason was clear. The clock had been ticking and the witnesses had now been held in silent isolation for over an hour and a half, while police were free to move around the house at will. At 5 a.m., Todd and Michael finally reached out to Kerry Sutton, a high-profile attorney located in Durham. During their preliminary phone call, she advised Todd to stay in the room with investigators to observe whatever they might be doing.

"But we're not allowed to leave the study," Todd told her.

"Okay," replied a perplexed Sutton. "Wait for me."

She arrived at the house twenty minutes later. And despite requesting to observe the investigators in action, she was, like all others, forbidden from doing so. She was whisked through by police to the library, where she consulted with Michael.

With Sutton present, police began to take statements. Todd and Michael refused, on the advice of the newly arrived lawyer. Once statements from the others were taken, Todd and Michael left with Sutton to her own private residence, three blocks away. It was at Sutton's home where the larger family unit would come together, finding a shared space in which to grieve.

The Petersons were finally out of the house. And with a new degree of calm in the air, the police could start to appraise the situation.

Here's what they knew so far: A woman was dead. Her body was stretched out across a hallway at the bottom of a staircase. A vast amount of blood was smeared and spattered on the back wall of the stairwell. But there was also blood where none should be: blood in the kitchen, blood on the frame of the front door, and drops of blood forming a trail down the outside front path.

The woman's husband was uncooperative and uncommunicative; the woman's stepson agitated and controlling.

It was 6 a.m., an hour and a half before sunrise. Dan George sighed and looked at his watch. As the lead forensic technician, he had now been waiting for more than three hours to begin cataloguing the scene. Time trickled slowly. Things were a little surreal. George had already been on duty for over thirteen hours, and he would remain on the scene processing evidence for nine more. He rubbed his eyes and blinked, preparing to read a piece of paper that was handed to him. The document he had been waiting for had arrived—a search warrant. He was now free to begin his work. He hauled in his video camera and popped on a pair of gloves and protective boots. George could now record the official crime scene video of the house and its surroundings.

He walked through the house and around the body for the next several hours with a young photographer, Angie Powell, trailing him. Her camera flash was jarring to his eyes. The whole process went on for what felt like forever. There was so much to film. Blood was on the front path. Blood was all over the front door. Blood was all over Kathleen. Strange things were in the kitchen. This looked like anything but a fall down the stairs. But the more he walked and the more he filmed, the more he found something he just couldn't make sense of.

Why was her body covered in *pine needles*?

And why was the front path totally littered with *that stuff*?

He turned the camera off, puzzled.

Outside the mansion, a couple of hours passed. The sun rose and the rain started falling. As the rain washed the house clean, Kathleen's corpse was carried out in a body bag. Peterson's lawyer, Kerry Sutton, returned to 1810 Cedar Street and watched from behind the police tape. She waited all day and all night—in the rain—until the mobile crime scene command unit cleared the scene. It took until 11 p.m. The house had been in the sole custody of the Durham police for twenty hours, during which time a total of thirty-nine officers had come and gone. What had *so many* officers been doing for *such a long period* of time?

Sutton entered, accompanied by a colleague, and made notes, took photos, noted uncollected evidence, and closed off the stairwell.

It was after midnight on December 10 when she eventually left the empty house. Most of Durham was asleep. Everything was still, quiet and dark once again. The inside lights were off, the floodlights were shut down, and the candles were extinguished. The trees rustled in the wind. The calm of night infused every inch of empty space. And the bats flew out from the attic again, chasing moths and fireflies.

CHAPTER TWO: A FALSE DILEMMA

THE END

Nearly two years after Kathleen's death, Michael turned to his children, who were seated behind him. "I love you... It will be all right."

With that, he was led out of the courtroom.

It was October 10, 2003. After more than thirteen weeks of defense and prosecution arguments, the jury deliberated for five days before returning its guilty verdict. Inside the deliberation room, it had been an even split at the beginning. But by the last day, things had turned 10-2 for a guilty verdict. The outlying two jurors were converted in the space of the final hour. It had been the longest trial in the history of the state. And Michael would spend the next 2,987 nights sleeping in a cramped Nashville, North Carolina, prison cell.

Principally, the trial hinged on carnage. A deceased woman lay splayed out at the bottom of the stairs. Blood was all over the house, and her injuries were brutal and strange. Twelve jurors (plus four alternates) spent weeks upon weeks getting an education in blood spatter patterns, cast-off stains, blunt force trauma, and neurochemistry. The scientific analysis of forensic blood spatter and transfer stains alone took up nearly twenty-five days of the trial. And it was all in an effort to answer one question: what killed Kathleen?

The jurors were faced with a choice between two alternatives. Was it an accidental fall down the stairs, as the defense had argued? Or had Michael brutally bludgeoned his wife, as the State had alleged? Lucky for them, the choice was simple and binary. If it wasn't one, it had to be the other. And according to one juror, the case was essentially closed the very minute he visited the Peterson home alongside his fellow jurors and poked his head inside that staircase. The enclosed space in the stairway, he said, was not a death trap. It was tiny, only forty-two inches across, quite contained, and anyone who fell could have easily gotten back to their feet again. No one could just slip to their death.

So that was that. And as Sir Arthur Conan Doyle wrote into the mouth of Sherlock Holmes, "When you have eliminated the impossible, whatever remains, however improbable, must be the truth." A fall was impossible. It couldn't have happened. And if it wasn't a fall, then it was a cold-blooded killing. If it wasn't one, it had to be the other.

It was all too simple. But things are never as simple as they seem. And even Sherlock Holmes makes mistakes. In fact, his famous axiom is misleading when it comes to choosing between competing theories. When you have eliminated the impossible, you really haven't done that much at all. This is easy enough to prove.

Imagine you have three theories: A, B, and C. Now imagine that you have somehow proved that A is impossible. Well, in such a case, you will still have B and C remaining, and they cannot possibly both be true. So, eliminating an impossible theory may leave us with multiple possible theories remaining. And how should we choose between them?

There are more problems with Sherlock's axiom than that. If you have only two theories on the table, A and B, simply showing that A is impossible does not necessarily prove that B is true. This would only be the case if you were sure that you had been considering all the available possibilities, however strange and numerous they may be. And we are rarely in such a position of omniscience.

So what does all this have to do with Kathleen? In the case of Kathleen's death, only the two most obvious explanations were considered at Michael's trial—either she fell down the stairs, split her scalp open, and died in a terrible accident; or she was beaten to death at the hands of her homicidal husband, who later staged the scene to look like some kind of accident.

Now, with Sherlock's axiom in mind, we should ask ourselves, "What if we discovered that both of these explanations were impossible?"

What if she *couldn't* have fallen? And what if she *couldn't* have been beaten to death? The consequence is obvious. We would have to start thinking outside the box. We would need to seek alternative explanations.

So if not A, and if not B, then *what*?

THE FALL THEORY

According to the defense, Kathleen just fell. She tripped on the steps and killed herself. Right? Or did she tumble down from the top of the stairs to the bottom? Many people are unsure about what exactly the scenario is supposed to be. So what precisely is the fall theory? And why did the defense believe they had any chance defending it?

The story of Kathleen's death, according to the fall theory, goes like this. Kathleen and Michael had been out by the pool, drinking a few glasses of wine together after having watched a comedy movie earlier in the evening. The pair had already had dinner, and were probably discussing the birthday of their adopted daughter Margaret, who would turn twenty the next day. After chatting for an hour or so, Kathleen declared that she would make her way to bed. She rose from her deck chair and left Michael alone, smoking his pipe and sipping (or perhaps sculling) his wine.

Kathleen had had a couple of glasses, taken a Valium, and, although she may have been far from sloshed, her motor control would certainly have been impaired.

Once inside the house, she attempted to climb the stairs which led to the bedroom. However, the combination of alcohol, sedatives, flip-flops, and stairs proved deadly. She slipped on one of the first two steps, hitting her head, lacerating her scalp, and causing a concussion. As she came to in a very confused state, she registered where she was and attempted to rise to her feet. But now the stairs were slippery with blood. As she tried to lever her body upright, her footing was lost and again she fell back, hitting her head on the sharp edge of a metal chairlift, which had been installed by a previous owner. Her attempts to lift herself to her feet resulted in blood being smeared and wiped around the walls of the stairwell. She called out to Michael and coughed and sputtered, spraying the blood that had fallen across her face over the walls. Finally, she attempted to get to her feet to reach Michael for help. But again, she slipped backward, hit the back of her head with a solid thump, and inflicted what would be the lethal injury. She was unconscious, slowly bleeding out, still breathing, but losing life rapidly.

Hours later, after nodding off beside the pool, Michael casually returned to the house without a care in the world. But upon entering, he found his wife drenched in blood at the bottom of the staircase. He called emergency services. She was gasping for breath. He got some towels to place under her head. It felt like the ambulance was taking an eternity. He gathered paper napkins to wipe her face of blood. Suddenly, the breathing stopped. He called again, but she was already dead. When help arrived, it is just minutes too late. Michael's clothing, a t-shirt and shorts, were now covered in bloody transfer stains from clutching his wife. When the paramedics got to the body, they were stunned by the large amount of blood. The authorities doubted that a fall could have produced such carnage. Within minutes, he was the prime suspect.

In a nutshell, that is the fall theory: Kathleen drank, Kathleen slipped, Kathleen died. In the midst of her multiple falls, she spread a vast amount of blood in the stairwell. When Michael found the body, his hands and clothes became wet with her blood. Having already fostered a sour relationship with the police, he was unlikely to get fair or impartial treatment. That is the theory. It sounds like a theory that could never explain the overwhelming amount of blood on the scene. And why was Michael behaving so strangely? And could a woman *really* inflict fatal wounds on herself by a series of shallow falls? Let us stop and ask: does the theory have anything to speak in its favor?

THE VIRTUES OF THE FALL THEORY

The fall theory sounds unlikely to the point of impossibility. No one is so unlucky as to slip multiple times at the base of a set of stairs, to inflict upon oneself horrific injuries, to die from such injuries, only to have one's own husband discover the event so many hours later after having remained outside, possibly asleep, wearing next to nothing on a winter's night.

However, the fall theory has several surprising virtues. Most importantly, it is the theory with the highest prior probability. In the USA alone, approximately twelve thousand people die from falls on staircases every year. It is a surprisingly common cause of death. Contrast this with spousal and intimate partner murder (approximately two thousand people per year) and the raw numbers paint a clear picture. Disregarding any particular piece of evidence, the fall scenario is six times more likely than a homicide scenario from the outset.

Yet there is a more impressive fact that the fall theory can account for. The theory also helps to explain one of the strangest anomalies surrounding Kathleen's death: she had no damage to her skull or bruising to her brain. The damage to Kathleen's head was almost entirely external, e.g., bruises on the scalp, abrasions, and lacerations. This fact alone is incredible if Kathleen was beaten about the head with some kind of weapon, which is what the State believed had happened. But this finding is not so unusual if her injuries resulted from a series of shallow slips and falls. Sudden contact with the sharp edges of the hard oak stairs would explain the lack of internal injuries while explaining the external ones.

The fall theory is also consistent with the family's narrative of an extremely close relationship between Michael and Kathleen. By all accounts, their relationship was idyllic and forged by a strong bond of love and care. There is no prior evidence of physical or psychological abuse (whether by Michael towards Kathleen or vice versa). And the fall theory is ultimately consistent with Michael's hysterical behavior and apparent shock response in the hours after finding her body. Simply put, there is no evidence of a pattern of violence between the two. And Michael's reaction to his wife's death appeared sincere. If Michael murdered Kathleen, his homicidal violence came seemingly from out of the blue, surprising even himself.

And even though there was a large amount of blood at the scene, little of the blood spatter evidence indicated a murder had taken place. Despite the sheer quantity of sprays and smears, the position of the blood spatter in the stairwell was surprisingly inconsistent with murder. Few cast-off patterns were found that were consistent with Michael swinging a bloodied weapon over his head. And despite the fact that Michael's clothes were stained with blood, the stains on the fabric were largely transfer stains. The stains were evidence of direct contact between Kathleen's clothes and his own. Only one small blood spatter stain was found on the inside of Michael's shorts. It was far too small, and in too restricted an area, to be consistent with the gargantuan amount of blood spray that Kathleen's head wounds would have produced during a homicidal attack.

The blood found on Michael's clothes speaks in favor of Michael holding Kathleen's dying body. And the pattern of the stains hardly supports the theory that he stood over her for a prolonged period, beating her skull repeatedly with a blunt object. His face and hair and clothes and shoes should have been profusely covered with blood spray. They were not. This is all evidence that she wasn't murdered. And if she wasn't murdered, the story goes, then she fell.

The Trouble with the Fall Theory

But the fall scenario is far from perfect. It has some serious problems. Indeed, some facts are totally anomalous if Kathleen truly just slipped on a few stairs after having one too many glasses of wine. Consider the blood droplets found *outside* the house on the front path. Consider the bloody smears coating the front door and its frame. Consider the trail of blood drops stretching out along the hallway between the front door and the staircase. Sure, a fall could generate a large amount of blood, but how could a fall make blood materialize in different rooms and even outside the house?

At trial, Michael's attorney David Rudolf argued that these bloodstains, discovered far from Kathleen's body, were all the result of accidental contamination. In the hours following Kathleen's death, her blood was spread around and outside the house by Michael's movements, by the footsteps of police, and by total incompetence with respect to containing a crime scene. There was blood all over the house because so many people had been moving all over the house.

But can this explanation work? There are reasons to be doubtful. Let's begin with the blood droplets found outside the house, along the front path, and on the front step. It is virtually impossible these resulted from accidental contamination. Why? Because the stains found in these areas had been left by something dripping blood. They were not smudges, scuffs, or smears. They were not caused by the contact transfer of blood from hands or shoes or medical equipment onto the path. The stains were caused by an object or person actively dripping fresh blood. And if we are to accept that most of the blood around Kathleen was already dry when discovered, it is impossible for an object dripping with wet blood to have been brought down the path after first responders arrived.

The drips outside the house are not the only problem. Some of the blood inside the house defied explanation. In particular, the smeared bloodstains on the back of the front door are very difficult to account for. The sheer amount of smearing across such a wide area is unlikely to have been caused by, say, the bloody hands of first responders opening and closing the front door. And why were there stains along the inside of the doorframe? Did some paramedic with heavily bloodied hands rub a series of smudges into the frame of the door? Why? For what purpose?

The fall theory struggles to explain all sorts of things. Take the needles, those anomalous pine needles scattered around Kathleen's body and stuck to her hands. Sure, there was a Christmas tree in the house that night. But it begs belief that immediately before succumbing to a fall, Kathleen fell onto the tree or that she covered herself in these needles for some reason we will never comprehend. According to Sergeant Fran Borden, there were not just a few of these needles, but "a lot" of them scattered all around the hallway in which the body lay. So how did these needles get there?

We can also think of the clumps of hair that Kathleen had pulled out from her scalp. They were found clutched in her hands. Why would a woman, slipping on a staircase, rip out her own hair from her head?

But the most difficult problem for the fall theory to explain is the blood on the walls of the stairwell. Although the blood on the walls was inconsistent with a beating, it was equally inconsistent with a fall. Over ten thousand individual spots of blood were counted, with many having been flung at high velocity. This could hardly be caused by the movements of an unconscious woman, even one writhing in the throes of death.

The fall theory, however it is formulated, just can't explain what happened to Kathleen. There are too many oddities and too many loose ends. So let us turn to the alternative.

THE MURDER THEORY

In his opening argument for the prosecution, District Attorney Jim Hardin faced the jury. He held up a long and narrow brass blow poke with a hook on one end. It was a fireplace tool that had been given to Kathleen many years before. And it was, he would argue, the weapon that had killed her.

"They said it's an accident, a fall down the stairs, and we say it's not," Hardin said. "We say it's murder."

"This case," he later added, "is all about things not appearing as they seem."

The Peterson family contended that their home life had been idyllic, stable, and loving. But this was a facade, argued Hardin. Tensions were seething beneath the surface. What looked to be a warm and supportive family was actually riddled with problems. Secrets and lies were unraveling. A crisis point had been reached. What sorts of secrets? And what was the crisis?

The secret was that Michael was bisexual. For years, he had been hiding this side of himself from his wife. While Michael insisted that Kathleen knew about his sexuality, there is no evidence she was truly aware of the details.

Even if Kathleen was aware of Michael's sexuality, it is doubtful she was aware of any extramarital encounters with men—encounters that appear to have been ongoing during the marriage. It was this fact, this secret, that was allegedly uncovered on that fateful night. "Like a storm cloud," as Hardin put it, "many pressurized conditions in the Peterson house began to converge, and on December 9th, 2001, they erupted."

How did bisexuality lead to murder? The prosecution's argument went something like this.

The time was 11:08 p.m. Kathleen received a call from a coworker at the telecommunications giant Nortel. The colleague's name was Helen Prislinger. The call came from outside Toronto, where Kathleen would be flying two days later to consult with the Nortel team. The conversation was brief and perfunctory. Prislinger heard nothing in Kathleen's voice to suggest drunkenness, fear, or anxiety.

Prislinger had called because she needed to email some sensitive documents to Kathleen that night. Over the phone, Prislinger heard Kathleen ask Michael for his email address (Kathleen had no access to her own work email from home). She heard Michael reciting his address in the background. Kathleen passed on the email address. And with that, the call ended. Prislinger would be the last person apart from Michael to speak with Kathleen on the night of her death. Sitting at her desk in Toronto, Prislinger finally sent the documents to Michael's inbox at 11:54 p.m.

The district attorney argued that Kathleen had opened Michael's inbox and discovered a lengthy and sordid exchange between Michael and a male sex worker. He was discussing the sexual services he was seeking and getting a quote for a rendezvous. Kathleen, reading the exchange, was aghast.

Confronting him with the illicit emails, the pair locked horns. As tempers rose over the next hour or two, Michael snatched the brass blow poke from the downstairs fireplace and cornered Kathleen in the stairwell. He thrashed at Kathleen with the improvised weapon and she eventually succumbed to repeated blows. Attempting to fend off Michael's attack, Kathleen smeared copious amounts of her own blood across the walls and floor. In his fury, Michael grabbed his wife's throat and squeezed. The attack rendered Kathleen unconscious.

Realizing the gravity of his situation, Michael raced to the laundry and gathered cotton towels and paper towels to clean up the scene. He returned to the stairwell and wiped some blood from its north wall. He then selectively wiped at two more small areas of skirting board. But before he had a chance to clean up everything, Kathleen regained consciousness and leapt to her feet. Michael dropped his cleaning equipment, took up the blow poke once more, and delivered the final fatal blow to Kathleen's head. She was now dead from a major concussive event.

Michael's plan had been upset. His focus now shifted to the murder weapon. It had to be hidden. He took the blow poke, dripping with blood, and raced outside to dispose of it. On his way, he left a trail of blood leading from Kathleen's body, down the hallway, out the door, and along the front path. On his way outside, Michael smeared blood around the back of the front door and inside the doorframe.

After disposing of the blow poke in an unknown location, Michael decided to stage the scene to look like an accident. He emptied a bottle of wine down the sink and neatly arranged two wine glasses beside the bottle. *Excellent. The police will assume she had been drinking,* Michael thought to himself. *They'll guess she simply fell.*

Having checked and rechecked the scene, organizing things how he thought they ought to look, it was nearly 3 a.m. when Michael rang emergency services, feigning distress. He invented a story about a fall. He cried crocodile tears. But the police saw right through it. And he was soon arrested for murder.

THE VIRTUES OF THE MURDER THEORY

The murder theory is complex and elaborate, but is much better at accounting for much of the available evidence. The distribution of blood inside and outside the house is well explained and we are given a clear motive for Michael's attack. Kathleen discovered something abhorrent about Michael—he was having affairs behind her back. The pair fought. Rage took over. He killed her.

The murder theory can account for the blood that was found outside the house. It can explain why we find drops of blood outside. It can also explain why the front door and its frame were bloodied. And as if this were not enough, there was a bloody shoe print on the back of Kathleen's track pants. It was Michael's tennis shoe: conclusive evidence, said the district attorney, that Michael stood over and even upon Kathleen as he beat her to death.

The murder theory is better at accounting for Kathleen's injuries. For example, Kathleen had broken cartilage in her neck—a common injury resulting from strangulation. And Kathleen had scratches and cuts on her face and hands that are hard to account for from a fall on the stairs. But if we assume that a sharp-tipped blow poke was involved during Kathleen's attack, then it could have been responsible.

The murder theory can also explain some of Michael's strange behavior. Why was he so hesitant to answer police questions? Because he was being deceptive. Why had he lawyered up so quickly? Because he already knew he was under suspicion. And moreover, there was a strange contradiction between Michael's initial statements on December 9 and his statements in all subsequent interviews. When Michael first spoke to the paramedics, he stated that he had come down from upstairs to turn off the outside lights and that he had found Kathleen's body upon returning. Yet in all subsequent interviews, Michael maintained that he was not even inside the house. He was outside the house, beside the pool, drinking, smoking, and possibly dozing. He only discovered Kathleen's body upon entering the house around 3 a.m. This is a radical change to Michael's alibi. And if Michael's alibi changed like this, we have good reason to believe he was hiding something sinister.

All of these points suggest the murder theory has more to recommend than the fall theory. It is little wonder the jury agreed on a guilty verdict. So what problems does this theory face?

THE TROUBLE WITH THE MURDER THEORY

Difficulties with the murder theory emerge when we analyze the prosecution's claims in detail. To begin with, there is no evidence at all that Kathleen discovered Michael's conversation with a male escort. In fact, there is some evidence that this didn't happen. The email from Helen Prislinger was never opened that night. This suggests that Kathleen did not open Michael's inbox on the night she died.

There is other forensic evidence that speaks against the prosecution's murder theory.

Take the claim that Michael cleaned up the scene. This claim was motivated mostly by a lack of blood on the north wall of the stairwell. It looked like it had been wiped clean. But there is reason to doubt that blood had been removed from this section of the wall. The area is not actually free from blood. A spray of blood spatter extends over the area that was allegedly wiped.

If the lack of blood on the north wall was the result of a clean-up, Michael must have first bludgeoned Kathleen unconscious, then cleaned for a while, then delivered the fatal blow, which sprayed blood over the supposedly cleaned areas. It was this strange feature of the blood evidence that forced the State to contend that Michael first beat Kathleen unconscious, then cleaned up, then killed her. It is a very unlikely sequence of events. Did Michael really believe that

Kathleen was dead, for instance, even though she was still breathing? And why didn't Michael continue to clean the scene after killing Kathleen?

The blood spatter was a problem, but it wasn't the biggest problem. The strongest evidence against the murder theory is that Kathleen suffered no damage to her skull or bruising to her brain. This is unlikely to the point of impossibility if Michael truly bludgeoned Kathleen's head with a weapon. Michael would have had to strike Kathleen's head with enough force to rip the skin on her scalp to pieces and kill her by a severe concussion, while simultaneously restricting the force of his blows so that only external damage was inflicted.

Michael's injuries were a problem too. That is to say, he had none. No bruises or scratches, no abrasions or torn clothing. Not even a stretched shirt. He had none of the kinds of injuries that would be typically found in the midst of a domestic assault.

And did Michael really stage the scene to make it seem that Kathleen had been drinking? We know that Kathleen had been drinking that night. Her blood alcohol level proved it. Yet we are asked to imagine that Michael planted wine bottles and glasses in the kitchen in an effort to make it seem that Kathleen had been drinking. But she had been drinking. So why?

And if Michael was so concerned with staging the scene, then why did he leave the front door of the house wide open and covered in blood? The fact that the door was like this when first responders arrived immediately raises doubts that Michael meticulously covered his tracks over several hours. We are supposed to imagine that Michael went out the front door, disposed of the murder weapon, then came back in through the door, leaving it wide open and bloodied. Why would he overlook such an obvious piece of incriminating evidence? Who leaves their own front door wide open at 3 a.m. on a winter's night? Who leaves their own front door smeared with bloodstains?

And lastly, there is the blow poke—the weapon used during the attack. We now know this could not have been the weapon that killed Kathleen. It was found during the final week of the trial. Not crooked or dented, not red with blood—just sitting there abandoned and collecting dust in the Petersons' basement. No alternative weapon was ever proposed. And it is difficult to imagine any other weapon that could do the job. It was the blow poke's combination of solidity and hollowness that made it the most likely candidate for the attack. It was hard enough to break the skin yet light enough to leave the skull and the brain undamaged.

The problems with the murder theory are varied. But then, so were the problems with the fall scenario. And if neither theory succeeds, then we are left without any compelling story about what killed Kathleen Peterson.

IF NOT A OR B, THEN WHAT?

Neither the fall theory nor the murder theory works. Both theories have problematic loose ends. Of course, almost all good theories have some loose ends. Seldom does a hypothesis explain everything. But in this case, the central problems are not explained. The very things that make Kathleen's death so unusual are not resolved. And although there are numerous reasons to doubt the two most prominent theories, the most central problems are these:

1. If Kathleen fell, there should not be so much blood around, and outside, the house; and
2. If Michael beat Kathleen with a weapon, her skull and brain should have been badly damaged.

There were blood drops around and outside the house, so Kathleen did not fall. And Kathleen's skull and brain were without injury, so this was no beating. In short, if you think she fell, then you can't explain the blood. And if you think she was murdered, then you can't explain how.

With these problems in mind, we must abandon Sherlock's axiom. Both of the most popular theories fail. We have no account of what happened. But then, what are we left with? We are left with no explanation at all. We must go back to where we began, with a dead woman at the foot of a staircase, her scalp sliced to shreds, with a husband pleading innocence, and with a large amount of blood at the scene—not just on the walls of the stairwell, but all over the house.

Was it a fall?

No.

Was it a murder?

No.

The odds are against either theory. If Kathleen fell, it was a fall like no other. If Kathleen was murdered, the circumstances were incredible. If you believe one of these theories, the probabilities are outlandish. Whatever happened to Kathleen, it was highly unusual. And so, we may need to consider more unusual explanations.

This is the point at which we must dispose of the false dilemma that plagued this case from the beginning. Here is where we must drop Sherlock's axiom. We have eliminated the impossible, and now we are lost. So if Kathleen was not murdered and if Kathleen did not fall, then what on Earth killed Kathleen?

CHAPTER THREE: THE OWL THEORY

LOSING A MOTHER

We remain in Durham, but we rewind the clock several decades. It is now the 17th of September, 1968. It is midnight, or thereabouts. A twin-engine aircraft—a slim Beechcraft Baron—is readying for takeoff. The Baron belonged to the Piedmont Aviation Company. One of the company's employees, Forrest Pollard Jr., sat in the pilot's seat. Beside Forrest sat Nancy Dalton, who worked as a stewardess. She had attended a basketball game with Forrest earlier that evening. Behind the pair was seated Julia Davis Pollard, the mother of Forrest. The Beechcraft Baron could fit six inside, but tonight the airplane was half empty. It was heading west to Winston-Salem, around eighty miles away. After a short wait on the tarmac, the runway was cleared and permission was given to depart.

Outside the airport's perimeter, there sat a lone car. The younger brother of the pilot casually leaned against it, watching the plane on the runway. He had dropped off the passengers earlier, and he was waiting to watch the dinky plane get airborne. The weather was calm and clear and cold. There were quiet stars sparkling overhead. At last, the silence was broken by the whirr of an engine, a mechanical growl which cut through the still of the night. The time was exactly 12:15 a.m.

The little plane moved along the runway and readied itself in position. The growl got larger and pushed the Baron along the tarmac. The small aircraft motored along faster and the cold air was sucked under its wings. The wheels, now turning at incredible speeds, no longer touched the ground. The younger brother watched as the plane ascended, majestic, making its way up towards those quiet stars. And the rumble of the engine softened. And altitude was gained. And that was that.

The young man sighed, went around the car, and opened the door to get in. He took one last glance, his hand resting on the chilly metal of the door handle. The Baron flew up a few hundred meters above the ground. It then veered extremely hard to the left. A clanking sputter replaced the growl. The plane then sank down through the sky, stalling, tracing an uneven and uncontrolled arc towards the earth. The brother of the pilot removed his hand from the door handle and held it over his mouth. The crack of the impact reached his ears well after he saw it happen. The broken craft folded in a field of grass just beyond the runway, its wings splayed like a wounded goose.

"Oh God, no! Please, God, no!"

Larry Pollard had just witnessed his own mother's death.

He sped his car across the tarmac as close to the wreck as possible. When his legs got him the rest of the way to the aircraft, things were dire. The three occupants were still strapped to their seats. Two of them were moaning and bleeding badly. Julia Pollard, Larry's mother, was nonresponsive. In a frenzy, Larry tore away debris and clutched Forrest's arm, wrenching him out of the craft. When he finally extracted him from the wreck, he did not recognize his brother. It was as though an axe had socked him between the eyes. Forrest collapsed on the grass, gasping. Larry turned his attention to the two women. Nancy had deep lacerations on her arms and was bleeding badly. She freed herself with difficulty and knelt beside Forrest on the grass in a state of shock. Julia remained limp and motionless in the back seat. Larry carefully removed her safety belt and carried his mother out of the crippled aircraft. He laid her down on the grass gently. She was not breathing. He tried to resuscitate her.

Nothing.

Larry drove away at full speed, seeking a telephone. The situation was critical. He saw the lights of ticket counters flickering through the airport's windows.

"Call an ambulance, now!" he shouted as he ran inside. An ambulance was called.

At the hospital, hours later, Julia lay on a hospital gurney. Larry watched as a nurse pulled a sheet over his mother's face. She did not have a drop of blood on her body. But her seat on the plane, unlike the two in the front, had no headrest. When the airplane hit the ground, her spinal cord was severed in two, killing her instantly. As for Forrest, he remained in a coma for months afterwards. He would eventually walk away from this accident permanently disfigured and with brain damage. Nancy, the youngest occupant, escaped with minor injuries.

CEDAR STREET

Now without a mother and caring for a disabled brother, Larry Pollard took over affairs at the family home, a large property at 1902 Cedar Street. He had only recently been reunited with his father, a state representative who had been imprisoned on a manslaughter charge in 1960. Larry would soon graduate from UNC Chapel Hill, but this would entail no change of scene. Home, for Larry, was always that piece of land, woody and idyllic, in Forest Hills. He had, after all, been brought there as a newborn.

In fact, in his younger days, little Pollard used to play with the neighborhood children on the adjoining property at 1810 Cedar. Capture the Flag and Cops and Robbers were perennial favorites. The grounds were eight acres of magic. Back then, it was known as Buchanan House, having belonged to relations of the influential Duke family of Durham. The children would hide under the trees, peek into the windows, and explore the grounds as though they were part of a great forbidden jungle. There was a spooky old bomb shelter to crawl in.

This wasn't like city life. Foxes and raccoons ran about in the undergrowth. The odd coyote would even make a visit. Wildfowl roamed at will. And, of course, there were the owls. Barred owls and barn owls would nest together in the old barn that sat along the property line. Through the nights, their hoots were the soundtrack of Cedar Street. Now in his fifties, Larry knew the neighborhood better than anyone else.

Oddly, for a middle-aged man, Larry had a peculiar sense of style about him. He was often seen in town with a brown fedora, which sat atop a mop of wispy gray hair. His speech was stentorian and grand, even in everyday conversation. And as for his character, well, he was a man of many values, perhaps too many: committed to Christ, committed to wife, committed to justice, and committed to (or rather, completely obsessed with) hunting and fishing. He was a strong-willed man—assertive and eccentric, a combination that was hard to define and sometimes harder to deal with. He was, above all else, an outdoorsman. And yet, on paper at least, he was actually an attorney who had worked in some of the most prestigious legal counsel positions in North Carolina. As a youth, he had risen to the rank of Eagle Scout. And one had the sense that this remained, even through adulthood, the core of his self-image.

1902 and 1810 Cedar were side by side. So did Larry know the Petersons? Obviously, he did, but not particularly well. They had been his neighbors for several years before the tragedy in 2001. A greeting would occur when they crossed paths for the morning newspaper. Pleasantries were exchanged across the back fence. Heavy things that needed lifting, or hedges that needed cutting, or a jumpstart on a car. That kind of thing. As far as Larry was concerned, the neighbors were fine. They caused no problems. They may have been woolly liberals with "progressive" ideas, but they kept on top of things and helped out when necessary. No problem.

Like the rest of Durham, Larry was often astounded—even stunned—at the gusto which oozed from Michael's newspaper column, critical as it was of Durham's politicians and police. Of course, Michael's writing was also extremely funny—sarcastic and parodic—but only at the expense of these figures of authority. Larry took this behavior for what it most probably was. As an eccentric himself, he respected Michael's strange ways, even if they manifested as a very "unSouthern" disregard for those fusty old virtues like *courtesy* and *deference*.

In one of the few meetings between the two men, Larry went to his neighbor to ask for help. He knocked on the door of 1810 Cedar and waited for it to open.

"Oh. Hello, Larry," Michael said, surprised.

"Afternoon, Mike. Are you in the mood to lift something?"

"Ha!" Michael laughed. "Heavy, is it?"

"You bet!"

"Even better then."

Michael followed Larry to his garage where a large box, almost like a coffin, was waiting. Larry lifted the lid, beaming, and Michael got a peek inside. A huge, stuffed marlin was waiting to be mounted on the wall.

"Sheesh, I didn't see that one coming," Michael said.

The fish had been Larry's catch in a tournament. It would spend the rest of its days mounted on the wall as a point of pride for Larry and an object of wonder for visiting children. Larry told Michael to be careful, as one man grabbed the tail end and the other the nose.

"Okay, on three... One, two, three."

The men nearly fell over. Having been stuffed, it was far lighter than either anticipated. They laughed, and then attempted the lift again, getting it up on the wall with ease.

On December 9, around the time Kathleen was dying, Larry was home watching football. He and his wife Brenda had returned earlier in the evening after dinner in the center of town. When they passed their neighbor's house, it was strongly lit with floodlights.

"It's lit up like the *Titanic!*" exclaimed Larry. Little candles were in the windows.

"They must be having a party," said Brenda as Larry slowed the car.

"Without moi?" Larry joshed.

But there wasn't a party. There were no figures moving about in the windows. There wasn't a sound. The floodlights had never been turned on before. It was an unusual fact about that night that Larry and Brenda remember vividly to this day.

The news of Kathleen's death was a shock to the Pollards. And when the trial began, it was almost uncanny for Larry. He himself was only twelve when his father was imprisoned for manslaughter. And it was a few years later when his mother died in that terrible accident. He was concerned for the Peterson children, particularly the two boys, as he witnessed them sitting behind their own father. The Peterson children waited for a verdict that would destroy their family. They would have a mother deceased and a father imprisoned, just as Larry himself had.

Two years passed between Kathleen's death and the start of the trial. And in the space of those two years, Larry's concern and interest had only grown. Like everyone else, the evidence perplexed him. Something just seemed wrong. He felt there were strange legal goings-on that made little sense. The trial by media that preceded the court case was obviously prejudicial, he felt. And why was this case being tried *in* Durham? Finding an impartial jury after two years of frantic media coverage would be impossible. His doubts and suspicions were not like those of a layman.

Larry's experience within the Special Prosecution Division of the North Carolina Attorney General's Office told him that the evidence in this case—and what it was supposed to support—simply did not add up. The prosecution, he felt, had no case for murder. And the defense, he felt, had no case for a fall. Both sides of the story failed to account for the evidence.

A THEORY FORMS

Since the beginning of the trial, Larry had followed the news closely. He had spoken with the Peterson children and reached out to help in whatever way he could. He found the whole affair baffling. He wanted a better idea about the circumstances of Kathleen's death. As an experienced prosecutor himself, it was in his nature to want to see the evidence clearly laid out. Larry had listened carefully to the legal arguments, and he knew only slightly more than what had been covered at trial. That little bit extra was simply local knowledge. Larry knew what Cedar Street was like. He knew the Petersons—not as characters in a media spectacle, but as a family of human beings.

He heard directly from members of Michael's defense team that the head wounds on Kathleen were not just extensive, but strange in their shapes and dimensions. His interest was piqued. He asked if he could be shown a photograph. Without needing to ask twice, a young woman belonging to Michael's legal team brought Larry a color photograph of the wounds on Kathleen's head. "Here," she said. "You see what I mean?"

Larry took the photograph and held it up close to his face. What he saw struck him as uncannily familiar. He lifted an eyebrow and pulled his neck back. Two trident-shaped wounds jumped out from the paper. "Why," he exclaimed, "these look just like turkey tracks!"

Larry was an avid hunter and had been since the age of six. His trophy room could boast, to name just a few, two stuffed black bears (one standing and growling, the other arranged to sit in a chair), two alligators (each over twelve feet long), a zebra skin, an impala, a bobcat, geese, ducks, and the heads of several deer. Larry was familiar with the different sorts of impressions left behind by game animals. He had tracked many of them before. The gashes he saw now had been described in the autopsy report as "tri-pronged lacerations" but that was medicalese. What Larry saw was a set of wounds remarkably consistent with bird tracks. He asked for the photo to be Xeroxed, and he stashed the black-and-white copy away in his pocket.

It was Larry's first inkling that a bird may have been involved in Kathleen's death. But turkeys do not kill, of course. He didn't really get what the marks could possibly mean. In fact, it was several weeks after he first saw the autopsy photo that Larry realized—given the late-night attack—the only candidate creature would be an owl.

An owl?

It was a strange idea that began to grow in his mind. Could it have been? Perhaps it was one of the barn owls or barred owls that were common on the heavily wooded land. So many oak trees surrounded the houses on Cedar Street. There was an old magnolia along the property line which was one of their favorite places to sit and watch, in the day and the night alike. He thought back to those days around Christmas in 2001. It was common around winter to hear the hoots at night, when new families of barred owls would start to build their nests. They were all around the Peterson home and had been there for fifty years.

An *owl*?

No… Not an owl. It was a ridiculous thought, and he knew it. *Sure*, he thought, *they may look like wounds an owl*

*could inflict, but who ever heard of an owl killing a woman?
And who ever heard of an owl killing a woman inside her
own house?* The whole scenario made no sense. He knew
the odds were vanishingly improbable. He disregarded his
hunch. It couldn't have been a turkey, of course. And it also
couldn't have been an owl.

A month or so went by.

Larry was in the basement of his home—the trophy
room, full of his prized hunts. He questioned himself and
he shook his head. He knew his idea was wrong but he
couldn't shake his instincts. The thought kept returning.
Those wounds looked exactly like turkey tracks. And if
Kathleen was attacked at night, then it could have been an
owl, at least in principle. Was there really no way to get an
owl inside the house?

Perhaps there was an open window. Yes?

It flew in and frightened her down the staircase? No…

Or perhaps Michael had captured an owl illegally.
Right?

It escaped inside the house and landed on Kathleen?
Preposterous…

Or perhaps an owl snuck in the house like a prowler…
Oh lord, it was all no use.

Larry tried to formulate a workable theory while all sorts
of bizarre ideas circled around in his head. It all seemed
pointless. His eyes suddenly fell on the head of a doe he'd
had mounted many years before after a successful hunt in
pouring conditions. His eyes met with the glassy eyes of the
deer and he felt the sensation of the deer looking back.

"Do you remember the night that you killed me?"

Larry was struck dumb and stared into the eyes of the
deer.

"Do you remember it was raining?"

Larry walked closer, hypnotized by the eyes of the deer.

"What happened after you shot me?"

Larry remembered the hunt all right. It was an exhilarating experience. He remembered the pounding rain and the trouble he had finding his way back to the deer carcass.

What are you telling me? Larry thought.

"Think. Think. Think," a voice repeated.

"I shot you and you ran," Larry finally answered.

"Where did I run to?"

"I don't know. Just *away*. You ran to find safety."

"Did I find it?"

"No, you died."

"Did you find me?"

"In the rain? Yes. I followed a track. I walked a line. I found the first drop of blood on the ground where I shot you. I followed the drips like a trail of breadcrumbs. They led me to your body."

"What was my body like?"

"Bloody. You were covered in blood."

In the downpour, Larry had worried that he would never find the deer as it scampered away. But the drips of blood formed a trail which led from the place the beast was shot towards the limp body. When he eventually found the deer, she was drenched in blood and now deceased, lying on the ground.

"Where was the first drop of my blood?"

Under the spot where you were first struck, Larry thought.

And that was it. That was the answer. It was so simple. It was Larry's eureka moment.

What if the State's case had everything back-to-front? What if Kathleen began bleeding outside, leaving a trail of blood *leading the way* to her body? What if Kathleen's first injuries were sustained not on the stairs, but on the path itself? What if the blood outside the house was pointing the way to her body inside?

"Of course!" Larry shouted to an empty room. "The attack happened outside…"

It all began to make sense, in increments. Why had Kathleen pulled her own hair out from the roots? More than sixty individual hairs were found clasped in her hands. What compels a person to do this? She was trying to pull a bird from her head! Why were there pine needles stuck to her hand and found around her body? Because the whole attack occurred outside! Why had all of Kathleen's serious injuries been restricted to the area above the shoulders? Because that's exactly the zone in which birds of prey focus their attacks! Everything was falling into place. Everything pointed to an animal attack that had happened outside, along the path and under the trees of the Forest Hills property.

The injuries to Kathleen's head could not have been sustained from simple blows by a thrashing metal rod. And there was no brain bruising, no skull fractures, only deep lacerations and slices to her scalp, tiny cuts and punctures to her face, and a trail of blood along the front path, right below where owls were always so happy to hunt. How could the prosecution explain the pine needles and hairs pulled out by the root? They simply couldn't. But Larry had the answer. It was all as though she had been trying to rip something away from her head as she struggled during an attack that began outside.

Larry was familiar with the territorial behavior of barred owls on the property. He had witnessed his friends and family being swooped at before. And it was well known that owls had harmed humans in the past. People had been injured before. Eyes had been lost. Scalps had been torn. But this was a more serious attack than anything he had ever heard of. Do owls kill? *Can* owls kill? "Am I really thinking this?" he asked himself.

By now, the trial was almost over. It was three days until closing arguments. Larry's revelation had arrived too late. He waited until the trial was over before he started the arduous task of presenting his new theory to the authorities.

LARRY'S THEORY

Larry only knew a little about the evidence contained in the case file. His theory was developed primarily to explain the drops of blood along the front path and Kathleen's strange head injuries. He could explain the hair pulled out by the roots and he could explain why there were pine needles inside the house around her body. But it seems there is much that this theory can't explain.

Could an owl truly be responsible for Kathleen's death? The odds would be staggering. If owls have ever killed humans, such an event is so rare as to be basically unheard of. How large would a "killer owl" need to be? No owl ever killed a person, right? So it would be unprecedented. Could this really be a possibility?

As a matter of fact, Larry didn't believe an owl killed Kathleen. Even to him, this seemed too farfetched to be the whole story. Sure, an owl may have attacked Kathleen with its meat-hook talons. But an owl could not be solely responsible for her death. There had to be more to the story.

So, Larry's theory went like this.

Kathleen speaks over the phone with Helen Prislinger at 11:08 p.m. on December 8. She gives out Michael's email address. Sometime around 11:30, both Michael and Kathleen retreat from the house to the poolside with a couple of glasses of wine. Lying on their deck chairs, they chat and relax at the end of a long day. They have had dinner, they have watched a comedy, and they are starting to wind down before bed. Michael has received some promising news about a Hollywood adaptation of one of his books and the pair are celebrating the news. All is well and life is good. After a couple of drinks, Kathleen declares that she will head inside, finish up a few odds and ends, and go to bed. Michael says he'll stay out a bit longer, sitting by the ambient light of the outdoor pool, smoking his pipe and drinking.

Sometime after midnight, Kathleen decides to set up the last of the Christmas decorations. She takes a small, white balsa-wood reindeer up in her arms and strolls down the path to place it beside the front gate. Larry had seen the reindeer there on the morning of the 9th, and he knew it had not been there the previous day.

When Kathleen stoops to set it down, she is abruptly struck from behind, not hearing the silent glide of a large barred owl. The owl's eyes have been attracted to the contrast between the white reindeer and the darkness of the night. Kathleen falls and screams, already bleeding from the head, but she is too far from the pool to be heard by Michael, who is relaxing or dozing. The bird slices her head with its sharp talons and pecks at her face with its beak. On its second attack, the bird's feet become entangled in her hair. Kathleen begins to run back to the house. She grapples with the owl before freeing it from her head, halfway along the path. She pulls out clumps of her own hair, with thirty-eight hairs in her left hand and twenty-five in her right. The shaken owl ascends back to the branches.

Now dripping blood and with severe injuries to her head, Kathleen flees up the front path. She leaves a trail of drops on the paving stones along the way. She smears blood on the door frame as she clumsily makes her way inside. She staggers into the house, continuing to drip fresh blood on the hallway's wooden floor. As she reaches the bottom of the stairs, presumably on her way to the upstairs bathroom, she faints from the shock of the attack. She is unconscious and now spilling blood at the bottom of the stairwell.

Once Kathleen regains consciousness, she attempts to rise to her feet. But the bottom steps have pooled with blood. Her bloodied feet slip on the very first step and she knocks the back of her head on the wooden molding. In her efforts to gain her footing, she grasps about with her hands, spreading blood profusely around the walls of the stairwell. She shakes her bloody hair, spraying blood around the enclosed space. She is unconscious once again, and this time she will not come back.

Larry sums up exactly what he believes happened to Kathleen on his own website:

> I believe an owl attacked Kathleen Peterson in the early morning hours of December 9, 2001, while walking toward her Durham, NC house … The deep gashes in her head were not accompanied by any evidence of blunt force trauma to her skull. The shock of being attacked, the sight of her own blood, mixed with fatigue, alcohol, and pills, caused her to faint by the staircase. Ultimately she died from blood loss while unconscious, hours later.[1]

Michael, who had been dozing beside the pool, finally wanders into the house around 2:30 a.m. He discovers his wife's body hours after she was first attacked. He cradles her body, staining his hands and shorts with her blood. He calls emergency services and states that Kathleen fell. It is only natural that he assumes this was what happened given the location of the body at the bottom of the stairs and the injuries to her head. He collects towels to place beneath her. He clutches her body tight, whispering her name through tears. He calls 911 a second time as soon as Kathleen stops breathing. Paramedics arrive shortly afterwards to find Michael kneeling beside her body, weeping. The medical team notices blood far from where it should be if she simply fell down the stairs: They find the drops in the hallway. They

---

1. Pollard, Larry. "The Owl Theory."
https://owltheoryorg.wordpress.com/

find the smears on the back of the door. They find blood outside the house. They doubt she fell. They call the police.

And so quickly, just a few minutes after help arrived, the two hypotheses were set in stone: either she fell or she was murdered. The investigators soon became myopic. Michael's fate had been sealed the very moment he dialed 911 in a state of hysteria. His fate was sealed when he uttered this single word: "fell."

VIRTUES OF LARRY'S THEORY

The owl theory has several surprising virtues that make it a stronger hypothesis than the fall and homicide theories. In particular, the two major problems that beset the fall and homicide theories can be better accounted for by an owl attack. Firstly, the claim that Kathleen's head injuries were inflicted not by a blunt weapon but by razor-sharp talons accords perfectly well with the fact that Kathleen suffered no skull fractures or brain bruising. Secondly, the distribution of blood both inside and outside the house is well explained by an attack that began at some point along the front path. It all makes sense if you assume that Kathleen's attack began outside.

If you accept that Kathleen either fell or was murdered, then at best you can explain one of these unsettling facts. Yet with the owl theory in hand, it is possible to account for both of these problematic pieces of evidence in literally one fell swoop. Both the blood on the path and the lack of brain injury can be accounted for.

The owl theory is also excellent at explaining the general appearance of Kathleen's injuries. The majority of Kathleen's lacerations, scrapes, and abrasions are focused on the areas around her scalp, eyes, and nose. Owls, in their prior attacks on humans, have often been witnessed to grasp the head with talons while pecking at the face.

Other incision-like injuries were discovered on Kathleen's elbows, which are also compatible with the grasps of talons.

And most famously, the owl theory can explain why pine needles were found stuck to Kathleen's hands and why she had pulled out her blood-soaked hair. It is natural to assume that if Kathleen did have an owl attached to her head along the front path, she would be wrenching it away with her hands, drawing hair from her head and pine needles from the bushes or from the feathers of the bird itself. Even more pine needles may have gathered on Kathleen's clothes as she fell to the ground on the outside path. So much of the evidence that simply can't be explained by the other two theories can be explained by the owl theory.

PROBLEMS WITH THE THEORY

But there are problems. And not small ones. To begin with, we now must posit two events, rather than one, to explain Kathleen's death. First, she is attacked by an owl. Then, she falls over in the stairwell, banging her head after fainting. If that is what is needed to account for her death, then we have doubled the number of unlikely events required to explain how Kathleen died.

These two events in question are hardly commonplace. It is extremely unlikely to find oneself the victim of an owl attack. And it is also unlikely to inflict fatal injuries on oneself by falling on a few stairs. So, far from bringing all of the evidence under a single umbrella, we are forced to assume that two incredibly unlikely events conspired to cause Kathleen's death. What terrible luck she had! It is akin to winning the lottery twice in a row. But the prize in this case was death.

Even if we set aside the probabilities involved, Larry's theory lacks the kind of forensic evidence we would expect to find if Kathleen was attacked by a bird of prey that became entangled in her hair. Most importantly, we should expect to find feathers all over the area where the attack took place. If Larry is right, and Kathleen was attacked on the front path, tussling with a relatively large bird of prey, then the front path should be littered with feathers; so many feathers, in fact, that they could scarcely have gone unnoticed by forty officers investigating the property for over twenty hours. Yet no officers reported discovering a large pile of feathers anywhere. Indeed, not a single whole feather was taken into evidence.

Apart from feathers, we might expect other trace evidence, such as owl droppings or blood at the scene, perhaps even part of a chipped talon or beak. On Kathleen's clothes, we might have found the imprint of a talon or a wing. And again, forty officers over twenty hours failed to report finding anything like this.

Larry's theory can explain a lot, but there are major gaps in his account. He can explain why blood is found outside the house. He can explain the unusual injuries to Kathleen's scalp and why there was no skull or brain damage. He can also explain why a reasonable jury would conclude that Kathleen looked like she had been attacked. After all, she had been!

But what Larry can't explain is why—if it truly was an owl—just why is there so little evidence of such an attack? Was this some sort of ninja owl? Did the owl cover its tracks, meticulously disposing of all the other predictable trace evidence? There must be more to the story.

LARRY'S OMEN
Larry's theory was still an embryo when he first let out a word of it to anyone else. His mother-in-law was told of the crazy idea during an out-of-town visit. Brenda watched on, waiting for her mother's reaction. "An owl?" said the old woman incredulously. "Well, that's a new one!"

With the fog of a mother's doubt hanging over them, Larry and Brenda packed their things and returned to Durham. As they were driving back home that evening, Larry's car struck something. He pulled over to check on the animal he had crushed, only to discover it had been an Eastern screech owl. He stood over the dead animal with a feeling of mystical incredulity.

"What was it?" asked Brenda as Larry returned to the car.

"Guess…" he answered.

Brenda's eyes widened. "That's a sign."

"You bet," he said, turning the key. The starter clicked over and the engine began to rumble. "And the owl returned to Noah in the evening," said Larry, "and behold, in its mouth was an olive leaf." The car trundled along the dark North Carolina highway—leaving the crushed omen in its wake—and its occupants now knew that the battle ahead was not just legal, but spiritual.

THE TRIAL ENDS

The guilty verdict was delivered on October 10, 2003. By now, the owl theory was barely a week old. The verdict had stunned and angered Larry. After hearing the news, he stormed from the house and began raking leaves in the yard, hopelessly attempting to take his mind away from the injustice of it all.

As Larry piled up leaves, a car pulled into the Petersons' circular driveway and ex-congressman Nick Galifianakis stepped out. Galifianakis, uncle of the comedian Zach Galifianakis, was a close friend of Michael. He had worked with Michael at length during the writing of the book *Charlie Two Shoes*. Galifianakis was also a friend of Larry, living only a few blocks away. The friendship between the two men had only deepened since the arrest. He came towards Larry and leaned over the fence.

"I guess you've heard?"

"Yeah," Larry replied as he angrily scooped up some yellow leaves.

"I'm about to see the boys."

"Okay." There was a meaningful pause. "You know," Larry began, "I'm convinced it was one of these damn owls."

"Come again?"

"The wounds, the blood, the hair, the pine needles... She was attacked outside."

"You think an *owl* killed Kathleen?"

"Yes. Because... Because..." Larry paused before trying to launch a convincing case. But where to begin?

There was a long pause, while Galifianakis dreamed up a pun. "So, it's a true hoo hoo dun it then?"

"I'm dead serious. She—"

"Look," Galifianakis interjected. "Let me go check on the kids first. I want to talk after. Don't head out anywhere."

An hour later, Galifianakis knocked on Larry's front door. The guest was brought into the parlor and given a tumbler of scotch. The two men sat across from one another and Galifianakis started the conversation. "Right. Tell me about this owl."

By the end of the evening, Larry was exhausted from outlining his theory, Galifianakis was astounded by what he had heard, and a bottle of scotch that had once been full was returned to the cabinet half empty. Larry had converted his first true believer. Together, they would launch this new theory. Galifianakis stood and left. Larry collapsed into bed.

The next morning, Larry woke early, nursing a hangover. It was the first day of battle. He got up, got dressed, and grabbed the phone from the wall. It was not yet 6 a.m. when the Durham sheriff was rudely awakened.

"Who's this?" asked the sheriff as his irritated wife rolled over and flipped the pillow.

"Coach, it's Larry."

The old sheriff had been Larry's high school football coach. The childhood designation had never disappeared. "Larry!" replied Coach. "What are you calling about?"

"I need to meet with you immediately. It's about the Petersons."

"Oh?" Coach's ears pricked up. "What about them?"

"I think I really need to talk to you about it in person."

Coach rolled over and looked at the clock. "Okay, look, I'll be in the office in twenty minutes. Meet me there."

When Coach arrived, Larry was already loitering around the locked front door of the sheriff's department, looking disturbed and on edge. Not knowing what could warrant such an early morning visit, Coach quickly led his old friend into the office. The two men sat opposite each other and Coach sensed the anxiety and stress that radiated from Larry.

Coach had a sudden, troubling thought: *Jesus Christ, he's not about to confess, is he?*

"Coach," Larry began. "Mike didn't kill Kathleen."

Fuck, thought Coach, quickly turning pale. *He actually is!*

"I think it may have been an owl."

Any esteem that the old football coach once had for the young athlete evaporated. Here was a middle-aged man dragging him into the office before dawn to tell him that a woman had been killed by woodland creatures.

"An owl?" double-checked Coach.

"Yes."

"As in birds?"

"Yes."

"As in feathers, wings, beaks?"

"Yes, yes, yes… Owl as in, well, an owl."

Coach checked the calendar. It wasn't the first of April. His eyes returned to Larry, now with a look of concern.

"You been drinkin'?" he asked.

"I know it sounds crazy, but listen."

Coach listened with patience to Larry's bizarre new theory. By the end, he had to admit, it had at least some merit.

"Well, it sure makes more sense than slipping at the bottom of a staircase," he finally conceded.

"Or bashing in someone's head with a metal rod while magically failing to damage the skull," added Larry.

"So," Coach asked, "what do you want me to do about it?"

"What can you do?"

"Well, to use some legal jargon, not a hell of a lot."

Larry leaned back and ran his fingers through his hair. "I'm thinking about approaching the DA. There's a chance I could file a successful motion for appropriate relief."

"You might need a stronger case. There are dog attacks. There are bear attacks. Give me an alligator or a shark, but an owl?"

Larry sighed.

"Alright," said Coach as he stood to leave. But then he paused as he foresaw the path of ridicule ahead of Larry. "Just, well, you know… Be careful, Larry, and Godspeed."

CHAPTER FOUR: LARRY'S LABOR

THE BIRTH OF RIDICULE
By December 2003, the newspapers had gotten wind of the new theory. The collective gasp of Durham was deafening. When the reviews came out, they were not encouraging.

> "Embarking upon a flight of fancy that famed oddball and movie director Alfred Hitchcock might have dreamed up after smoking a dime bag of wacky weed, Pollard and Galifianakis—hereafter referred to as the *Duh-namic Duo*—contend that an owl caused the gashes to Kathleen's scalp."
> *The Raleigh News and Observer*, December 16, 2003

> "The theory has succeeded in little else but spawning jokes."
> *The Durham Herald-Sun*, December 28, 2003

> "Thanks to Larry Pollard and Nick Galifianakis for the *big laughs*."
> *The Durham Herald-Sun*, December 18, 2003

> "To say an owl flew into the house and did it is absurd."
> *The Durham Herald-Sun*, December 23, 2003

"No feathers, no biological evidence of an owl's presence—none of this strikes a chord of reason in the bird of prey theory."

The Durham Herald-Sun, December 15, 2003

Larry had certainly expected some pushback in the wake of his revelation, but this went far beyond anything he could have imagined. The response was not just dismissive or doubtful. It became almost childishly cruel. Gleeful mockery filled the papers. Within a week, Larry had become a human joke.

The level-headed among North Carolina's journalists focused more impartially on the shortcomings of the theory. "No feathers or other evidence of a bird attack were inside the house,"[2] noted a reporter for the *Rocky Mount Telegram*. It was the kindest of the reviews.

Those early days were a dreadful time for both Larry and Brenda, and it is no surprise their marriage was strained as a consequence. Together, the pair had already dealt with the deaths of loved ones, serious illnesses, the trauma of infertility, and countless legal woes. But this new stress in their lives was a horrible and unfamiliar one. It was a pointing and a laughing that they could feel all over, wherever they went. It was the loss, not of money or health or material things, but of standing. "For better, for worse," Brenda would remind herself daily. "For better, for worse."

A LETTER TO HARDIN
A letter was delivered to Jim Hardin on December 5, 2003. It was signed by Larry and Galifianakis. It asked Jim, a man

---

2. AP. "Whoodunit? Writer's Friends Say Owl Killed Wife." Star News Online. December 13, 2003. https://www.starnewsonline.com/story/news/2003/12/14/whoodunit-writers-friends-say-owl-killed-wife/30534246007/

they considered a friend, to consider reopening the case in the light of the new theory. This was not to occur.

"It's absurd," Hardin told reporters shortly after receiving the letter. "Nothing in the evidence in any way suggests that there is any validity whatsoever to the theory. It's one of the most ridiculous things I've ever heard."

Hardin's response was entirely predictable. The request to reopen the case was declined.

Larry arranged to meet with Hardin in the aftermath of this public response. He wanted to present his case in person rather than through the impersonal medium of written text. Instead of sitting down and discussing the matter, Hardin escaped out a back exit of the district attorney's office, leaving Larry waiting clueless at reception.

Surprisingly, Michael's defense team was no more enthusiastic than Hardin. When interviewed by the *Herald-Sun*, one of Michael's attorneys, Thomas Maher, made it clear that the defense had no part in the theory and would not be pursuing it.

When Larry approached the lead attorney David Rudolf, the reaction was not so different. "You want to argue that an *owl* killed Kathleen?" he asked, eyebrow cocked high. Rudolf eventually conceded that had the idea crossed his mind before trial, it may have been an angle for the defense. But all focus for Michael's future appeal was now placed on more specific procedural problems that had infected the first trial. The defense was not going to veer towards such an extraordinary explanation. In any case, Larry's attempts to convince were largely fruitless, falling on deaf ears. All attempts to persuade were met with laughter or mockery.

Still, Larry could not be dissuaded. He spent hours upon hours discussing the new theory with ornithologists, reading reports of owl attacks, and researching the literature in the North Carolina State Museum of Natural Sciences. The longer he looked, the more credible evidence he found in support of the theory. But even so, this was not the kind of evidence that would convince the district attorney. And by now, the media had reduced the theory to an urban fairy tale.

As one newspaper columnist put it: "A more plausible explanation for what happened on the fateful night that Kathleen died is a visitation by a harpy."[3] Larry's magical hypothesis was on a par with the ancient Greek tale of Jason and the Argonauts. In both cases, the columnist argued, we were dealing in the stuff of myth.

For Larry to gain any credibility, more evidence was needed. It was not enough to point to the head injuries. It was not enough to suggest that Kathleen began to bleed outside. It was not enough to point to prior owl attacks on humans. Larry needed a smoking gun. And he would find it.

THE SMOKING FEATHER

After a few years, things quietened down. The public mockery abated, even if it was always there in the background. Michael's case, if it was mentioned in the papers, no longer found its way to the front page. It was four years after Larry's letter to Hardin had been dismissed when the owl theory briefly made headlines again.

The renewed interest came from the actions of a great horned owl. Chris Cox and Byron Unger, business partners, were attacked in separate incidents in the carpark of VMR Graphics, halfway between Durham and Raleigh.

"I thought someone had hit me in the head with a baseball bat," said Cox, who bled badly from the head.

"Almost took my eye out," said Unger.

The whole thing had been recorded on surveillance video and was eventually shown on the local news. After the owl attack footage went public, journalists who had

---

3. "Search for the Killer Owl." *The Herald-Sun.* December 15, 2003.

previously mocked Larry's theory began to worry that they might find themselves eating their own hats.

When the footage aired, Michael himself was alerted by fellow prisoners. "Mike!" they shouted. "Come look at the TV!"

Michael went through and watched as the owl could be seen kicking Cox right in the back of the head before swooping away unseen. When Cox turned to fight his assailant with his fists at the ready, the entire rec room exploded with laughter. "Sure looks like that neighbor fella mighta been on ta something!" said a voice amongst the jeers. Michael managed a wry smile.

The recording of this owl attack, so close to Durham, caused some to soften up to Larry's theory. But many remained unconvinced. The theory had always faced the objection that if an owl were involved, feathers would have been recovered from the scene. Since feathers weren't recovered, there was no owl. Indeed, Larry knew that this objection was a strong one. There must be at least some evidence remaining of the owl. Could Kathleen be exhumed to test her scalp for the presence of owl DNA? Of course, that was never going to happen.

In a second letter to Hardin, much shorter than the first, Larry made a simple request: for the State to confirm or deny whether any feathers were discovered during their investigation. It was sent away to the district attorney's office. The reply Larry received was both perfunctory and dismissive:

> Dear Mr. Pollard,
> We thank you for your concern regarding yada yada.
> There were no feathers discovered during yada yada.
> We are confident that the jury made the right yada yada.

Yours somethingly…
Etc.

Larry smelled a rat, and he had the means to flush it out. Having spent many years with the NCSBI's Special Investigations Division, it was an old friend who greeted Larry as he strolled into the building.

"Well, hello there. Long time no see!"

"Hello, Jamie," replied Larry. "How are things?"

"Fine, fine. How's the wife?"

"Coping, sure. Definitely coping. See the game?"

"Overtime! What in the name of..." They both shook their heads in unison and the small talk was brought to a close. "So what can I do ya for?" asked Jamie.

"Do you have the trace evidence report for the Peterson case?"

"Sure do."

"Can I get that?"

"Of course."

Some formalities were formalized and it was a matter of weeks before Larry held the trace evidence report in his hands. A couple of minutes of reading was all it would take to contradict the signed letter of the district attorney. He whisked through the pages like he was dealing cards. He scanned it with excitement, so quickly that no human language could possibly be discerned. At last, Larry turned back to the first page, steadied himself, and went through the report line by line.

On the first page of the report, a few lines down, reference was made to a microscope slide containing a strand of Kathleen's hair, with full description on page three. Larry flicked through to the description. This stated that the slide held a single hair. The hair had been sent through to the SBI from the medical examiner's office. It had been pulled from the root. Its color was noted as straw. On the hair, dried blood was noted; in that blood, a feather.

Larry looked at the word, like a beacon, with one hand on his forehead.

Feather.

He read it again and again.

Feather.

Feather.

Feather.

Had he forgotten how to speak English? "Feather" meant feather, didn't it? There was a feather. The office of the district attorney had lied. He threw the papers down in anger. Galifianakis was the first to hear the news.

From here, a checklist of permissions from a range of authorities went in circles. Writing to the DA's office, Larry was told he would need the attorney general's permission to see the slide, in whose ownership it presently stood. Writing to the attorney general's office, he was told that it was not with them, but with the Durham police. Asking the police, he was told it was a matter for the district attorney. At last, Larry and Galifianakis arrived at the district attorney's office, with both the original letter request for feathers as well as the SBI report.

Hardin was no longer the district attorney. The new man behind the desk was David Saacks. Larry approached Saacks and pointed a finger at the twin words on different documents: the "feather" he had requested and the "feather" on Kathleen's hair. Within an hour, Saacks arranged for the slide to be brought to the office from the police evidence store. With bated breath, the slide was unsealed from its packaging and, just like that, nearly five years after he first conjectured a bird of prey, Larry held the smoking feather in his hand.

There was just one problem.

It couldn't be seen. The feather was microscopic and could not be observed with the naked eye. The slide was held at this angle and that angle, under lamplight, close to the eye, far from the eye—but there was no hope. All that was visible was a strand of hair and a piece of glass. Arrangements were made for the delivery of a microscope and the assistance of an expert. With the office of the district attorney now converted into a makeshift laboratory, everyone had a go at peering down the lens. Everyone saw it vividly. From the hair shaft, a spindly feather stuck out. There were little black dots surrounding it that couldn't be discerned. But the feather itself was easily seen. This was observed at 200x magnification.

"Can we increase the magnification?" Galifianakis asked.

At 400x magnification, everyone in the room saw that the SBI report had made an error. This was not a feather after all. It was *two* feathers. Two distinct microscopic feathers jutted out from the hair shaft. The black dots remained indiscernible. When 800x magnification was applied, the team saw that the black dots were red. They were flecks of blood that had dried, acting like glue, keeping the feathers attached to the hair shaft. Not only had feathers been found, but they were found in blood.

Larry had discovered the smoking gun. So what to do with it? Naturally, these pieces of evidence needed to be tested in some way, to determine if they really were from an owl.

The aptly named Dr. Carla Dove was an ornithologist centered at the Smithsonian Institute in Washington, DC. Her expertise lay primarily in the forensic analysis of feathers. But not for murder cases. For the most part, her work was done for airlines. She was the world's leading authority on the topic of bird strikes, i.e., when birds are sucked through the engines of aircraft or battered against their hulls in flight. In her most active moments, she was looking down a microscope, analyzing feathers and feather fragments. Through the aid of a lens, she could identify different kinds of birds even from tiny pieces of material. She soon received a telephone call from Larry.

She was as surprised as anyone else to hear the details of the case, but as a person well familiar with the ways of owls, her doubts were weighed equally by knowledge of their strength. She did not dismiss the theory out of hand, but neither was she convinced. "Send through the slide and I'll see what I can do."

The slide itself could not be sent as it belonged to the State. But Larry had been sensible enough to have photographs taken on the day at the district attorney's office. Having been sent the images, Dove could confirm that the two microscopic remnants were indeed feathers, but could she confirm anything more specific? That hinged on what remained of the feathers.

A bird's feather has two parts: one, the part with hooklets that have a particular color, pattern, and texture; and two, the downy part that lies beneath the exterior feathers. The down feather (or even the down at the base of a feather) has diagnostic characteristics that can lead to group identifications. Very often, it is possible to determine which particular group (or taxonomic order) of birds a downy feather belongs to just by looking for the characteristic features. This is what Dove was hoping for when she observed the photograph, but the features that would have been specific to a particular group of birds simply were not present in this photograph. The feathers were not complete—they were broken fragments—and the clues that were needed were missing.

The objects on the slide were certainly bird feathers. That much she could confirm. But to get any further information, she would need to get the slide itself. The feathers would then have to be prised away and submitted for DNA analysis. Robert Fleischer, the head of the genetics lab at the Smithsonian, was happy to perform that test. But all up, the process would cost tens of thousands of dollars, and the transfer would require the additional permission of the State. As such, the analysis never went ahead.

Instead, Larry sought out the opinions of further experts so a better case for the theory could be mounted in case a retrial was ever ordered. If such a retrial occurred, then the feathers would be requested and tested. The State would have no authority to refuse such a request.

LARRY'S ANGELS

Before the feathers were found, Larry was seen as a crank. He had spent years in the wilderness of public opinion, ostracized by friends, family, and the media alike. It had been a lonely time, but he had not been entirely alone. He had Brenda to depend on, of course. He had Nick Galifianakis. And there were others who had helped along the way.

Back in 2003, during the filming of *The Staircase* docuseries, crew members often chatted with Larry when he emerged in his own backyard. The film editor, Sophie Brunet, eventually heard about Larry's theory from other members of the film crew. Her interest was piqued and she sought him out one evening. She spotted him in the yard and snuck up on him.

"Pssst," whispered Brunet over the fence, acting out a secret transaction. "What is all this business about the owls?"

"Hah!" exclaimed Larry, who had not heard her approach. "Oh, so you've heard... Well, it explains the wounds to Kathleen pretty well, don't you think?"

"Sure it does," Brunet answered. "But owls aren't really aggressive, are they? How often do owls actually attack people?"

Larry got a glint of mischief in his eyes. "Come with me," he said, waving a hand. He led Brunet to the wooded property line, towards a large magnolia tree where he knew some owls had newly nested. "Take a walk over there," Larry directed Brunet.

Brunet ventured beneath the trees with her shoulders hunched. Larry began to imitate the calls of the owls in the trees. He saw their heads begin to bob as their eyes fixed on the movement below. A pair of pale-yellow wings opened. Down flew a silent missile, aimed at Brunet. She ran back to Larry. And the bird, satisfied, returned to the tree. She accepted Larry's reckless demonstration, and would later become an avid proponent of the theory.

Was Brunet's opinion about Michael's innocence impartial? Perhaps not. She had already become romantically involved with him. The relationship began in the midst of the filming of the docuseries and lasted nearly fifteen years. Despite this love affair with the Devil, Brunet is still alive and quite unmurdered. To this day, she is a supporter of the theory that a bird of prey attacked Kathleen.

Brunet began to research the topic of owl attacks on humans. And her contribution to the owl theory accelerated after she read the story of the Gilbert family from the state of Montana.

That story began in 2006 when Cy Gilbert found himself standing face-to-face with a female grizzly bear and cub. With the boy locked in her eyes, the animal growled and shifted her massive paws. Cy shook in horror. The bear stood on her back legs and roared. Then, before Cy had a moment to react, the bear set her paws down again and calmly lumbered away from the young teenager. For two years, Cy had been the one with the *legend of the bear* to boast about. It was a story he loved to tell the extended family, especially at Christmas gatherings. "I survived an encounter with two grizzlies," began the story. "And even when they were nothing more than a couple of dots on the horizon, I was still shaking."

"Again! Again!" his young cousins would cry.

But on a winter's day, two years after the bear encounter, his younger brother Austin would claim the new bragging rights.

Austin was only twelve years old. He was with his parents, who were cross-country skiing in Glacier National Park, just south of the border with Canada. While he was standing in deep, cold snow, a great horned owl swooped down, latched onto his head, punctured the skin, and scraped his face. After a short tussle between the youth and the feathered beast, it let go its grasp and flew away. Luckily, Austin required no stitches. He was, in fact, the park's second victim of a horned owl in two days. A guest at a nearby hotel had been twice swooped upon while out for a walk on a nearby trail.

"I survived an encounter with a territorial owl," the new story began. "And even when it returned to the branches, I was terrified it was going to get me again."

Everyone loved the new legend except for Cy, whose story was now pale in comparison. Indeed, Austin's story would soon make headlines in the local paper, *The Missoulian*.

Before the ink would meet the paper, an ornithologist from Montana named Kate Davis received a call from a reporter who wanted to gather her expert opinion. Davis was the founder of the educational foundation Raptors of the Rockies and had worked with a variety of raptors for over thirty years. She was exactly the kind of expert the *Missoulian* needed to talk to about an owl attack. She told the paper[4] a bit about the fluctuations in owl aggression throughout the year, especially its links to territoriality around the breeding season. What happened to Austin, she noted, was not all that surprising. Owl attacks were far from unheard of.

4. "Owl Attack Leaves Boy With Cuts and a Tale." The Missoulian. https://missoulian.com/news/local/owl-attack-leaves-boy-with-cuts-and-a-tale/article_1b0973f5-a576-5cda-a795-263679b4e709.html

With that one simple interview, a ball began to roll. The *Missoulian* interview caught the eye of Brunet, who phoned the ornithologist from Paris. During the course of their conversation, Brunet explained to Davis the nature of Kathleen's death, Michael's subsequent trial, and Larry's new theory. Brunet tried to express to Davis the strangeness of the wounds on Kathleen's head. "They look like what I'd imagine an owl scratch to look like," she said. "But I'm no ornithologist and I can't know for sure."

An hour after hanging up the call, Davis did a little experiment.

Davis' educational institute was home to a resident barred owl named Graham. Carrying her oblivious experimental subject towards an upturned metal bowl, Davis proceeded to mold a layer of clay over its base. She then sat the clay-covered bowl on the ground under the bird as though it were the scalp of a person. Lifting the unsuspecting bird over the bowl, she released her hold, causing Graham to attempt a grasping landing. The marks he left behind were photographed and sent to Brunet. The French film editor was evidently impressed with the result. In return, she sent over Kathleen's autopsy shots via email. Comparing the two, it was a positive match.

Through the postal service, weeks later, Davis received a DVD set of *The Staircase,* which she binged twice in immediate succession. Only afterwards did she realize she had missed the entirety of her planned viewing for the prior two weeks: the Beijing Olympic Games. The case had gripped her attention to the virtual exclusion of the outside world. And now, like Brunet and Galifianakis before her, she was a true believer, one of Larry's angels.

THE MOTION FOR APPROPRIATE RELIEF

Five years had passed since the trial had ended. Michael agreed to adopt Larry as his attorney after an emotional meeting through a pane of glass and across a telephone wire. This meeting occurred shortly after the footage of the owl attack at VMR Graphics had aired. A Motion for Appropriate Relief (MAR) was finally submitted in the middle of 2009, citing the newly disclosed feathers. Importantly, the motion was premised on the fact that since an additional feather had been discovered on the microslide, there was now new evidence available that had not been available during trial. The new discovery should vacate the guilty verdict.

The importance of the feathers' discovery could not have been realized during trial, but only in the light of the owl theory, which was brought to public knowledge after the trial had ended. Larry urged that the MAR should be granted in order "to prevent a fundamental miscarriage of justice to the defendant, to his family and friends, and to the citizens of the State of North Carolina."

Predictably, the MAR was shot down by the Court. Despite the surprising discovery of the feathers, the owl theory was "speculative," according to the State, and totally without merit. The State argued that because Michael had already filed a prior MAR that made no reference to an owl, it was an illegitimate claim to present in a new motion. As the State worded it, Michael had been "in a position to adequately raise the ground or issue underlying the present motion but did not do so."

Larry was dumbstruck by this response. He replied to the ruling: "Just when to advance a theory of defense, like when to issue an indictment, is a balancing act weighing the amount and strength of the evidence at hand." It was not until mid-2009, when the MAR was submitted, that Larry had the ammunition available to properly defend the owl theory. This was six years after the first inklings of an owl attack had even crossed Larry's mind.

Four affidavits were attached to the MAR. The first was from Robert Fleischer at the Smithsonian's genetics lab, stating a willingness to test the feathers. The second was from Dr. Alan Van Norman, an owl fanatic and neurosurgeon who had previously worked as a US Army surgeon. Van Norman argued that two lacerations on Kathleen Peterson's scalp were arranged as a pair and that each laceration had "the appearance of a trident with three limbs converging to a point at roughly 30 degrees from each other and a fourth limb converging to the same point at nearly 180 degrees from the center limb of the other three limbs." This was all consistent with an owl's talons.

As an expert in raptor behavior, Kate Davis' affidavit was grounded in her everyday working life. She had seen, more times than she could count, the damage that talons inflict. Indeed, she had fallen victim to such cuts before. To that effect, Davis wrote an affidavit for Larry which argued that the damage to Kathleen's head resembled an owl attack: "It is my professional opinion, based on 37 years of experience, that Mrs. Peterson's wounds are consistent with wounds inflicted by birds of prey on people and on animals."

Dr. Pat Redig, Professor of Veterinary Medicine at the University of Minnesota and Director of the University's Raptor Center, concurred with Van Norman and Davis. At the time, he had nearly forty years of experience and, perhaps more relevant to this case, in his private life, he was an avid falconer. He knew only too well how birds of prey attacked their targets.

All these experts agreed that the wounds to Kathleen's head were well within the repertoire of larger birds of prey. As a testament to the incredible strength of these birds, Redig included the following grotesque anecdote in his affidavit:

> Our clinic once admitted an emaciated great horned owl (starved out) to which was clinging the carcass of a headless dead barred owl, whose talons were embedded in the breast muscle of the horned owl.

Apparently, the horned owl decapitated and killed the attacking barred owl, but was unable to free itself from the tightly clenched talons of the barred owl.

A serious attack on a human being was far from impossible. Although rare, it was well within the capability of larger owls to inflict significant damage on adult human beings. And if Kathleen was first attacked outside, before fainting in the stairwell, then the attack could easily have precipitated her death. The combination of an attack with concussion and blood loss would be sufficient to kill Kathleen.

In addition to the new feather evidence, the MAR appealed to two other problems in Michael's first trial: ineffective assistance of counsel and prosecutorial misconduct.

Larry argued that Michael's defense counsel was ineffective because they had "refused to listen to the owl attack theory as an exculpatory explanation of the source of the wounds on Kathleen Peterson's body when they had a duty to pursue all such exculpatory evidence." Larry had first informed Rudolf about the theory in 2003 but Rudolf dismissed it out of hand. The defense had, like a much larger bird, buried its head in the sand.

The second claim—that there had been prosecutorial misconduct—was one Larry held close to his heart. It was clear that he was still stinging from those early days when childish mockery ruled and had even been deployed as a tactic by esteemed legal authorities. "After a conviction," Larry noted, "the prosecutor is bound by the ethics of his office to inform the appropriate authority of … information that casts doubt on the correctness of the conviction."

Hardin had told the media that the theory was "ridiculous." And the new MAR was dismissed as representing a "chimerical" and "phantasmagorical" theory.

These were the specific adjectives the State chose to use when trying to justify why Hardin had fled out a back exit of the district attorney's office rather than meeting with Larry.

Larry blasted all this behavior as unethical. "Inherent in its duty is that the prosecution not ridicule the new information, cast the information in a false or misleading light, or try to maliciously and without merit, discredit the people or persons who are conveying the information that casts doubt on the correctness of the conviction."

That, Larry thought, *would be the last time they would reduce his theory to a joke.* But in truth, it would be the last time within the legal system that Larry had the opportunity to defend his neighbor, vindicate his owl theory, and assert his dignity. Larry had no idea at the time, but the fight was drawing to a close.

Michael Out

Seven years after the failed MAR, Brenda Pollard looked at the telephone as if it might jump off the wall and bite her. She hesitated for a long time, deciding whether or not to pick it up. Larry was out of the state and it was certainly not her responsibility to tell him. But then, who would tell him? If she called, he would be enraged. But if she didn't call, he would also be enraged, only a bit later. After an eternity of deliberating, she picked up the receiver and took a deep breath.

"Larry," she said. "Michael's taking the Alford."

"He *what*?!"

"He is taking the Alford, Larry."

There was a pause while Larry looked at the ground, which felt like it was falling away. "They told me—"

"I know," Brenda interjected.

Larry scratched his brows with frustration. He groaned as that simple word—*Alford*—erased more than a decade of work from his life. The owl theory would never see its day in court. Brenda tried to calm Larry, despite the anger she herself also felt. They had lost their chance to regain their standing.

You see, by now, Michael had already been out of prison for about six years. On December 14, 2011, Judge Orlando Hudson ordered a retrial. And after eight years inside, the writer was finally out. Michael was held on a $300,000 bond and would need to wear an electronic bracelet. At the time, nobody could care less. Michael was no longer incarcerated. There was rapture among the diehard believers, dismay among the skeptics. Larry had been over the moon with the news. After all, at a new trial, Michael could finally make the defense that a bird of prey had attacked Kathleen.

Michael's long-standing attorney, David Rudolf, had been the one who succeeded where Larry failed. Rudolf had made an MAR that appealed not to owls or feathers but instead secured reasonable doubt about one of the State's expert witnesses. During the trial, the State relied on the blood spatter expertise of SBI Officer Duane Deaver. But as had become clear from a litany of prior cases, Deaver was a habitual liar: a crook in cop's clothing. He often twisted evidence to secure convictions for the State. And because his testimony was riddled with probable untruths, a major pillar on which the State's argument rested was found to be rotten and corrupt. "Is a new trial required?" Judge Hudson asked rhetorically. "The answer is yes."

In the years that followed, preparations for a second trial were underway. But by 2017, Michael could no longer depend on the pro-bono legal arrangement with Rudolf. Additionally, a wrongful death suit brought by Kathleen's daughter, Caitlin, had seen her awarded twenty-five million dollars in damages. Michael was in a tough position, facing a retrial with no real resources to fund it.

Larry had been advised that despite all these hardships, Michael would not settle for a deal with the State. He would see it through to the end. Michael would clear his name and the owl theory would be at least one part of what did it. It was all to play out at the retrial. The feathers would be tested. The jury would see it all laid out. And yet behind closed doors, Rudolf had been negotiating with the prosecutors to find a way to end it all.

The outcome was something called an Alford plea. In essence, this meant that Michael would plead guilty before any new trial began while still protesting his innocence. Alford pleas are acceptable within almost all of the United States. They act as a legal device for those who claim to be innocent but who accept that a reasonable jury would likely find them guilty. To Kathleen's sister, Candace Zamperini, the distinction made little difference. She had been convinced of Michael's guilt ever since she first saw the vast amount of blood in the stairwell. "The correct ending to *The Staircase*," barked Zamperini, "is that Michael Peterson was correctly charged with murder and he is pleading guilty today." She said this at Michael's Alford hearing while darkly eyeballing the cameras of the French documentary crew.

For Michael, however, the affair was clearly more a matter of realpolitik. There were grandchildren to see, relationships to reforge, and only a little amount of (healthy) life left to live. A retrial would be time-consuming, expensive, and would only reopen wounds that were in the process of healing. Given the many examples of corruption that riddled the first trial, it was unlikely a future trial would be played by the book. Rudolf summed up his client's motives like so:

> Mr. Peterson is not guilty. He never was guilty. He is not admitting that he was guilty … He does not feel that he got a fair trial based on the conduct of the law enforcement officers the first time around. And he is simply not willing to play again at what he perceives to be an unfair or crooked table …

He is entering this plea because it is 15 years on. He served 8 years for a crime he did not commit. He is 73 years old. And he has no faith in Durham law enforcement being interested in the truth as opposed to being interested in convicting him, twisting the truth for that purpose. That's why we are entering this Alford plea.

The hearing occurred on February 24, 2017. The adjusted charge which Michael now faced was manslaughter, with a maximum sentence of eighty-six months in prison. Having already served ninety-eight months in the Department of Corrections, Rudolf noted to the judge that Michael must be sentenced to time already served.

"All right," Judge Hudson concluded at the hearing. "The Court does find that he has served his time and he is free to go."

He was free.

It is telling that Michael let out no smile or celebration. There was no cacophony of cheers from the benches. Nobody embraced. Instead, Judge Hudson's words were followed by the gentle sigh of a man who had simply had enough. And with Hudson's final words, the conclusion had been reached. Everybody rose from their seats as the honorable judge left the room.

Larry rose also. He had been sitting alone in the front of the chamber, directly behind Michael and Rudolf. Despite the fact that the truth would never be out, he had taken a moment to smile with his eyes quietly shut, just at the moment that proceedings were brought to a close. It was clear, at that moment, he had made peace with Michael's decision. Even if Larry found the decision distasteful, he had to accept that it was Michael's choice. The writer had chosen to swallow a dose of pride to secure freedom. Larry Pollard took two steps forward and gave the free man a solid slap on the back, which echoed across the courtroom like a blown bulb.

"Thank you," said Michael, turning to Larry—no longer his attorney or neighbor, but a friend.

CHAPTER FIVE: OWL ATTACKS

ARE THERE ANY?
Despite the claims of Larry's ornithologists, a life-threatening owl attack seems like the sort of thing that you might find in fantasy or fiction, but never in real life. It seems like the sort of thing that Alfred Hitchcock and a dimebag of wacky weed might produce. Yet surprisingly, even Hitchcock's famous film was informed by facts rather than fictions. He had done at least a little research into the numerous attacks launched by birds on humans.

"Even the most extraordinary events in our story have a basis in fact," he once told the press. "Why, just a year ago, there was an incident in La Jolla, Calif. in which a thousand finches invaded a home in a period of a half-hour. The man and woman tried to light a fire to smoke them out but the birds caught their wings on fire, flew against the drapes, and burned the house down."[5]

Whether or not Hitchcock's tall story is true, a campfire tale about kamikaze finches is not really a genuine or concerted attack on human beings. One can only guess that the flock of finches—if it ever existed—was lost or confused. Nevertheless, crows, blue jays, magpies, hawks, eagles, and seagulls have all been well-documented as deliberately attacking and injuring humans. And most of us have, at one time or another, been dive-bombed by

---

5. "Birds Shoot Back in Latest by Hitch" *Progress-Bulletin*. April 9, 1962. p.9.

territorial birds seeking to defend their nests. Most of us run for cover, instinctively, to avoid getting pecked. Perhaps this shows that we are a bit too skittish. After all, most of us have escaped unscathed, if a little rattled.

But owls, for some strange reason, have managed to salvage a different reputation among most modern human communities. Owls are wise. Owls are cute. Owls are cuddly. Owl was Winnie the Pooh's teacher, mentor, and friend! Far from considering owls as an enemy or a fearful predator, we still take owls to be, by and large, something like the teddy bears of the sky.

Yet owls, in the mythologies of other cultures, signify something quite sinister. In India, the eagle owl is known by some of the following monikers: the bird of evil omen, the death owl, the ghost owl, and, most ominous of all, the devil bird. The idea that owls are themselves ghosts is a common theme among various cultures worldwide (in Indonesia they are called *burung hantu*: "ghost birds"). And the view that owls are harbingers of death is common in many cultures around the globe. Yet these views are foreign to most modern Western folk, who continue to see the owl as a soft and lovable creature—wise, watchful, and entirely harmless.

So despite the well-known phenomenon of aggressive bird attacks on humans, one of the biggest hurdles for the owl theory to overcome is that it continues to seem insane to most people. How could an adorable, fluffy owl attack, let alone kill, a fully grown woman? It is not in their nature! They are harmless! Indeed, the following reaction is extremely common: Why stop at owls? Why not a werewolf? Or little green men?

Well, there is a pretty big difference. We all know that owls exist, but few of us believe in werewolves or little green men. But the people who bring up werewolves are just trying to point out, with a little bit of hyperbole, that the probability of a fatal owl attack is close to zero. Owls are as likely to have killed Kathleen, they think, as a bogeyman.

But are the probabilities as bad as all that? Is a fatal owl attack really so unbelievable?

HUNTING BEHAVIOR

Owls are powerful and effective hunters, and they are equally aggressive in defending their territory. The two largest and most ferocious owl species common to North Carolina are the barred owl and the great horned owl (the latter is sometimes called the "tiger owl" for its orange stripes, its ferocity, and its monstrous claws). Both species are light and agile, as most birds tend to be, with the former coming in at just under a kilogram (around two pounds) while the latter tops the scales at 1.5 kilograms (2.8 pounds). The barred owl has a wingspan of around 100 centimeters (40 inches), while the great horned owl's wings can stretch out to nearly 1.5 meters (nearly five feet). When extended, the toes of the great horned owl's foot spans—from digit to digit—a full 20 centimeters (8 inches).

Also common in North Carolina is the Eastern screech owl, a much smaller species (around 150 grams or 6 ounces), which despite its size, is highly aggressive towards humans. This particular species belies the idea that because owls are small and undeniably cute, they are therefore harmless. Some victims of these tiny feathered creatures have lost eyes or required stitches. It is unlikely, however, given its tiny stature, that an Eastern screech owl could be responsible for the kind of carnage that Kathleen endured. So let's focus on the two larger species: the barred and great horned owls.

To make clear just how powerful these birds of prey can be, compare them to some domestic dogs. Pit bulls are infamously dangerous and temperamental animals. The reason for their notoriety has to do primarily with their jaws, which exert a bite force of around 250 pounds per square inch. It is estimated that more than 280 people were killed by domestic pit bull attacks between 2005 and 2017 in the United States.[6] Once locked in its jaws, a human being has little chance to escape. But compare a pit bull's bite with the grip force of the talons of the larger owls, and the pit bull's abilities pale.

The great horned owl's talons have a grip force of anywhere between 400 and 500 pounds per square inch (compare this with the grip force of your own clenched fist, and the great horned owl's clasped foot is anywhere from six to ten times more powerful). The smaller barred owl has a grip force about equally as powerful as the pit bull's bite. Moreover, owls' talons lock onto their prey, as all owl species have what is called an "avian digital tendon locking device." In layman's terms, this is like a ratchet attached to each toe. So, when the toes are constricted, they are, in a sense, ratcheted shut. The ratchet within each toe needs to be deliberately let loose before the grasp can be relaxed. With adaptive features like this, it's clear what fearsome predators they make. Owls may not weigh much, but they pack a mighty punch.

Both the barred and great horned owls are largely nocturnal, hunting mostly at night. However, they are not exclusively nocturnal. The eye of the owl is adapted to hunting in very dark conditions. With extremely poor color perception, owls view the world almost entirely in black and white. But their night vision dwarfs our own. In the black of night, an owl's eyes can process anywhere from ten to one hundred times more light than our own eyes can in the same conditions. Despite the common myth that owls are blinded by the light in daylight conditions, that is not the

---

6. "U.S. Dog Bite Fatalities: Breeds of Dogs Involved, Age Groups and Other Factors Over a 13-Year Period (2005 to 2017)" DogsBite. org. May 2018. https://www.dogsbite.org/reports/13-years-us-dog-bite-fatalities-2005-2017-dogsbite.pdf

case. Just like us, an owl's pupil constricts and it squints in bright light conditions to limit the amount of light hitting the retina. They are as capable of hunting during daylight as they are at night. In fact, quite a few attacks on humans have occurred during the day.

Unlike other birds, owls have highly specialized feathers with soft, comb-like serrated structures along their edges. The sound of their wings is muffled by the soft edges of the feathers, allowing them to swoop upon their unsuspecting victims in virtual silence. Their flight is almost entirely without sound. Few humans attacked by these birds ever heard any warning. This unique feature of their feathers comes at a cost, however. Unlike the feathers of other birds, owl feathers have a relatively fluffy texture, and so they largely lack the preening oil that keeps the feathers waterproof. For this reason, you won't often find owls hunting in the rain.

When hunting in their usual habitats, the primary food sources of the two larger owl species include rodents such as rats, mice, and rabbits, as well as smaller birds. They will also launch attacks opportunistically on other wild animals. Porcupines, raccoons, bats, foxes, and even skunks often find themselves on the menu (as you might guess, owls have a very poor sense of smell). Larger animals still—such as sheep, horses, and deer—have also been targeted.

Naturally, as owls find their territories increasingly swallowed up by the expansion of human settlements, domestic animals have come to be a new focus of their attacks. This has been particularly the case with regard to stock animals on farms and inside barns and coops, such as chickens and turkeys. But worryingly for pet owners, domestic cats and dogs have been increasingly targeted.

Despite the many well-documented cases of owls attacking domestic animals, there remained (until recently) a strange skepticism, even within the zoological community, that owls engage in this behavior. An interesting example of this skepticism can be found when, in 1974, a series of cat mutilations occurred on the outskirts of Los Angeles. A couple of years following the first reports of this phenomenon, Reverend Jack Blankenship witnessed an owl attacking a cat in the very same part of the city. The cat, in this case, managed to escape from the owl's talons. But the very next morning, a cat's mutilated body was found beneath the tree where the same owl had been perching. Yet when interviewed by the *Sacramento Bee* about what was happening to cats in the area, the director of the Los Angeles Zoo, Warren Thomas, was quoted as saying: "The likelihood of an owl going after a cat is basically nil."

That was nearly fifty years ago. Nowadays, however, it is well-accepted that owls will prey on cats and dogs alike. In 2016, the US Department of Agriculture released a report in which the reader was warned: "Owls are highly opportunistic predators. Small dogs, cats, kittens, and caged pet birds left outside and unattended occasionally are at risk of attack and predation. The frequency and severity of such incidents may increase during winter when food is scarce."[7]

As for domestic dogs, smaller breeds make easier targets. But even large breeds have succumbed to owl attacks. For example, in Nebraska, in 1891, a Gordon setter was reportedly killed after a great horned owl swooped down and pierced its neck with its hooked talons.[8] The owl was shot by a rancher in the midst of the attack, but not before it managed to kill the dog. This particular breed of dog typically weighs around 30 kilograms (66 pounds), and stands around 66 centimeters (26 inches) tall. Owls are certainly capable of downing prey far larger than themselves.

---

7. Washburn, B. 2016 "Hawks and Owls" Wildlife Damage Management Technical Series 6, 17. https://digitalcommons.unl.edu/cgi/viewcontent.cgi?article=1005&context=nwrcwdmts
8. "An Owl Kills a Dog." *Sidney Daily News*. January 19, 1891. p.4.

More recently, it is easy to find examples of smaller breeds being killed by predatory owl attacks. In 1993, on the evening of New Year's Day, Dorothy Verthein, a resident of La Crosse, Wisconsin, opened her front door to let in her pet Pomeranian. She was bewildered when the door flung open and knocked over a large bloodied owl on the front step, which flew back up to its perch in the pine trees. Her Pomeranian was dead in the garden, bleeding from the neck. Just two years later, in January 1995, Bandit (a poodle-Pekingese cross weighing 11 kilograms [25 pounds]) was carried off by a great horned owl in Greenville, Maine. His body was dropped by the owl and retrieved by his owner. But Bandit had already been killed during the attack. Dogs, particularly smaller breeds, make easy pickings.

Whether the attacks are territorial or part of broader hunting behavior is unclear. In any case, both territorial and predatory attacks follow a similar pattern. Territorial nesting behavior begins for the barred owl in late autumn (usually around November) each year, while the great horned owl begins to nest shortly after. This typically sees a lone male occupying a nesting site and beginning courtship displays to entice nearby females. Once a pair has nested, eggs are incubated for approximately one month before hatching. The parents' hunting behaviors increase after this time in order to feed the fledgling owlets. If nesting often begins around November, then the first hatches in North Carolina would usually occur in December, the very month that Kathleen was killed. The overwhelming majority of owl attacks on humans occur across late autumn and early winter. So the date of Kathleen's death is perhaps no surprise.

"I never heard a thing, not a sound, because they don't make any noise. I didn't know until I was banged in the head." *CBC*, March 10, 2021
    Carly Blake, Labrador
    Owl: great horned owl

"It felt like getting hit with a board, like someone was trying to knock me out. There was no warning; it came out of nowhere. I screamed and looked back, seeing the legs of a large bird while I cowered and crossed the road. Then the owl swooped in again, going for my ponytail." *Skagit Valley Herald,* September 29, 2020
    Brigan Coard, South Carolina
    Owl: barred owl

"It felt like someone hit me with two fists. When they hit you, it's like a rocket … It's a classic attack, they come at you from behind. It locked its talons in the back of my skull then the front talons came over and latched onto the top of my skull." *Skagit Valley Herald*, September 29, 2020
    Greg Cooper, South Carolina
    Owl: barred owl

"It was like a huge electric shock ran through my body, but also like I got hit in the head by a two-by-four all at the same time … Or maybe a strike of lightning." *USA Today*, January 19, 2015
    Ron Jaecks, Oregon
    Owl: great horned owl

"He dug his claws in, knocked me four or five feet … The whole right side of my face went numb from the impact. My nose started to bleed.

It was the hardest I've ever been hit in the head."
Bennington Banner, December 17, 1981
Jeff Torrey, Maine
Owl: great horned owl

Descriptions like the ones above are typical of owl attacks in North America. The owl swoops upon its unsuspecting victim from behind, usually knocking them to the ground with the attack. Comparisons are made to being struck from behind by a baseball bat or wooden board. The impact is incredible. Notably, the first four attacks described by the victims above are from within the last couple of years or so. And also notably, the attacks were carried out by the two larger species of owl common to North Carolina.

In their attacks, owls usually mount a swift initial offensive blow to the head from behind, followed by further strikes aimed at the eyes and neck. Swooping in silence towards their prey's head, they extend their legs, bringing both feet together, opening the toes wide, to collect their victims like the clamp of jaws. For the most part, the injuries inflicted on humans fall on the scalp, neck, face, and hands (the latter are typically defensive injuries).

Owl attacks, although seemingly rare, occur every single year in North America. Most victims escape with only minor injuries, such as puncture wounds to the scalp or abrasions to the face. But many require medical care. Carly Blake, quoted above, was attacked by a great horned owl. Her wound required a suture. In 1982, a series of owl attacks in Scranton, Pennsylvania, ended with one woman requiring eight stitches to close a three and a half-inch gash in her head.[9]

Many attacks can be mended with a few stitches or a dressing. But others have been less lucky. Professional wildlife photographer Mike Darter lost an eye in 1999

9. "6 Owls Killed in Clark's Summit after Attacking Residents." *Times-Tribune*. June 7, 1982. p.3.

while on a hunting trip when an owl swooped on his head. More recently, in 2018, twelve-year-old Beckett Shanahan suffered a severe concussion and serious lacerations to his face and head after an encounter with a hostile owl while sledding alone near Medford, Massachusetts.[10] He was delirious after the attack, believing that the bird had carried off both his mother and sister. He spent four days in the hospital and required morphine. He has since fully recovered, with one hell of a story to tell.

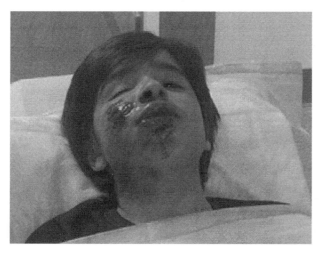

Beckett Shanahan's injuries. Credit Michael Shanahan.

These are just some recent examples of owl attacks in North America. If we look further back through history, we find a veritable mountain of cases. In 1962, Airman Melvin Hill was airlifted to the hospital after a vicious attack from a great horned owl in Quebec.

"I didn't know what hit me," he said. "All of a sudden, I was tangled up with a maze of feathered wings and talons." While he was knocked down, the owl plunged its talons into his throat, missing his jugular vein by two inches. He suffered numerous injuries to his face and head,

---

10. *Boston Globe*. April 1, 2018. p.A48-49.

which required medical care. He spent nearly a week in the hospital.[11]

In Alberta, 1932, thirty-five-year-old Albert Hughes lost an eye to an owl's talons. He was hospitalized for his injuries.[12] In Edmonton, 1946, Bill Currie was temporarily blinded and later hospitalized after an encounter with a great horned owl, which left four deep gashes on his scalp.[13] In Washington, 1926, Henry Rushmier was disfigured for life after a great horned owl attached itself to his face, refusing to release its hold even after being killed by Rushmier's brother.[14]

In 1965, Ida Cronk, a Nebraska native, was hospitalized after what must have been a particularly traumatic attack. At dusk, she heard a thump against her front door. Opening it to investigate, she found an owl acting dazed and flopping about. Not knowing what to do, she brought a broom to the door and attempted to shoo the owl away. The owl, now aggravated, latched onto her leg with so much force that she could not remove it. The owl's claws tore through her leg, puncturing an artery and causing severe blood loss. She grabbed the bird around the throat and managed to choke it to death. She was rushed to the hospital.[15]

The most common serious injuries affect the eyes, which are often lost. In 1969, sixteen-year-old Kathryn de Riever suffered injuries to the cornea and lens of her right eye when a great horned owl lunged at her in her San Diego

---

11. "Ottawa Airman Target of Vicious Owl Attack." *Ottawa Citizen.* November 10, 1962. p.10.

12. "Owl 'Hypnotizes' Man; Claws Out One of Eyes." *The Republican Leader.* May 5, 1932. p.8.

13. "Northerner Nearly Loses Eye in Attack by Vicious Owl." *Edmonton Journal.* January 29, 1946. p.1.

14. "Great Horned Owl Buries Claws in Man's Face; Vicious Bird Released Hold Only When Killed." *Spokane Chronicle.* April 8, 1926. p.5.

15. "Attacked by Owl." *Scotia Register.* February 4, 1965. p.7.

driveway. The same owl had attacked three other members of her family in a single evening.[16] In 1907, Mrs. George Burke lost her left eye (and possibly her right as well) after a barn owl attack in York, Pennsylvania.[17] On February 13, 1928, a four-year-old girl most likely lost both eyes after an attack by a large owl in Quebec.[18] Another youngster to have his eyes attacked was six-year-old Tyler Tharp from Iowa. In 1989, he was attacked while cycling in a driveway. He underwent hours of surgery to salvage the sight in his left eye after the great horned owl's attack. The surgery was unsuccessful. The eye was lost.[19]

The attacks described here, although more brutal than most, are fairly typical of owl attacks in North America. Notably, the majority of attacks occur between October and March. The majority of injuries are focused on the back of the head and around the neck. Lost eyes and deep lacerations to the scalp are the most common serious injuries. Concussions and whiplash are also common. And the injuries are such that they often require immediate medical attention.

Moreover, owl attacks often continue over a long period of time, despite the actions of humans to defend themselves. Owls will often make multiple swoops at their victims even if they find their "prey" behaving aggressively in return. Being hit or kicked or battered only seems to further rile the frenzied birds. Many attacks have been noted to continue for half an hour or longer, long after the bird itself has sustained injuries.

---

16. "Girl Attacked by Horned Owl." *Albuquerque Tribune.* July 3, 1969. p.26.

17. "Blinded by an Owl". *The News.* August 1, 1907. p.3.

18. "Child, Attacked by Owl, May Lose Both Eyes." *San Francisco Examiner*. February 14, 1928. p.4.

19. "Boy Home, Playing, Mad at Owl." *The Gazette.* May 12, 1989. p.1.

Despite their apparent fragility, the birds are by no means easy to kill. For example, Jeff Torrey, attacked in 1981 by a great horned owl, managed to dislodge the bird from his head before grabbing both legs and whacking the creature's head more than a dozen times against a wooden fence. The owl went limp, apparently deceased. Torrey flung the owl's body to the ground and ran inside to his wife. From the window, a minute or so later, the couple witnessed the owl regain consciousness, hop up to its feet, and casually flee the scene. Other accounts include birds with bullet wounds persisting in their onslaughts, even while the life is leaving their bodies.

Other factors can play a role. Owls seem particularly willing to attack when their human prey is:

1. Fast-moving (e.g., on a bike, jogging, or skiing);
2. Wearing a hat/helmet or having long hair (particularly ponytails);
3. Encroaching on the territory around the nest site;
4. In the company of dogs or other domestic animals;
5. Small statured (e.g., a woman or child);
6. Mimicking the owls' warning hoots (this is taken by the owl as provocation).

There are a couple of other surprising points to make about owl attacks on humans. Firstly, owls are willing to venture inside barns, houses, and both stationary and moving cars to pounce upon their victims. They do not seem to be averse to entering confined spaces. There are several historical reports of drivers losing control of their vehicles during attacks in which owls have flown through open windows to reach their victims. And some attacks have even been noted to have occurred exclusively indoors when owls have flown through open windows into bedrooms or public buildings to attack their victims.

Secondly, among the numerous stories that can be found in the newspaper archives, many of the attacks consist of multiple owls attacking a single victim. Most often among the larger species, two owls (presumably the male and female of the nest) will team up in their attack. But attacks have been known to happen in much larger groups, with as many as eight owls taking part in a single attack. These "parliament" attacks are more prevalent among the smaller breeds, such as the common barn owl and Eastern screech owl.

When the victims sustain serious injuries, they often require hospitalization. They often come away with permanent injuries. They often live with new respect for and fear of the mighty birds. Yet despite all this, they usually live out the rest of their lives. They usually aren't wounded in a life-threatening way or killed during the attack. Usually, but not always.

THE FIRST SERIOUS ATTACK

One of the more horrifying accounts comes from Zanesville, Ohio. The details are sketchy and possibly unreliable, as the attack occurred in 1905, during an era of lesser journalistic standards. But newspaper reports from the day indicate that a man named Harvey Fredericks—a young employee with a touring wild animal sideshow—was severely maimed by a snowy owl as he removed it from its enclosure after it had been incarcerated for weeks. The snowy owl is, on average, a slightly larger bird than the great horned owl, having a wingspan of anywhere between three and five feet. There is little doubt that such a bird could inflict significant harm on a human being.

In the course of the owl's attack, it tore an artery in Fredericks' arm, as though a knife had sliced right through.

His chest was also mauled by the owl's talons, exposing the rib bones beneath. These sorts of injuries may sound unbelievable, but can be found in more recent cases. So there is some reason to think that the wounds may have been as severe as reported.

Although there are no reports of Fredericks' death from the time, a doctor who treated the man expressed pessimism about his survival. The shock of the encounter combined with severe blood loss was so severe as to jeopardize his life. The prognosis was poor: if he would not die from his wounds, he would die from blood poisoning shortly after. This was, for all we can tell, an extremely serious attack on a human being. There is, unfortunately, no further information to be found about this case.[20]

THE SECOND SERIOUS ATTACK

There has been another attack that was nearly fatal.

West Alexander, Pennsylvania, is a small farming community at the border with West Virginia. At present, the population consists of only a few hundred people. But it once was, before the realignment of state roads in the 1920s, a growing rural settlement. As many as twenty-five stagecoaches a day once stopped there on the line between the two states. It has since fallen by the wayside.

Let's visit the community during its heyday. The time was June 1911. The weather was fine and clear. It was broad daylight when Phillip Cruzen, a wealthy, older farmer, strolled through his front yard. It was a day like any other. As he walked along his path, a sudden flash of feathers covered him. All at once, his face and scalp were punctured by the talons of a large barred owl. Bloodied and in disbelief, he was knocked to the ground. Believing that the bird must have collided with his head by accident, the old man

---

20. "Owl Badly Maims a Man." *Lawrence Daily Journal.* June 21, 1905. p.2.

slowly climbed back to his feet to assess his injuries. As he regained some composure, the bird launched its second attack. It swooped down again, plunging its talons into his neck. From this grotesque perch, it repeatedly pecked with its sharp beak at his face and eyes.

Lying on the grass of his front lawn, he was now unable to see. The blood that poured from the splits in his scalp covered his face and eyes. Although he was effectively blind, he felt the bird's claws still clutching his shoulder and continuing its attack. He attempted to defend himself, hopelessly grabbing at the owl, as it delivered several sharp jabs to his right eye. The eyeball burst. Over the course of an hour or longer, during which Cruzen feebly attempted to fight back, the owl mauled his head and body, drawing an incredible amount of blood. He fell unconscious. The owl hissed and attacked regardless, clawing Cruzen's motionless body and biting his face as he lay bleeding.

He was discovered by a neighbor hours later, prone and unresponsive in the yard with the aggressive owl still there, beating its wings and screeching in a fearful display. The neighbor returned with a rifle, shot the bird, and Cruzen, covered in blood, was moved inside his house. Concussed, in shock, and terribly wounded, he received medical attention from a visiting doctor over the days that followed and the doctor was skeptical that he would recover from his injuries. The old man did recover, dying in 1930 at the age of seventy-seven.

After the attack, the barred owl responsible was measured. When its wings were stretched out, it had a wingspan of nearly three feet (one meter). This was no monster owl. As a matter of fact, this is a relatively small wingspan for an adult barred owl. Indeed, it may even have been a juvenile.[21]

---

21. "Fierce Battle with Owl in Pennsylvania." *Norwich Bulletin*. June 30, 1911. p.1.

A Fatal Attack

If Kathleen Peterson was killed in the midst of an owl attack, she was not the only recorded case. It may come as some surprise, but yes, owls do kill.

It was early August 1985. On the side of a highway, just outside Los Banos, California, several policemen walked around Robert Brian Schmidt's mutilated corpse. He wore a torn knit shirt and blue pants. He was thirty-five years old and nearly six and a half feet tall. This was a strong man—a regular trucker—with bare gums on his top palate; his false teeth were stashed away in a trouser pocket. When discovered, his face was found to be plastered with grass and straw and gravel. Small twigs stuck out from his moustache. Blood was smeared across his mouth and his nose. Red drips flowed down his temples, and red ants crawled all over his skin. His forehead, in particular, was deeply gashed. The grisly discovery had been made by a fellow trucker nearly twelve hours after his death. The scene was very unusual. The county coroner would need to be brought in. At first glance, this all looked suspiciously like a homicide.

Schmidt's big rig was found some distance from the body, still idling in neutral on the side of Interstate 5. The motor was purring over quietly while the driver lay dead a couple of hundred yards away. The investigators were utterly bewildered. Schmidt lay there with his chest and arms scored with deep cuts. He had lost a lot of blood. His ankle was twisted inwards, stuck fast in position by rigor mortis. There was no other evidence of foul play. For all that the police could tell, the trucker had parked, exited the vehicle, walked along the side of the dark road, and possibly fallen victim to a cowardly hit and run (one which just happened to leave very unusual injuries).[22]

---

22. "Trucker Found Dead on I-5, Apparently Victim of Hit-and-run." *Fresno Bee*. August 10, 1985. p.12.

Schmidt had been traveling from Los Angeles to his native San Jose. He was just over halfway along his journey when he had pulled over in the middle of the night. Why had he done this? He had apparently exited the vehicle, expecting to return to it shortly. He must have believed that he would be getting back into his truck within a few minutes to continue the drive back to San Jose. But, of course, he never did. Something stopped this from happening. So why did he leave his vehicle, and what had caused his death?

The evidence soon pointed away from the preliminary hit-and-run scenario. Schmidt's injuries were entirely external, and not a single bone in his body was fractured or broken. His blood work disclosed no illicit drugs or overdose. The best hypothesis the police could form was that this was an animal attack. The numerous linear scratches and slices that covered his neck, face, chest, and arms just weren't consistent with any other cause. At the autopsy, the medical officers removed his shirt to find a deep Y-shaped wound that cut down to the ribcage. His chest was riddled with cuts. His clothes were ripped and a series of what the coroner described as "chicken scratches" covered the length of his body. His elbows were bloody and his forearms bore classic defensive injuries. And strangely, the hood of his truck had been discovered with a prominent dent in the hood.

Given the timing of Schmidt's death, the police speculated that he had collided with an owl on the road.[23] He must have had a hell of a shock, and he may have even felt a bit guilty. You see, according to his family, Schmidt was a serious animal lover. They guessed that he had probably pulled over to check on the injured creature. As he approached the animal—perhaps lifting it up into his arms to bring it to some sort of shelter—the frightened bird

23. "Trucker May have been Attacked by Owl." *Fresno Bee.* August 17, 1985. p.11.

panicked. It plunged its talons into his chest, ripping through the muscle. Presumably, Schmidt was unable to tear the bird away before falling unconscious or into a state of shock. He would then die from his injuries.

Although this was the theory police were working with, it seems difficult to swallow. How, after all, did an owl survive a collision with a truck? Surely, an owl would not survive the impact of a big rig traveling at highway speed. Right? As a matter of fact, it is not that surprising at all. This sort of thing occurs surprisingly frequently. There are a couple of recent events that can be cited.

Just after Christmas 2016, a Canadian man, Adam Marton, was speeding in his Chevy Silverado (an SUV weighing two tons) at one hundred and twenty-five kilometers per hour (approximately seventy-seven miles per hour) on a highway in Saskatchewan. He admitted that he was traveling well over the speed limit. As his vehicle trundled forward, he collided with a great horned owl. "This bird flew right out of the ditch right into my grille,"[24] Marton said. He assumed he had killed the bird. *Poor bastard*, Marton thought as he continued forward.

A few hundred yards down the road, he decided to pull over to inspect the damage to his truck. But there was no damage to see. Instead, two large, feathered wings covered the front of the vehicle. The bird had gotten stuck inside the grille.

Marton brought his hands to the vehicle and heaved at the wings, eventually dislodging the creature.

> I put it on the ground and noticed it was still breathing and then it just followed me with its eyes … It turned its head and everywhere I went,

---

24. "'Owl roadkill season': Another Great Horned Owl Hits Truck, Survives." CBC, December 27, 2016. https://www.cbc.ca/news/canada/edmonton/owl-roadkill-season-another-great-horned-owl-hits-truck-survives-1.3912814

it looked ... I asked it if it wanted to come in the truck, come in the box. Then it kind of looked at me, shook itself off, hopped into the ditch and then took off.[25]

The situation is almost impossible to believe: an owl, struck by a two-ton truck traveling at incredible speed simply got up and flew away, seemingly unharmed. This may sound like a miracle. But it isn't a miracle at all.

In fact, less than a week before Marton's encounter in Saskatchewan, an owl had been struck on a highway in a very similar style by a car in the neighboring Canadian state of Alberta. This time, the driver, Jennifer Thomas, did not pull over to inspect her car, despite having hit the bird while traveling at the speed limit. She assumed the bird had been run over. *Poor bastard*, she thought.

The bird had not been run over at all. It was, once again, lodged inside the grille. Thomas kept on driving, oblivious that she had acquired a new passenger. The bird survived for several hours wedged in the grille before it was discovered, perfectly alive and unharmed. It seemed miraculous, but again, it wasn't. Owls are remarkably hardy animals. And this one, a great horned owl, was released back into the wild the very same night it was pummeled by a car on a highway.[26]

Given these examples, it is far from surprising that Robert Schmidt's big rig may have hit an owl that survived without injury. Perhaps it got wedged in the grille, or perhaps it simply bounced off the bumper. Either way, the

25. "'Owl roadkill season': Another Great Horned Owl Hits Truck, Survives." CBC, December 27, 2016. https://www.cbc.ca/news/canada/edmonton/owl-roadkill-season-another-great-horned-owl-hits-truck-survives-1.3912814.

26. "'Fairy Tale Ending': Owl Saved After High Speed Collision with Truck." CBC. December 21, 2016. https://www.cbc.ca/news/canada/edmonton/fairy-tale-ending-owl-saved-after-high-speed-collision-with-truck-1.3907189

best theory to account for Schmidt's death was that he found an owl after some accident and tried to retrieve it. The owl, not realizing it was in the arms of a good Samaritan, mauled and killed Schmidt.

The trouble with all this was that no one would ever believe that an owl killed Robert Brian Schmidt. It was the only plausible theory the police had to work with. But how could they work with such a theory? It was patently ridiculous. Even an owl that hadn't been hit by a truck couldn't kill a human. And certainly, no injured owl could kill a strong and healthy thirty-five-year-old man (especially not a man of such stature, standing nearly six and a half feet tall!). Merced County authorities were bewildered about what had happened. And they were far from equipped to judge the probability of a fatal owl attack. With this doubt in mind, the county coroner, Joe Sabo, reached out to ornithologists at the nearby Fresno Zoo. He inquired whether a fatal owl attack on a fully grown man was a possibility. The zoo laughed off the theory. Within a week, the coroner concluded that although an owl attack had clearly precipitated Schmidt's death, it was not what had finished him off.

Still, Sabo was somewhat unsatisfied with this verdict. He inquired whether toxicologists could test blood serum for rattlesnake venom. Apparently, he speculated that during the owl attack, Schmidt may have also trodden on a rattlesnake. These two events together might have been able to explain his death. There were two small puncture wounds on Schmidt's thigh, just one inch apart, that were compatible with this theory. But the toxicologists could not perform the necessary test, and there was no other evidence of a snake's involvement. In any case, the punctures were perfectly compatible with the sorts of puncture wounds that could be inflicted by needle-sharp talons. And even if Schmidt had been bitten by a snake during an owl attack, it takes several hours, and usually, several days, to die from a snake bite. And the larger the individual, the less likely a fatality is to occur.

So what caused Schmidt's death? The coroner was bewildered. The best theory he could come up with went like this.

Schmidt collapsed during an owl attack. He fell unconscious, perhaps from fear or confusion. At thirty-five years old, and with no other preexisting conditions, the investigators doubted an owl could have killed the man. Despite the extent of his injuries, the Fresno Zoo's ornithologists were adamant that owls don't kill. But their verdict was based mainly on the fact that there was nothing poisonous about an owl's scratches. They did not consider whether an owl was capable of mauling a person to death. The coroner was forced to conclude that Schmidt died, not from an owl attack (even though one had occurred), but from unknown causes. Ultimately, the media were told that the cause of Schmidt's death was shock.

It may pay to explain what it means to die from shock. Most people equate shock with a state of fear or panic. So, you might think that the claim is that Schmidt was quite literally scared to death. Indeed, perhaps he was. But in the medical sense, *shock* is a more specific term. Shock is defined as a sudden lack of blood flow to the organs and brain.

In the case of Robert Schmidt, a healthy thirty-five-year-old man, the assertion that he died from shock tells us next to nothing about the immediate cause of his death. The coroner's conclusion is a bit like a shrug of the shoulders. The man just, well, *died.* He was attacked by an owl, he was wounded, and then, he died. In one sense, he was killed by an owl, but in another, less informative sense, he died from a sudden lack of blood flow to the brain.

If you want a more detailed explanation, it most probably goes like this: Robert Schmidt was attacked by an owl on a California roadside in 1985. He had collided with the owl a few minutes previous and was hoping to bring it to some kind of shelter. The mauling that followed was lengthy and brutal, and led to a sudden lack of blood flow to the brain, which caused his death. The attack was sufficient to cause Schmidt's death.

Or, more succinctly, an owl killed Robert Schmidt.

CHAPTER SIX: INJURIES

THE AUTOPSY

"Mushrooms," said North Carolina's Assistant Chief Medical Examiner Deborah Radisch. "They look like canned ones." She poked about for a few more seconds, but as her hand reached into Kathleen's stomach, she retrieved little else that was identifiable.

Radisch had incised a T-shaped cut across Kathleen's chest. The rib cage had been cracked open and the internal organs were exposed to view. Checking internally, Radisch found no sign of damage or injury. The liver was intact. The kidneys were sound. The bowels were in good shape. Her bladder, it should be noted, was virtually empty. Kathleen was a fit and healthy forty-eight-year-old woman. Nothing was diseased. Nothing was ruptured or bruised. If Michael had murdered her in a mad rage, he had landed no blows to the abdomen or waist. No forceful punches or kicks had been inflicted. No bones were broken.

Radisch prodded at the mushrooms, now in a small dish. "Maybe they were in some sort of stew... They've been partially digested," she said. Kathleen had eaten within the last six hours prior to her death. One of the last emails Kathleen had sent to her sister contained a recipe for mushroom soufflé. Had this been her final meal?

"The bladder is empty: Urination immediately prior to death." This was an important observation that would explain the dilution of the bloodstains around the crotch of Kathleen's sweatpants and on Michael's shorts.

As far as Radisch could tell, this must have been an ordinary night for Kathleen. Her toxicology examination had shown that she'd had a couple of glasses of wine. She'd taken a small dose of Valium, probably shortly before bedtime. She had eaten dinner. Wearing only a sweatshirt and sweatpants, it is reasonable to assume that Kathleen had already changed into her casual, pre-bed attire. She had no evidence of long-term trauma or physical abuse on her body. And so it must have been a pretty normal night, Radisch supposed. That is, right up until the moment Michael killed her.

The conclusion of her autopsy report read as follows:

> In my opinion, the cause of death in this case was due to severe concussive injury of the brain caused by multiple blunt force impacts of the head. Blood loss from the deep scalp lacerations may have also played a role in her death. The number, severity, locations, and orientation of these injuries are inconsistent with a fall down stairs; instead, they are indicative of multiple impacts received as a result of beating.

These were the words the jury would read. And it is difficult to underestimate how forceful they must have been. A medical professional, going beyond the clinical diagnosis of the cause of Kathleen's death, went so far as to point the finger directly at Michael. Not just blood loss, not just concussion, not just blunt force trauma, but a beating was the cause of death.

We now know, from communications between the State's investigators and Radisch, that she was dissuaded from emphasizing the role that blood loss played in the death of Kathleen. The role of "concussion" was emphasized at the behest of the authorities. But most probably, Kathleen had actually bled to death.

THE SCALP

A member of the medical examiner's office, Kenneth Snell, arrived at the Peterson house around daybreak on December 9. He was granted entry by an officer, who noted his name in a register. The police had been operating without oversight on the scene for hours. They had contained the house, barred entry to the crucial areas, and they were coming up with ideas about homicidal beatings. But they were no experts in forensic pathology. No jury would accept the investigators' testimony without the additional say-so of a trained expert.

The forensic team was waiting to receive a legally sound opinion on the cause of death. And now, their man had arrived. Upon entering the mansion, Snell suited up in booties and gloves and went to assess the state of the body. He, like everyone else, was stunned at the sight of so much blood around the body. "Jesus," he whispered to himself as he looked up and down at the walls awash with red. He approached the corpse. Kathleen's head now lay directly on the bottom step. The towels Michael had used to cradle her head were gone. Someone had already removed and disposed of them. When? And more importantly, why? They were never taken into evidence.

Lifting Kathleen's head, Snell was able to see a four-inch-long laceration at the back of Kathleen's skull. It was a severe injury.

"What do you think?" lead forensic technician Dan George asked.

"It's a very deep cut," Snell said. "Certainly possible from a fall, but we'll need to do the autopsy to really know for sure." He placed Kathleen's head gently back in position, taking care not to disturb the deeply lacerated scalp and hair.

Shortly after, Snell and another forensic technician, Eric Campen, lifted Kathleen's body into a black bag. They hammocked Kathleen down the hallway a few feet towards an area with better lighting. Placing her body down gently, Snell now had a better view. As he moved her head from side to side, he found still more lacerations on her head. At least four, so far as he could tell. But he could not determine what these wounds really meant without a more careful analysis. Snell noticed that when the body was first moved into the body bag, the blood on Kathleen's clothes dripped down onto the floor, proving that much of the blood was still wet. This fact was also noted by Campen. Drops of blood fell from the body along the length of the hall. The blood was not dry, despite the earlier assumptions made by paramedics. It had merely looked dry.

The zip was pulled up over her face and this morbid cargo was taken away by mortuary services at 8:30 a.m. She was transported to the Office of the Chief Medical Examiner where the autopsy would take place.

"I mean, if it's not from a fall down the stairs, it's from a beating with some kind of thin, rod-like object," Snell told detectives.

The detectives listened with enthusiasm. "A rod-like object" they echoed, nodding. Now they had something to look for.

At its new location, Kathleen's body was lifted onto the stainless-steel autopsy table. She was, by now, very cold and pale. Rigor mortis stiffened her limbs. After carefully noting the external condition of Kathleen's body, Radisch held up a fistful of hair and shaved the back of Kathleen's head, exposing the deep lacerations to the scalp. Some were so deep that they had caused avulsions—the skin could be lifted as a flap.

When Dr. Radisch saw the wounds on Kathleen's scalp, she raised her head to look through a window, behind which stood the police photographer, Angie Powell. Powell had been watching the proceedings and was waiting to take the autopsy photographs. Radisch raised her eyebrows high and mouthed "oh my gosh" to Powell. The gashes were unlike anything she had ever seen before.

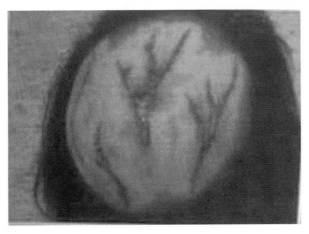

Kathleen's head lacerations, as shown in an autopsy photograph.

The wounds were certainly unlike anything a fall could inflict. The shapes of the cuts were too strange. And two of the lacerated areas struck Radisch as extremely peculiar. During the trial, both the defense and prosecution admitted that these wounds were anomalous. They were hard to explain by appeal to any available theory. They were oddly symmetrical, trident-shaped, and side by side. They were Larry's "turkey tracks."

Radisch measured each of them and noted their dimensions in her report:

> There is a tri-pronged linear laceration measuring 3" vertically, with the upper lateral prong measuring 3/4", upper medial prong 1 3/8", and lower prong 1 5/8". The greatest width of the laceration is 1".

Two and one half inches medial to the first laceration is another tri-pronged laceration with avulsion. This laceration measures 2 1/2" horizontally and 4 1/8" vertically.

The largest trident wound was four inches from top to bottom. This is coincidentally around about the same length as the extended toes of a barred owl from tip to tip. And there were two of them side by side.

To the left of the trident-shaped injuries were two linear lacerations, one of which measured four inches, while the other was closer to five inches. What is interesting about these four injuries is the similarity in their sizes, all measuring approximately four to five inches in length. This suggests that if Michael had caused the gashes to her scalp, he was strangely accurate, strangely consistent, in his delivery with each blow.

How could these trident-shaped injuries be explained? At trial, the prosecution argued that these were blunt-force impact wounds produced by the fireplace's blow poke. But how could a blow poke, long and narrow, produce two (almost identical) trident-shaped wounds, side by side? We must imagine that Michael struck Kathleen in such a way that her skin suddenly split into a trident formation. And of course, we must imagine that Michael managed to perform this magical feat twice. Or we must imagine that Michael used the hook at the tip of the blow poke to carefully carve this strange trident shape into Kathleen's scalp while she was still alive for some occult reason that we will never understand (and that he did so twice, of course, for the sake of consistency). In either case, explaining the injuries as a beating was close to impossible.

During the trial, Jim Hardin asked Radisch whether the fireplace blow poke could have caused the lacerations. He passed her the four-foot-long hollow brass tool. She twirled the hook at the tip. She turned the poker in her hands and turned over the question in her mind.

"Yes," she eventually replied, thoughtfully, as though the answer could have gone either way. "This item has weight to it, but it is not solid."

That was the State's explanation. As an improvised weapon, the blow poke was capable of working magic. It was the "rod-like" instrument Snell had advised detectives to seek out. Kathleen had been struck by something solid but light. To inflict a couplet of trident-shaped wounds that exposed the skull beneath, all that was required was a thin metal rod. So said the prosecution's stellar expert witness.

The blow poke is very unlikely to have caused Kathleen's injuries. Some have considered the idea that Michael did not use the blow poke at all. An as yet unknown weapon may have caused the trident-shaped lacerations. But it is difficult to think of any household object that could inflict the trident-shaped wounds that Kathleen had on her scalp. There may exist some sort of forked garden tools or rake-like household items that could come close, but even a forked weapon would not inflict two identical wounds that have all the forked tips meeting at the center. If any weapon was responsible for these wounds, it would seem to be dynamic or mechanical, like a hand-operated claw of some sort.

Could the defense explain the wounds? Not at all. They had nothing better to offer than the prosecution. Each of the "turkey tracks" stamped on Kathleen's scalp was the result of a single impact in each case, they argued. The moment that her head hit the molding or the metal chairlift, her skin had ruptured into the same formation—twice. Again, it was like magic. But as with most magic tricks, this one was ultimately misdirection.

If Kathleen fell and repeatedly hit her head on the edges of the steps or on the metal chairlift or on the wooden molding, then we have no reason to expect such consistency between the two head wounds. Far from exhibiting any degree of randomness, the trident wounds are extremely similar, on the same plane as one another, and side by side. Two random whacks to the head, each inflicted by varying forces of gravity, will not produce two identical trident-shaped splits to the scalp. It is magical thinking.

As Larry was the first to recognize, the best explanation for the wounds to Kathleen's head is not that she was beaten across the head. And a fall would not explain these strange splits to her scalp either. The best explanation is that a bird of prey caused the strange injuries in a single lunge: two incredibly powerful feet with needle-sharp talons grasping at Kathleen's head and etching through to the skull beneath.

The lacerations were caused by the owl's talons, which first punctured Kathleen's scalp at four points, before being brought together to a center point as the owl attempted to grasp its prey. The fact that the two wounds are nearly identical and side by side is a consequence of the fact that owls have two feet, identical in form, side by side.

As for the two linear wounds to the left of the trident-shaped lacerations, these are precisely like what is typically inflicted by owls in their initial swooping attacks on humans. Carly Blake, an owl attack victim from Newfoundland, had an almost identical slice on her head after being swooped upon by a great horned owl. It is reasonable to think, then, that these slice marks may have been the first injuries inflicted on Kathleen's head, with the trident wounds inflicted as part of a secondary attack, during which the bird became attached to Kathleen's head.

THE ELBOWS
The wounds on Kathleen's head were not the only injuries found. Indeed, the wounds on her head were not even the strangest of her injuries. Inexplicably, each of Kathleen's elbows had anomalous puncture wounds. These wounds,

like the ones on her head, were again nearly identical in each case. Three deep punctures, arranged like the points of an equilateral triangle, were found on each elbow. Radisch noted their position on her diagram of the body.

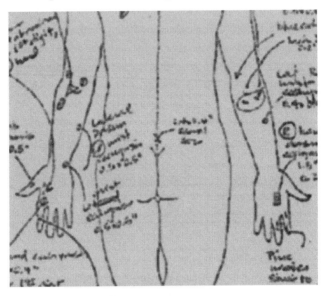

The locations of Kathleen's elbow injuries,
as described in the autopsy report.

Like the wounds to her head, it is difficult to account for the elbow injuries with either the homicide or fall theories in hand. How could Michael have inflicted such injuries? And what on the stairs could have pierced three holes into each elbow? So what caused these injuries to Kathleen's elbows?

At trial, the prosecution once again lay the blame on the blow poke. In this case, the sharp tip was thrust at Kathleen's body six times, leaving six stab wounds on her elbows. But if Michael had inflicted this series of injuries on Kathleen, we must once again view him as a strangely meticulous killer. Blow poke in hand, Michael supposedly thrust at each of Kathleen's elbows, three times apiece. He carefully arranged his stabs so the wounds would be found in two equilateral triangular formations.

This explanation is, once again, totally implausible. Michael did not murder his wife with such keen attention to detail. Michael was not a maniacal mathematician. He did not kill Kathleen in a blind rage, all the while keeping at the forefront of his mind such abstract notions as symmetry and repetition.

Michael did not inflict the puncture wounds. And neither were they inflicted during the course of a fall. The best available explanation is that a bird of prey grasped each of Kathleen's elbows at some point during an attack, with its three forward talons piercing the skin. It is very easy to imagine how the lunge of talons could inflict these injuries. And it is extremely difficult to imagine how they could be sustained during a fall or a beating.

But even if the punctures were inflicted by a bird of prey, why the elbows? And why both of them? Did the owl get behind her back and spread its legs, grabbing both elbows in an attempt to hold down her arms? That's obviously ridiculous conjecture. After all, owls typically bring their feet together when they lunge at their prey; they do not spread their feet apart. So even the location of these puncture marks seems difficult to explain by pointing at a bird of prey.

But as a matter of fact, the elbow injuries are naturally explained as defensive injuries, incurred most probably when Kathleen was covering her head with both arms. She was most likely facing the owl when, at some point, it jumped at her head. She protected her face with both hands placed on top of her head. In so doing, she presented both elbows, side by side, to the forward lunge of the owl's talons. Covering her face with her forearms, her elbows bore the brunt of a frontal attack, an attack so typical of all owl species—one aimed directly at the eyes.

Illustration of Kathleen's defensive stance.

It is an elegant explanation that can account for all six injuries with one single blow. And this explanation is clearly more sensible than anything the homicide or fall theories could provide us with. Is it realistic that Michael would land six individual stab wounds on each of Kathleen's elbows? Is it reasonable to believe that a fall could inflict this damage? Or is it more likely that a bird of prey landed a single blow to a cowering Kathleen? If a raptor caused the injuries, it was just one blow—one lunge—an entirely predictable result of Kathleen defending herself from an owl attack.

THE THROAT

One of the most incriminating injuries on Kathleen's body was found inside her throat. Her left thyroid cartilage was fractured with a small associated hemorrhage. This posed a serious problem for the defense. It is an injury that is highly suggestive of strangulation. It was a disturbing discovery that was extremely difficult to explain without supposing that somebody had strangled Kathleen. And if somebody strangled Kathleen, then Michael was the obvious culprit. Many proponents of the homicide theory point to the fractured cartilage as conclusive evidence of a beating. Radisch herself, while giving her testimony at trial, argued that the fracture was clear evidence of strangulation.

And Radisch was right. A fractured thyroid cartilage is highly correlated with strangulation. However, it is not unique to strangulation. As a matter of fact, thyroid fractures have been documented as occurring from all kinds of minor trauma to the neck, including whiplash, sneezing, and even from simply swallowing. So although the injury is suggestive of strangulation, it is not the only possible cause. Even if extremely improbable, this injury could, in principle, be explained by the fall theory. If Kathleen tripped on the stairs and landed neck-first against a step, for example, then this could explain the broken cartilage. If Kathleen coughed in an unusual way during her demise, then this could explain the fracture. It would be an unusual injury to sustain without strangulation, but not impossible.

Nevertheless, given the state of Kathleen's body, it all seemed to point in the direction of strangulation. Kathleen appeared to have been attacked as she cowered in the staircase. And as we all know how common strangulation is during homicidal attacks, it all pointed directly at Michael. But the fractured cartilage ended up being far more problematic than first thought. Analysis of the injury was complicated by a puzzling lack of any associated trauma to the neck. The cartilage was fractured and there was a small bleed as a result. But nothing else suggested she had been strangled.

At trial, Rudolf interrogated Radisch, trying to unpack her conclusion that the fractured cartilage was evidence of manual strangulation.

"In cases of manual strangulation," he began, "there is something like a galaxy of related injuries that you would normally look for, are there not?"

"There are." Radisch nodded.

"Most commonly, you might find external bruising on the neck?"

"That's correct."

"Or fingernail marks?"

"Yes."

"Or marks from the fingers themselves?"

"Yes."

"Or internal bruising?"

"Yes."

"Or pinpoint hemorrhages in the eyes?"

"Yes."

"Or congestion in the face?"

"Yes."

"None of that was present here?"

"No."

Rudolf paused to retrieve a textbook from the side of the bench. "Would you agree with the following?" he asked before turning to a page. "'If there is no bleed, the fracture must be post-mortem. But if there is a small bleed, then the lesion can be either antemortem or post-mortem. Naturally, the findings must be taken in conjunction with other evidence of neck injury. If there is other evidence, then the bleeding can be accepted as an antemortem injury. Conversely, the solitary finding of a fractured thyroid cartilage, even with associated bleeding, is not sufficient evidence of antemortem trauma to the neck.'"

Radisch turned up her nose at the quotation. "What's the reference?" she asked, flipping the interrogation on its head.

"Do you know who Bernard Knight is?"

"He's a British forensic pathologist."

"A well-respected forensic pathologist?"

"Yes."

"So it's fair to say that there are some well-respected pathologists who would disagree with your finding."

"Yes."

So, the injury may even have been a post-mortem artifact, caused by incising the neck area during autopsy, or by moving Kathleen's body when it was in a state of rigor mortis. Either one of these explanations might explain why we would find a fracture to the cartilage which occurred after death. And the absence of other injuries to the neck and face indicates that even if the injury was sustained pre-mortem, it may not have been not sustained during an act of strangulation.

Of course, such an explanation is not particularly convincing for those who are committed to the view that the fracture was violently inflicted. So if the injury was sustained during a violent attack, how can it be explained by the owl theory? It seems like a lost cause. Murderous humans often strangle their victims. But an owl can hardly have clasped Kathleen's throat between its soft feathery wings and squeezed. If Kathleen was strangled, and if humans are the ones who strangle, then Kathleen was killed by a human. With an injury so typical of homicide, Michael is the obvious culprit. His grip must have been around Kathleen's neck when she was brutally throttled.

Could such a fracture result from an owl attack?

Yes, it could. The powerful feet of an owl are perfectly capable of breaking a fragile and thin cartilaginous joint in the neck. As already noted, the grasp of a barred owl's talons is as powerful as a dog's jaws. And there is even an injury on Kathleen's neck which appears to be consistent with a talon scratch. A small puncture or cut mark, approximately a quarter of an inch long, sits along the line of the thyroid bone, albeit on the right side rather than the left. The cut is visible in the crime scene video and it is documented in the autopsy notes. This injury suggests that if Kathleen's neck was clutched or hit by something, it may have had at least one sharp point at the tip. And unless Michael had unusually long and strong fingernails, it is unlikely that this puncture was caused by him grabbing Kathleen's neck.

If the fracture was caused during a violent strangulation event, then the grasping and piercing motions of the owl's natural weapons are sufficient to explain this fact. Despite it seeming fanciful that an owl may have choked Kathleen during an attack, this would hardly be unprecedented. As already noted, it is common for owls to direct their attacks at the face and neck. Kathleen would not be the first to have been clasped around the throat. Remember the airman, Melvin Hill, whose jugular vein was nearly pierced when an owl grabbed him by the throat in 1962? And remember also that with a grip force several times stronger than human hands, an owl's foot is perfectly capable of fracturing the thyroid cartilage; the soft cartilaginous structure in her neck would have been snapped by a grip force several times stronger than Michael's hands could have ever achieved. Kathleen would have had no chance of pulling the incredibly strong digits from her throat.

THE FACE

Kathleen's face was not bruised or battered. Michael never punched or stomped on her head. Her nose was not broken or even bleeding. Instead, there were a large number of smaller, incision-like injuries. Kathleen's face was covered in many small cuts, scrapes, punctures, and abrasions— eleven in total— few very deep, and the majority located around the eyes. It is all, once again, perfectly consistent with an owl attack and inconsistent with a beating or a simple fall down the stairs.

Nine of the cuts on her face were within inches of her eyes. There were three abrasions, in a line, sitting above her right eyelid. There were three cuts, again in a line, on the area just above her left eyebrow. Two smaller scratches were made on her lower left eyelid, each lying about an eighth of an inch from her eyeball. Then, on the bridge of the right side of her nose, close to the corner of her eye, was a puncture which, although small, had bled badly.

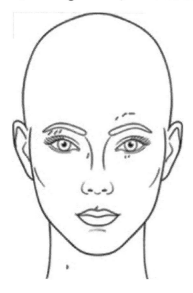

Illustration of the small cuts dotted across Kathleen's face.

The injuries are unlike anything seen in a typical domestic assault. Michael landed no punches to the face. Michael left no black eye or bleeding nose. We are supposed to imagine that in his out-of-control, homicidal rage, Michael never struck her face at all. The shapes and dimensions of the punctures on her face are inconsistent with the clawing of fingernails, yet consistent with the sorts of injuries typically inflicted by owls. Kate Davis testified to this fact in an affidavit she supplied for Larry in his Motion for Appropriate Relief:

> The abrasions, contusions, and puncture wounds on Mrs. Peterson's face and arms resemble those caused by a raptor's weapons, the talons. In a lifetime of handling owls and hawks, I have seen a fair amount of these. One wound on her face, in particular, has a triangular shape on the surface,

consistent with the deep puncture wound caused by an owl's talon, which is curved in the anterior surface and flat or de-curved on the posterior side. Again, I have seen and had many identical wounds. A colleague was struck in the face by a spotted owl (close relative of the barred) with three puncture wounds on her brow and one below the eye, similar to those found on Mrs. Peterson.

So according to Davis: the general placement of Kathleen's facial injuries was consistent with an owl attack, and the curiously triangular shape of an individual puncture mark was identifiable as precisely the sort of impression a talon would leave.

If you grant that an owl was involved in Kathleen's death, these injuries are not only easy to explain but predictable. Owls routinely aim their attacks at the head, and more specifically, the eyes. Almost every victim of owl attacks over the last hundred years sustained similar injuries. And while Kathleen narrowly avoided any damage to her eyes, the cuts around them are a visual testimony to a typical owl attack.

THE BODY

Other injuries were found on Kathleen's body, but none were very serious or important. A round bruise or abrasion ran across her left shoulder blade, approximately three inches in both length and breadth (six centimeters). Radisch describes the injury like this: "On the back, there is a large 3"x3" contusion with central pressure mark over the left scapula."

That sounds like the sort of injury that might be inflicted during a beating. But the State itself determined that this contusion had been impressed on Kathleen's shoulder blade post-mortem—an artifact of her upper back pressing against the wooden step for hours before the autopsy. It had nothing to do with how she died. Apart from this large bruise on her back, the rest of Kathleen's body was without any serious injury.

There were a series of small bruises and light abrasions dotted across her hands and fingers which are typical defensive injuries. They are totally unlikely to have been sustained during a fall. But they are perfectly compatible with either the homicide or owl attack theories.

The most fascinating feature of Kathleen's body, however, is not the bruises. Indeed, there was only a handful of these. What are truly fascinating are the items that were recovered from her body. Of course, there were the fistfuls of her own hair in her hands. But there were also foreign objects stuck to her skin and hair that tell us more than any injury could. On the back of Kathleen's right hand, Radisch discovered two pine needles caked in blood. And in her hair, possibly embedded in a wound, a splinter of something resembling wood or metal was retrieved.

All of this debris, together with the investigators' testimony at trial that Kathleen's body was surrounded by pine needles, strongly indicates that some portion of Kathleen's attack must have occurred outdoors. It also suggests that she was trying to pull something away from her head and pulled out countless hairs in her fruitless attempt. This is all inconsistent with the homicide theory but is an integral part of the owl theory narrative.

So what do Kathleen's injuries suggest as a totality? Clearly, they are not suggestive of a typical homicide. Homicidal attacks, particularly rage-induced ones, typically result in a range of injuries across the body. And yet all of Kathleen's serious injuries were restricted to the head and neck. All of the blood that spilled out around her body came from cuts above the neckline. Most of the bruises on her body were restricted to the hands and are clearly defensive injuries. Yet not a single large bruise or serious wound was found on her face, legs, or abdomen. No punches to the face. No kicks to the stomach. No thrashing at the legs or buttocks. It is nothing at all like a homicide. Michael's attack, if it ever happened, was unleashed quite uniquely on the back of Kathleen's head, to the virtual exclusion of any other part of the body. The pattern of the injuries— their shape, dimensions, severity, and placement—is all consistent with an owl attack. Her injuries are much more difficult to explain by appeal to a rage-induced beating. If you believe that Michael killed Kathleen, you must admit, he was a killer like no other.

CHAPTER SEVEN: OWL TRACES

NOT ENOUGH EVIDENCE

Kathleen was not killed by Michael. Kathleen did not fall on the stairs. Kathleen was killed by a raptor. She died during a prolonged and bloody ordeal, the likes of which few of us can possibly imagine. She would have fought with all her power against the incredible strength of the owl's lethal claws. She died alone but for the feathers brushing against her face.

But then, a prolonged struggle between an adult woman and an owl is unlikely to occur without a trace. So where is the evidence? Sure, Kathleen's wounds were compatible with an owl attack. Sure, the distribution of blood was compatible with an owl having attacked Kathleen. But it is one thing to say that a theory is compatible with the evidence, quite another to say that there is evidence that points directly at an owl attack.

Yet so far, the only positive evidence produced for the theory has been the two fragments of feathers found in Kathleen's hair. This evidence was not included at trial. Certainly, it was a surprising discovery. It was Larry's coup. And although the species of bird could not be identified, it was still a victory for the owl theory. A *small* victory.

The thing is, two feather fragments are insufficient evidence of a bird. Tiny bits of feather can be explained away as debris from the house. The feathers could have come from a ripped pillow or duvet. If a bird was involved, the evidence should go further than this. There should be whole feathers (and many of them), perhaps some owl DNA or blood at the scene, and even splats of owl droppings or chips from a beak or talon. This is especially so if Kathleen put up any kind of fight against the bird. Yet the jury heard nothing of any evidence like this. And nothing was documented by police. Without this kind of evidence, the owl theory sounds like nothing short of desperation.

But there is other evidence. The feather fragments are not the only evidence that points uniquely at a bird of prey. There is much more evidence that few are aware of. Some of this evidence was even hidden from view. Once this evidence is properly understood, it confirms, beyond a reasonable doubt, that a raptor was responsible for Kathleen's death. It also suggests that the true nature of Kathleen's death was something authorities wished to hide from a very early stage in the investigation.

DROPPINGS

White splatter stains of some kind of substance were found on the bottom step, directly under where Kathleen's head had lain. The white splats were deposited on top of the blood, so they must have been left there either during or very shortly after her attack. The white splats exactly resemble bird droppings.

This is an incredible coup for the theory that a bird attacked Kathleen. It is a piece of evidence that, surprisingly, Larry himself never mentioned. But then, perhaps it is clear why Larry failed to recognize the importance of the white splats. Larry's theory has always been that Kathleen was attacked outside. When she later ran inside and collapsed in the stairwell, Larry guessed the owl was already long gone.

But the splats are strong evidence that a bird was inside the house. So Larry's theory has to be adjusted to incorporate the surprising evidence. Once we make this adjustment, it can be seen that there is far more evidence of a bird inside the house than outside.

Before examining these strange white splats, let's get a bit of an overview of the digestive system of the owl. Owls are rather unusual among birds, in that their digestive processes have two aspects. They routinely eat small mammals and birds, the bones of which they cannot digest. To remedy this, owls digest only the soft tissue of their meals. The bones, beaks, and claws of their prey are, quite literally, barfed up later. They excrete pellets from their throat, containing these indigestible portions. The pellets resemble small turds. It's no pretty sight to behold. But apart from this unique talent, owls are much like other birds. They poop. They produce droppings, white in color, watery, and generally unpleasant. They are indistinguishable from the droppings of any other bird. Sometimes the poop has a hint of green or brown mingled in. When they deposit something closer to pure white, this is called a "mute" by ornithologists.

The bottom step of the staircase, showing mutes over the blood. Crime scene photograph.

And that's what is so fascinating about the bottom step. The white splats are identical in appearance to mutes and are found on the most important step of the staircase—the one on which Kathleen's head was resting when she was discovered. Moreover, the mutes are over the bloodstains. They can only represent something related to Kathleen's death. They had to be deposited there either during her demise or very shortly after. The splats are not small and some of the substance has even been smeared in with the blood, creating a morbid pink paste.

Every investigator knew the white marks were there. So how on Earth were these strange stains explained?

In short, they weren't explained. Yes, the stains were mentioned at trial. But incredibly, the State claimed to have never tested the white substance splattered over Kathleen's blood. This is so unbelievable as to most likely be false. The white splats were of some kind of liquid substance. And given the prosecution's account of the night, which revolves around the narrative that Michael cleaned up the scene, the State could have performed a chemical analysis which would have proved definitively that the white stains were made by some sort of cleaning product. It is unbelievable that no test of this substance was performed.

What did the defense think of the white splats? The stains infuriated Michael's defense counsel. How had they gotten there? What was their source? So far as the defense was concerned, Kathleen had fallen. She had not been carrying a glass of milk when she fell. And they rejected the idea that Michael cleaned the scene. So there was absolutely no reason for white stains of anything to be sitting on top of the blood.

With no hunch that a bird may have been involved in Kathleen's death, the best explanation the defense could think of had to do with luminol. Luminol is a chemical applied in the forensic analysis of blood. It is an enhancement reagent sprayed in a thin layer over any areas where blood is suspected to exist, despite being invisible to the naked eye. When applied, luminol glows in the presence of hemoglobin and alerts forensics to the existence of a probable bloodstain.

When luminol is not glowing, it is a whitish or pale-yellow substance. In many ways, the visible appearance of luminol does resemble the appearance of the splats on the bottom step. It was Major Timothy Palmbach from the Connecticut Division of Scientific Services who testified at Michael's trial that the splats were evidence that the State had carried out a secret, undocumented luminol test.

Tom Maher, one of Michael's attorneys, questioned Palmbach about the stains. "Do you have an opinion as to whether that residue is in fact luminol?"

"In my opinion," Palmbach answered, "the whitish residue that is dried and splashed at the bottom of the stairs is consistent with dried luminol reagent."

Surprisingly, when Rudolf questioned the police investigators about the substance, they agreed that the substance was consistent in appearance with luminol. "Does that show how luminol would look when it gets dry after application?"

"Yes, it does, to an extent," forensic technician Eric Campen replied. "I can't tell what brought about those marks," he continued, "but we didn't apply luminol on those walls. We never did."

Campen was not the State's only witness to agree that the substance resembled dried luminol.

"When you spray luminol and it dries, it leaves a whitish film, doesn't it?"

"Yes, it does," Dan George answered.

Rudolf passed George a photograph of the bottom step. "Do you recognize that?"

"Yes, that's the lower steps."

"And do you see the luminol residue down there?"

"I see a staining down there, yes, sir."

"My question was, do you see luminol residue there?"

"Oh, yes, sir. I do see that."

"And even over here." Rudolf pointed to a different spot of white. "There appears to be another spot of luminol residue?"

"Yes, sir."

Everyone agreed that the white splats on the bottom step were consistent in appearance with luminol. But if it was luminol, this would entail that the police had carried out a secret luminol test. If the results had been kept from the defense, this would amount to serious misconduct.

For that reason, District Attorney Jim Hardin immediately pushed back at the allegation when he finally got his time to question Dan George. "Mr. Rudolf showed you a photograph that's marked as Exhibit 147 … You've indicated that neither you nor Mr. Campen nor anybody else who was processing that scene put luminol in that stairway. Is that your testimony?"

"That's correct."

"Do you have any idea who put luminol in this stairway, if that's what it is?"

"No, sir."

"So anybody could have done this?"

"Yes, sir."

"Are you aware that Mr. Peterson has hired numerous experts to look at this stairway?"

"I wasn't."

"If he had, could those experts have put luminol in the stairway?"

An exasperated Rudolf shouted from the bench, "I object to that as an outrageous allegation!"

The objection was sustained.

But all this talk of luminol was a red herring. No application of luminol was recorded in this area. And no luminol test would be so clumsy as to leave behind great white splats of the substance. Not only were there splats, but the white substance, whatever it was, had also become smeared with the blood. It is totally implausible that the stains were caused by a luminol test. It is, of course, possible that this was the cause of the stains, but such an explanation relies on the assumption that the technicians on the scene were so beyond incompetent that they were unable to perform a simple luminol test without, quite literally, spilling the bucket. Rather than spraying a thin film of luminol in an even distribution, the investigators went full Jackson Pollock, tipping over the luminol container and wiping it around on the floor.

But if we assume that an owl was in the stairwell when Kathleen died, the splats are without any mystery. It is predictable that an owl in a high-stress situation will defecate. And the color and consistency of the white splats are entirely consistent with this hypothesis. To quote the raptor expert Kate Davis, the droppings at the foot of the staircase appear genuine and "very typical of a nervous bird."

The droppings are a predictable finding if a bird was involved in Kathleen's death. And the droppings are compelling evidence that the attack must have persisted inside the house. Given a choice between the two hypotheses, the appearance of the white splats is more consistent with the random defecation of an owl as opposed to the careful and systematic application of luminol. More importantly, this evidence tells us something incredible about Kathleen's death: Her attack was not restricted to the outside path. She did not run inside and faint in the stairwell, as Larry believed. The owl attack continued inside. Kathleen died in the stairwell while tussling with a large bird of prey.

As incredible as this piece of evidence is, it is not the only evidence that a bird was inside the house when Kathleen died. When all the evidence is seen as a totality, the picture that emerges is crystal clear.

TALON

At trial, it was called State's Exhibit 12, a very unassuming name for such a crucial piece of evidence. The technician Eric Campen had been its discoverer. He had wrenched the solid shard from the wood of one of the lower steps on December 10. It was stuck hard, stamped into the wood with immense force. The object was found beneath a circular clot of blood.

Campen sat on the stand, as the district attorney questioned him about the exhibit. The jurors could see Campen was extremely proud of his discovery. He had uncovered the State's Holy Grail. It was a key piece of evidence in the case against Michael. According to the prosecution, State's Exhibit 12 was a chip or a shard from the implement which had been used to murder Kathleen. It was a piece of the murder weapon. It would prove beyond doubt that Michael had bludgeoned Kathleen.

Hardin brought out the little container in which the exhibit was held and passed it to Campen. The exhibit was fastened securely with layers upon layers of thick red evidence tape. On the outside of the container, Campen's writing in a Sharpie pen was read to the jury. "Discovered at 18:32—item in blood." It was, they would argue, conclusive evidence of a weapon. Campen clutched the parcel in both hands, like a small treasure.

Hardin asked, "Now, did you actually process that item at the scene?"

"I collected it, yes," Campen replied.

"Did you give that to Mr. George?"

"Yes, I did."

"If you would please, describe to the jury what you took out of the blood and why you did that."

Campen stood, approached the jury, and explained. "There was a little circle of blood that this small item—that I'm getting ready to show you—was pulled from."

"Why did you do that?" Hardin asked.

"I knew there was something there. The top of it was covered in blood, you see, but there was a bump there. So, I lifted it up with the tip of my finger. And I found that on the opposite side of it, it was a silvery color. I could not determine what it was. So I collected it to be analyzed," Campen explained.

"If you would please, open what's marked as State's Exhibit 12."

Hardin passed Campen a pocket knife. He took the knife from Hardin and started to cut the tape. He fumbled, struggling to cut through the thick red tape which had been wound again and again around the delicate exhibit. He cut and hacked at the tape. It took nearly two minutes to finally lift the lid. The jurors were on the edges of their seats.

At last, voila! The lid was lifted.

Hardin leaned in, squinting. Campen prodded at the cotton wool inside as if searching for something. The two men held the container at different angles, trying to find the shard recovered from the steps. But to the surprise and shock of both Campen and Hardin, the evidence container was completely empty. The expectant jury was right in front of them, waiting.

The two men did not know how to proceed.

State's Exhibit 12 had vanished.

"Is there anything in there?" Hardin whispered to Campen.

The jury was sitting, still waiting for the exhibit to be presented with a flourish. Nothing was taken out of the container. Nothing removed. The jury waited. The two men fidgeted. The jury sat back, a little perplexed, entering their third minute of uncomfortable silence. It was clear that something had gone terribly wrong.

"Is that what was… Umm… The fle…"

"This… err…"

The two men's words intersected each other as they struggled to say anything at all. What the hell had happened?

The all-important shard of the murder weapon had vanished without a trace. Despite having been bound in layers upon layers of evidence tape, the object was no longer there. It had been removed.

Hardin, at last, found his words again, but it was clear he lost his train of thought. "Is that what... Er... Was.... Err... the fleck was contained in... In the case that is marked State's Exhibit 12?"

"Yes, there *was* a fleck or a small round piece of either metal or wood... I'm not sure what it was—it was silver in color—that I placed in this container and it *was* definitely sent to the state lab for analysis." There was another pause before Campen continues. "And it is not, as you can see, it is not in this container. So I... With it sealed up... I have no idea where it is."

Campen returned to the witness stand, confused. An unnerved Hardin returned to the prosecution bench and proceeded to scull rapidly from a polystyrene cup. The men eagerly moved on to the next question, desperately pretending that nothing of much consequence had just occurred. But they knew all too well that something extremely serious had just occurred.

What was State's Exhibit 12? And how had it gone missing? It was a small shard of *something*. It had been plucked from the wood grain. It had been stamped with tremendous force into the fifteenth step of the staircase, three steps up from Kathleen's head. It was a sharp-tipped piece of some kind of hard material—gunmetal grey on its exterior—probably wood or metal, but hard to tell.

The State's theory was that during Michael's thrashing of Kathleen, a chip from his weapon had become lodged in the wood of the stairs. It had broken away from the implement and remained stuck hard in the step. It could have been metal or it could have been wood. Campen wasn't sure when he found it. Whatever it was, it was tremendously solid. Either way, it was a sharp foreign object, pierced into the steps. And now it was gone.

Not much more was said about State's Exhibit 12. With the object now lost, its evidential value was totally diminished. The only available photo of the object was terribly overexposed and no detail could be made out. The jury had no way to observe the object, so they probably didn't linger on its meaning. And perhaps this was just how the authorities wanted it.

Luckily, in the years since the trial, the object has been described by eyewitnesses. In a 2018 interview with *Wired* magazine, lead forensic technician Dan George described the object in more detail. It was "a sixteenth of an inch long," he said. "A curved shape and looked almost like a mini-talon."[27] The descriptions from George and Campen are, in every respect, identical to how the chipped end of a barred owl's talon would appear. The talons of these birds are gunmetal grey, solid, and curved with a sharp tip. If State's Exhibit 12 did represent a chip from a talon, then it is obvious why such a sturdy material would be indiscernible between metal and wood.

In his interview with *Wired*, George subsequently backtracks from his use of the phrase "mini-talon." He makes clear that the object could have been anything! Perhaps it was a fingernail, he cautions, or a chip from one of the dog's claws. But, of course, given the dimensions and coloration, the idea that this was anyone's fingernail is preposterous. And how does a fingernail become embedded with force in a step? And if George truly believed that the object may have been compatible with the chipped claw of an English bulldog, then he is in some sense conceding that the object fits the bill: it resembled the chipped claw of a

---

27. "Did the Owl Do it? Behind the Staircase's Wildest Theory." Wired. June 13, 2018. https://www.wired.com/story/the-staircase-netflix-owl-theory/

large animal. So why was there a chipped claw stamped into one of the bottom steps under a clot of blood?

It is little wonder that in the midst of a chaotic battle in the stairwell, the bird's repeated attempts to maim Kathleen would damage its own talons as they were repeatedly battered against both her skull and the solid oak stairs. A talon punctured the wood grain, fastened in, and cracked away from the root of the claw. The owl, the true killer, left a calling card.

If State's Exhibit 12 was ever tested, such a test must have exposed who the real culprit was. But this evidence could never make it to trial. The owl's talon disappeared before it could lead anyone to the real murderer. The talon shard was hidden from view. Where it is now, more than twenty years after Kathleen's death, is anyone's guess.

CECA

The digestive system of owls is unusual among birds. As has already been noted, they produce pellets of undigested bone and hair, which can often be found around their nests. As also noted, the droppings produced by owls are similar in appearance to the droppings from other bird species. But owls expel more than pellets and mutes. In high-stress situations, they are prone to discharge a tarry substance resembling chocolate sauce from twin sacs in their gut called the avian ceca.

Anyone who has handled these animals is familiar with the secretions. For the most part, owl droppings are white with smaller spots of brown or green. But every now and again, the ceca discharge will be released. The odor, according to handlers, is utterly offensive. The smell is described as somewhere between ammonia and sulfur. It is an extremely strong and very distinctive chemical smell. The stench of ceca is so powerful that it is often the best evidence of its presence.

And surprisingly, as the investigators surveyed the Peterson residence on their first night of investigation, it was not only their eyes that were alerted to strange evidence. Twice that night, the noses of the forensic team were alerted to the presence of a strange and unusual chemical smell. It was Duane Deaver who first noticed a distinct and powerful odor emanating from the kitchen sink. "You have to come here and smell this," he told his assistant Eric Campen. The two men stood by the edge of the sink and inhaled deeply. The chemical smell was overpowering.

Two years later, at Michael's trial, Deaver would describe his olfactory experience as having been simply of "the odor of alcohol down the sink." His testimony made up part of the State's argument that Michael had staged the scene to look like an accident. Michael supposedly poured wine down the drain so that empty bottles would be seen on the countertop. This was all in an effort to make it seem that Kathleen was soused on the night she died. But there are strong reasons to doubt that wine was what Deaver was smelling down that drain.

First, consider how weak the odor of alcohol is when it rises from a glass of white wine. This is not like gin, vodka, or scotch. The alcohol content in a bottle of Moet & Chandon, for example, is a relatively meager twelve percent. If a full bottle were poured down the drain, then only three-eighths of a cup of pure alcohol content found its way down the plughole. Now consider the speed at which alcohol evaporates when exposed to the air. Deaver arrived on the scene more than fifteen hours after Kathleen's death, and it was many hours after he first arrived that he noted the strong chemical odor coming from the sink.

By this time, any alcohol remaining in the wine would have diminished by a dramatic margin, anywhere between three and five percent. And yet, according to Deaver, he was able to smell the strong odor of alcohol coming from the sink, when by now, the alcohol content of any wine remaining in the U-bend would have stood at between seven and nine percent. It is simply implausible that old booze would generate such a strong chemical odor.

Moreover, Christina Tomasetti, Todd's date on the night of Kathleen's death, testified to witnessing Michael opening the bubbly at approximately 10 p.m. And unless Tomasetti herself was part of some dark conspiracy to eliminate Kathleen, there is no reason whatsoever to doubt her testimony on this fact. No less important, the autopsy report established without doubt that Kathleen had been drinking on the night that she died. The wine was opened for drinking. The wine glasses had clearly been used. There is nothing to corroborate the idea that what Deaver was smelling down the drain was alcohol. And given how weak this odor would be, there is reason to doubt his testimony (unless he had some sort of superhuman sense of smell).

Despite it seeming fanciful that ceca discharge was in the sink, there is a good explanation as to how it may have gotten there. Remember that Michael washed his hands in the sink right in front of the officers on the scene. He was told to stop. Now, he may have washed his hands just because they were covered in blood. But equally, he may have washed his hands because they had become foul-smelling, coated in a mixture of Kathleen's blood and ceca. And if this was why he was washing his hands, then it is clear why Deaver could detect a chemical smell so many hours after Kathleen's death. The smell came not from alcohol but from the pungent secretions of the owl. If Michael was clutching the body long before the investigators arrived, he would have transferred at least some of the ceca discharge (which had been discharged onto Kathleen) to his hands and body. The chemical odor of ceca would be much more noticeable than the faint odor of old wine.

Indeed, there is more evidence that Michael may have transferred ceca discharge to his hands and body. Michael's clothes were collected into evidence early on the morning of December 9. Upon collection, a "strong smell" was noted to come from the clothing. At the time, it was assumed this was the smell of heavy perspiration combined with Kathleen's blood, which was now dry. And although it may be reasonable to think that the smell was nothing more than the whiff of body odor, if we assume the odor on Michael's shirt was coming from ceca discharge, then we can explain the offensive smells on the shirt and in the sink as having one and the same cause.

If an owl was involved in Kathleen's death, then the panicking bird would almost certainly have emitted fluid from the ceca sacs. This tarry emission would have become smeared into the blood on Kathleen's hair and on her clothes. If Michael clutched Kathleen's body for a period of time before investigators arrived, and we know that he did, then it is unsurprising that he also transferred the substance to his own hands and body.

The existence of ceca discharge may also be confirmed by the descriptions of the appearance of the blood in the stairwell. According to the testimony of the arriving paramedics, the blood appeared too dark to be fresh. It was not bright red, and it lacked the sheen or luster that fresh blood typically has. Instead, the blood was dark and appeared coagulated. And yet much of the blood was still wet when the medical examiner moved Kathleen's body down the hallway. If black ceca discharge had been mixed in with the blood from Kathleen's head wounds, then the blood would appear darker and have a muddier, coagulated consistency, just as though it were dry.

FEATHER FRAGMENTS

Of course, there was also the feather evidence Larry had discovered. He had found two microscopic feather fragments. The samples had been sent to the trace evidence team by the medical examiner's office. The feathers were found on a hair sample, which was one of the more than sixty hairs that Kathleen had wrenched out from her own scalp.

The feathers were a predictable finding if a bird of prey was involved in the death of Kathleen. And most importantly, the district attorney had denied their existence long before Larry had taken matters into his own hands. The feathers were evidence that Durham's authorities knew of the existence of at least some feathers and wanted them kept away from the public eye at all costs. Indeed, the district attorney's denial itself constitutes some of the strongest evidence of an active conspiracy at work in this case.

So just how strong is Larry's feather evidence? How far does it go to prove that a bird of prey was involved? In one sense, it is extremely strong evidence. The existence of feathers at the crime scene had never been part of public knowledge in this case. And yet Larry, by the power of sheer deduction, had predicted their existence. The fact that the district attorney had lied about their existence only buffers Larry's argument. Had the feathers been of little consequence, then denying their existence seems counter to reason.

Still, there are many who think that the feathers are of no evidential value. Perhaps Kathleen had a small rip in her duvet. Perhaps Kathleen's pillow had holes. Perhaps anything besides an owl. And who knows, maybe the hair on human heads collects this sort of debris all the time. Dust, bits of paper, threads of cotton, food, sand, or feather fragments would be among the most typical kinds of debris. Thus, the finding of the feather fragments might have been entirely typical for a microscopic examination of human hair. Far from demonstrating that Kathleen was attacked by an owl, the debris might prove only that she had regular hair with regular debris.

And shouldn't there be, after all, more than only two fragments of feathers? If you think of a cat with a bird, the result is usually feathers *everywhere*. Yet Kathleen supposedly wrenched and heaved at a large bird of prey that had embedded itself into her scalp—tussling for at least a few minutes—and all that remained were two microscopic feather fragments? Not even a whole feather anywhere?

Really?

Larry himself was skeptical that this objection was a strong one. In most recorded owl attacks, he argued, few feathers if any were ever left behind. For example, in the documented attacks outside VMR Graphics, no whole feathers were left. The owl swooped, the owl mauled, then the owl flew off before its victims ever knew what had hit them. In other similar recent owl attacks, such as those that had befallen Carly Blake and Greg Cooper, the victims likewise saw no feathers in the aftermath of their attack.

But this attack was, very clearly, more vicious than those that had afflicted any of the victims listed above. Unlike the other cases, the owl had attached itself to Kathleen's head and she had clearly tried to pull it away. There should have been many feathers drawn from its body which would have been found in Kathleen's hair and hands. If the attack happened on the front path—and if there was any degree of a fight—then feathers should have been found all around that area. And if the attack continued inside the house, lasting up until the moment Kathleen died, then there should have been numerous feathers in the stairwell.

Naturally, some feathers may have been collected during the investigation which were never identified as such. The preponderance of unidentified "fibers" collected from inside the staircase may be examples. Still more feathers may have been deliberately destroyed or mislabeled. The disappearance of State's Exhibit 12 (alongside other examples of suspicious police activity) makes this a live possibility.

In any case, Larry's account cannot be the whole story. Even if we assume that an owl attacked Kathleen on the front path, then the two feather fragments cannot be the only feather evidence. Kathleen can hardly have pulled so many hairs from her head without pulling numerous feathers as well. The fact that only a couple of fragments were recovered is, in its own right, extremely suspicious.

CHAPTER EIGHT: BLOOD

WHY THE BLOOD MATTERS

Within minutes of discovering Kathleen's body, it was obvious to first responders that a fall was not the cause of her death: Blood was on the front path. Blood was on the frame of the front door. Blood was around the kitchen. Blood was in all sorts of places where it simply shouldn't have been. And the sheer quantity of blood was itself an enigma. Within the stairwell, more than ten thousand individual blood spots covered the walls. How was blood thrown so profusely against so many surfaces?

It is crucial, then, to try to understand how Kathleen's blood came to be found in so many places. But the possibility of crime scene contamination makes this task even harder than it seems. A veritable legion of officers, paramedics, and firemen had wandered through the house before the first crime scene photographs were taken. And who knows where Michael went—or how much blood he had spread around—before the paramedics first walked through the open door? There is always the possibility that a particular stain here or there is not relevant to the question of how Kathleen died.

We should begin with generalities before getting into specifics. The defense's blood spatter expert Henry Lee made the following metaphor at Michael's trial: when we venture into a forest, we first want to get an impression of the overall feel of the environment before closely examining any individual tree. So what was this forest like?

In the stairwell, there was a gargantuan amount of spray and spatter—indeed, far more than is usually found in a typical homicide. Thousands of blood spots were sprayed across the walls at high velocity, many at near-horizontal angles. Given that Kathleen lay in the stairwell where the majority of the blood was found, it is overwhelmingly likely this was the site of her death. This much is obvious. She was not murdered elsewhere and then moved to the stairwell.

Additionally, the bloodstains in this area are smeared, wiped, and cast at various strange angles. There was a lot of movement in the stairwell during her death. Given the breadth of the stairwell (a mere forty-two inches across) and given the general distribution of blood, it is unlikely that any person could have stood inside the stairwell beating Kathleen. It was for this reason that the prosecution alleged that Michael stood outside the stairwell, bludgeoning Kathleen with the blow poke as she cowered within.

So, speaking generally, we can be confident about these facts:

1. The stairwell was the site of Kathleen's death.
2. There was a large amount of rapid movement or tussling around the bottom four steps of the stairwell.
3. No other person stood inside the stairwell beating Kathleen.

These were facts about which both the defense and the prosecution agreed.

There are other facts about which we can be reasonably confident. For example, the existence of blood droplets far from the site of Kathleen's body (on the outside slate paving stones and on the front step) is extremely suggestive that it was deposited at some point either shortly before or shortly after her death. Kathleen's blood was dripping outside before it had had time to dry.

According to the fall theory, this blood was mere contamination. But it is exceedingly difficult to suggest that contamination can account for large, wet blood droplets so distant from Kathleen's body. According to the murder theory, Michael left these drops along the path as he fled the house seeking to hide the murder weapon. This theory is easier to comport with common sense, except for the fact that no hidden weapon was ever discovered despite an exhaustive search of the property. According to the owl theory, these drips are the all-important clue indicating that Kathleen began bleeding outside. In its initial swoop at her head, the owl sliced her scalp, wounding her and causing her to race inside in terror. She leaves a trail of drips that leads from the front path to the front door.

The blood outside the house is extremely informative. But there is blood elsewhere that paints a stronger picture of what happened that night. For instance, the blood on the back of the front door is of crucial significance. The defense argued it had been deposited there either by the movements of first responders or by Michael himself as he stumbled around the house awaiting emergency services. The prosecution argued that Michael had indeed left the stains, but only in his mad rush to hide the weapon. So what caused the heavy blood smears on the back of the front door?

The Front Door

At least three arriving officers independently noticed, to their bewilderment, that there was blood smeared on the inside of the front door. This watered the seeds of doubt from the very outset. A woman was dead at the bottom of the stairs, yet her blood was on the front door. And since the first responders were the first people to see the blood, it had to be deposited there before they arrived. Therefore, its source had to be either Michael or Kathleen.

According to the murder theory, Michael left these bloody marks on his way out the door. With bloody hands, he pushed open the door, leaving tremendous blood smears all over its interior surface.

Is this explanation plausible? There are two reasons to think not:

> 1. If Michael was concerned with cleaning up the scene (over the course of several hours), he would hardly forget to clean up the large bloody wipes he left all over the back of the door. And he would certainly not forget to close the door behind him.
>
> 2. The smears themselves are too profuse and clumsy to be explained by the simple operation of opening or closing a familiar front door. It is as though something large and moving has fallen against the door.

So, the bloodstains on the back of the open front door are not well explained by the simple mechanics of opening a door, and the stains are very unlikely to have been overlooked by Michael in the course of his clean-up and staging of the scene. Both of these facts indicate that it was most probably Kathleen, not Michael, who left the stains there. So how did Kathleen leave these stains?

To answer this question, we should look at the door itself. The transfer and drip stains are all contained in an area approximately twelve inches high and six inches wide. The blood within this zone appears wiped and smudged. Importantly, there were no handprints or fingerprints. Instead, it is as if some blood-soaked object was wiped across the door diagonally, in a broad curve that extends down towards the lock. So, something soaking with blood was pressed against the door as it arched along a curve, leaving red smears on its interior surface.

Blood wiped on the back of the front door.
Taken from the crime scene video.

Since there were no handprints or fingerprints, it is unlikely that Michael left the stains as he opened the door. For the prosecution to argue that he was responsible for the marks, we must assume that it was his bloody clothes or arms that wiped along the back of the door. But this is implausible on its face. Firstly, Michael's clothes were almost entirely free of blood from the waist up. Therefore, his shirt could not possibly have wiped a large blood smear onto the door. Secondly, most people who have lived in the same house for many years are capable of opening a front door without colliding with it or clumsily rubbing themselves on its interior face. It is a very simple action to hold a doorknob, turn it, and push. Were Michael's abilities to exit a door so seriously impaired on the night of the murder? He had been drinking, sure. But even so, it is difficult to comprehend how so much blood got on so many parts of the door and its frame.

There is also a strange lack of blood that needs to be explained. Directly above the lock, there is no blood. There is a clean semicircle around which the blood is evenly dispersed. It looks like somebody held a protractor above the lock before spraying blood over it. Why is there a circular shape, free from blood, just above the lock?

It is unlikely that the blood was smudged onto the door in this precise pattern. It would be extremely difficult to leave behind a perfectly clean, circular boundary under which there is no blood to be found. Instead, the pattern suggests that something round did indeed stand between the lock and the blood source. The pattern suggests that the lack of blood in this area is a blood spatter "shadow." There is not much in the shadow's shape to single out any particular kind of round object. However, it could be compatible with the top of Kathleen's head. If she were crouching on the inside of the door, with her head level with the lock, then the blood pattern would be just as expected. The front of Kathleen's head would be in the way of the source of blood—the wounds on the back of her head.

Apart from the blood smears on the back of the door, blood was smeared on the door's wooden frame and around the interior latch. If blood was found on the internal latch, then we can deduce that the door was most probably partly open when Kathleen's blood was smudged across it. Had the door been closed when Kathleen fell against it, the latch would have been shut and therefore protected from any bloodstaining. The bloodstains on the door were left behind while the door was partly open.

If the shadow around the lock represents the top of Kathleen's head, then we can infer that Kathleen was crouching or kneeling, with her eyes at the same level as the lock, while the door was partly open. And we can deduce that some kind of frantic activity smeared blood on the door frame, the latch, and the back of the door while she was in this position.

The Stairwell

The forensic team faced a Herculean task: how to perform an analysis of the ten thousand blood spots and stains within the stairwell. The job would take years to complete. The stains were so numerous and extensive, the first blood spatter technician to arrive on the scene, Rebecca Reid, passed on the offer to analyze the scene. "This is way beyond my expertise," she offered as an explanation. Indeed, the assortment of different stains, sprays, and smears was so voluminous, so anomalous, it may have been beyond any investigator's abilities to comprehensively explain. It was perhaps the most debated aspect of the entire case against Michael.

With so many blood marks to examine, the scene was unlike almost any other homicide by beating. Even the most brutal bludgeoning deaths seldom generate this much spray and spatter. And strangely, the angles at which much of the blood had been flung were bizarre. There was virtually no evidence of any blood having been flung above the body by a weapon swung overhead. On the contrary, hundreds of bloodspots had been cast against the steps at ninety-degree angles, parallel with the steps themselves.

The analysis would require an expert of the utmost standing. With Reid having refused to analyze the scene, Agent Duane Deaver from the Environmental Crimes Unit was brought onto the scene. Deaver arrived a few hours after the lead forensic investigators. He came at the recommendation of the North Carolina Bureau of Investigation (NCBI) and claimed to have acted as an expert witness in over sixty criminal cases (a claim which was later found to be a fabrication).

Deaver arrived at 5:07 p.m. on December 9. Almost twelve hours had passed since the first forensic investigators had begun their work. He donned protective clothing and boots, then proceeded to make some initial observations. He paced around the house in silence. *Christ*, he thought as he realized how difficult the job would be.

Deaver began by making a crude diagram of the scene. He then noted, as best he could, the various kinds of marks and stains within the stairwell, which included transfer stains, cast-off stains, wipes, and smears. The sheer number of different impressions was difficult to process. But he immediately noticed three areas were very odd.

The first area was a large portion of the upper north wall, around two feet wide and one-foot high, which appeared almost entirely free from blood. In the notes he made at the time, he described this area as a "shadow." In other words, his first impression was that the reason this patch of wall was free from blood was that some object had stood between Kathleen and the wall, which had blocked the blood spray from reaching the wall. The second and third areas Deaver found odd were found opposite of step 17. They were in the corners of the step and they were also free from blood. These two blood-free areas were much smaller than the first, measuring just a few inches across and barely an inch in height. One of these clean patches was across a skirting board. The other patch, directly opposite the first, lay on the riser of step 16. In Deaver's initial notes, he did not refer to either of these two areas as the result of wiping or clean-up. It was only in later summaries of his findings that Deaver made the claim that the clean patches were evidence Michael had attempted to wipe the blood from the steps.

It was a bizarre explanation for the two "wipe marks." Why had Michael chosen to be so selective in his cleaning? Imagine you are Michael Peterson. You have just murdered your wife, leaving all the walls around her body bright red. You realize that unless you clean up the scene, and rapidly, you will probably spend the rest of your life behind bars. What do you do?

Illustration of the location of the two small "wipe marks".

Naturally, you race to the utility room to collect paper towels or sponges and cleaning products, like Ajax. You then return to the stairwell and, quick as a flash, you carefully wipe away a few inches of blood from the bottom half of one skirting board. You then step back and observe your work. *That won't do*, you think. *It's not enough.* You cock your head, wondering how to improve on your handiwork. At last, you realize that you have only done this on one side of the step. *Better keep things consistent*, you think before proceeding to wipe away blood in an identical manner on the opposite face to the first. "That's better," you say.

Of course, this explanation is insane and incomprehensible, but it was the very claim of the prosecution. Michael had selectively wiped these two tiny areas, despite leaving the rest of the walls covered in blood. What possible reason could Michael have for behaving like this? Presumably, it seems, he must have believed that there was something extremely incriminating in these two particular areas lying on the two opposing faces of a single step. What could have been so incriminating about these areas? It is hard to think of anything. And why were these areas so symmetrical? Why two wipe marks, very similar in their dimensions, directly across from one another, tracing a line along the opposing edges of the bottom of the very same step?

One of the wipe marks. Crime scene photograph.

If there was nothing incriminating to be found in these two very specific places, then we must assume that Michael had entirely lost the plot. Despite the vast amount of blood all over the walls and steps, despite leaving over ten thousand bloodstains in the stairwell, Michael focused all his energy on wiping away blood from a few inches of one step. Could he really believe that such a minor amendment to the scene would save his skin? Did he not realize that such a strangely patchy clean-up would only do more to incriminate him?

Despite these problems, it seems difficult to account for evidence of wiping without supposing that Michael tried to cover his tracks. Most people can think of no other explanation for the wipe marks. What other explanation is available? If the area was wiped, and everyone seemed to admit that it was, then it follows unproblematically and unquestionably that somebody wiped it. Right? Well, perhaps, but it need not have been Michael.

At trial, Michael's lawyer, David Rudolf, argued that these areas could have resulted from Kathleen writhing in the staircase. The sleeves of her shirt, for example, could account for the wiping as she struggled to rise to her feet. Moreover, Henry Lee, the defense's expert on the matter, argued that these areas could equally have been caused by Kathleen's buttocks or torso. Perhaps the wipe marks had been made when Michael pulled Kathleen's body down to the floor from the few steps above. There were other ways that the wipe marks could have occurred. These are all possibilities.

But although these explanations are possible, they all seem rather implausible. We must ask why the two wipe marks are so very similar and found on opposing faces of a single step. The wipes are inexplicably symmetrical. They appear controlled and exact in their placement, hardly the result of a scramble at the bottom of the stairs.

But there is a more elegant explanation for the nature of these anomalies in the stairwell. If Kathleen was attacked by an owl along the path, and subsequently ran inside with the owl still attached to her head, then her struggle with an owl within the stairwell itself can explain the wipes. It was not the sleeve of her shirt or her hands. It was none of the actions of Kathleen at all. An owl, now in the stairwell with Kathleen, would have been beating its wings rapidly. And in the same way that the illusion of an angel in the snow can be made on a winter's day, the tips of the owl's beating wings repeatedly wiped at the two opposing surfaces, creating an angel in blood. Remember, an owl's feathers are not waterproof like those of other birds. With each bat of its wings, the blood was licked up by the tips of the owl's feathers. This is not a deliberate clean-up. The wipes were made by the wings of an owl, beating against the opposite sides of step 17.

This explanation finds further support in the fact that most of step 17 was free from blood. If Kathleen's wounds were pouring blood onto the floor, the blood had seemingly been stopped on its way. The best explanation is that something was on this step which acted as a barrier between the floor and the blood from Kathleen's head. The body of a bird of prey prevented blood from reaching the step.

If Kathleen fell in the stairwell, or if she was beaten about the head, then blood should be all over the two bottom steps. But it isn't. The fact that there is very little blood on step 17 is highly suggestive of the fact that something lay between Kathleen and the staircase when she died.

Other findings in Deaver's report are consistent with an owl attack within the stairwell. Deaver found evidence that indicated impacts to Kathleen's head had occurred very high above the steps. These impact spatters could not have resulted from contact with the steps themselves. There was no way they had resulted from a fall. It was seriously bad news for the defense. So how did Deaver discover that impacts had occurred at such a height?

Deaver selected forty-two individual spots of blood on the walls. He then applied a method called "stringing," wherein long nylon strings are attached to the flecks individually and then pulled together in line with their angle of impact. The end of each string was taped to a rod placed vertically on the steps. The aim of this method is to draw back from several flecks of blood to a common source. Performing this analysis, Deaver found that the strings converged at two points: one point was eighteen inches above a step; the other was eleven inches above a step. One of these impacts had occurred barely two inches from the wall of the stairwell. This simple test demonstrated that at least two impacts to Kathleen's scalp occurred not on any particular step, but in mid-air. It was terrible news for the theory that she fell.

While this was bad news for the fall theory, it is not bad news for the owl theory so long as we assume that a bird was inside the stairwell with Kathleen in her final moments. If the owl's talons hit Kathleen's head while she crouched on the stairs, then we would expect impacts in the general areas found by Deaver.

Other strange bloodstain anomalies in the stairwell point to an owl. In his more detailed analysis of the stains in the stairwell, Deaver noted something extremely weird. Despite the fact that Kathleen was meant to have been writhing at the bottom of the stairs, Deaver did not find any handprints nor did he find fingerprints. What he found was a series of what he described as "fingerlike marks" on the stairs and on the walls of the stairwell. Some of these marks were even found to curl around the noses of the steps, landing on the surface underneath. Deaver never committed to the claim these marks were made by human hands or fingers; in fact, he deliberately held back from making this claim. There is reason to think the marks were not made by human hands. Every set of fingerlike transfer stains Deaver found had only three or four digits. He never found a print with all five fingers. All over the steps and the walls, he found numerous fingerlike prints having at a maximum four digits.

Why would he use this term? Why not simply call them fingerprints or finger marks? What else is "fingerlike" but fingers? Of course, it is possible that what Deaver found in the stairwell were finger marks left by human hands. He just never found a complete handprint or an identifiable human fingerprint. Perhaps Deaver was using uncharacteristically cautious language. But the preponderance of bloody imprints that had only three or four digits is suggestive of a non-human origin.

Owls have four digits on each foot. Moreover, owls tend to arrange their dexterous grip in one of two different formations. They can shift their feet so that three talons are facing forward, one facing backwards, in a trident-shaped pattern. They can also shift two digits to face forward, leaving two behind, in an arrangement typical for hunting (this arrangement is sometimes called the "square of death"). So, the existence of three- and four-digit fingerlike marks throughout the stairwell is not just consistent with owl feet, but consistent with the typical configurations into which they arrange their digits.

But the strangest anomaly of all was not the fingerlike marks. The strangest feature of the blood in the stairwell was the lack of any bloodstains under Kathleen's head. Before Michael inserted the towels beneath her head, Kathleen's wounds lay directly over the bottom step—step number 18. Her scalp was ripped and the skin was lying limp against the step. Blood oozed from her head, soaking her hair and her sweatshirt. Yet on the very step that held her head, directly beneath the wounds, no blood was found.

Think about that again, carefully. In the area which should have held the largest amount of blood, there was none at all. Kathleen's head lay on the bottom step, and the bottom step was almost completely clean. Whether Kathleen fell or whether she was murdered, that is simply impossible. We have a situation in which a woman bled to death from serious head wounds, with no evidence of the fact on the step beneath her head. The walls were red with blood, but the steps themselves were relatively clean. They had not been wiped and they had not been cleaned up. There just wasn't anything there!

Could the towels which Michael inserted under Kathleen account for the lack of blood? This explanation cannot work for the simple reason that her head had laid on the steps for a long time before the towels were inserted.

So what could have been between Kathleen and the floor which blocked the flow of blood? Notably, there is some blood on the bottom step. It is simply restricted to the edges of the step. The blood in these areas traces an outline of whatever object was between her head and the bottom step. It is within this boundary that we find a shadow which is almost perfectly wing-shaped.

A wing-shaped object was under Kathleen's head when she was bleeding out.

If the fall theory is correct, then there was nothing wing-shaped in the stairwell with her. If Kathleen was bludgeoned to death, it was not with a wing-shaped object that was later resting beneath her head. The best explanation for a wing-shaped blood shadow on the bottom step is that a bird's wing under Kathleen's head blocked the flow of blood onto the floor in her dying moments.

So, there are various facts about the distribution of the blood in the stairwell that are well explained by a bird's presence: The one-inch-tall wipe marks on the opposite sides of step 17 can be explained by the tips of beating wings. The preponderance of "fingerlike" transfer stains is consistent with the feet of an owl. And the lack of blood on each of the two bottom steps can be accounted for if we assume that something large was attached to Kathleen's head as she died.

These are all specific features of the blood spatter evidence well explained by the existence of an owl in the stairwell. But if we step back from these individual trees and view the forest for a moment, we find a more holistic explanation for the vast amount of blood sprayed across the walls of the stairwell.

With more than ten thousand individual specks, splatters, and cast-off impressions, the scene was much bloodier than even the most brutal homicides. According to the prosecution, Michael struck Kathleen across the head less than ten times. Ten strikes to the skull could not explain this much blood. But in contrast, we might wonder, how many times an owl would have beaten its wings during its attack? If the wings were soaked with blood, then the inordinate amount of blood, sprayed at various strange angles, makes a lot more sense.

In attempted reconstructions of the murder, the NCSBI had spent several thousands of dollars building a one-to-one scale model of the stairwell. In the enclosed space, Deaver struck a blood-soaked mannequin head thirty-eight times with a blow poke. He grabbed the dummy head and bashed it against the ground multiple times, attempting to recreate the blood spatter in the staircase. Both attempts were abject failures. There was nowhere near the same degree of staining covering the walls. His attempts were failures because the stains were not caused by spray from Kathleen's head wounds. The cast-off patterns that drenched the walls were caused by beating wings.

THE KITCHEN

Officer Juanetta McDowell had called Criminal Investigations almost as soon as she arrived at the scene; she called Sergeant Fran Borden. As soon as he arrived, he noticed blood in the kitchen area, seeing blood in the kitchen sink first. A sprinkling of red liquid was found here. It was one of the first observations that made Borden skeptical of Michael's claim of an unfortunate accident. So how did it get there?

Drops of blood in the sink are far from unexpected. We know that Michael washed his hands. He was asked to quit by Detective Terry Wilkins and immediately complied. And this event occurred before Borden arrived on the scene. There is nothing at all surprising about flecks of wet blood found in this location. It was simply surprising to Borden, who knew nothing of the hand-washing episode.

But Borden noticed other red marks on the faces of some of the kitchen cabinets. This supposed blood transfer was supposed to support the idea that Michael had staged the scene. According to the prosecution's story, Michael went to the cabinets after killing his wife and retrieved two champagne flutes, which he placed beside an empty bottle of wine. It was all part of his attempt to make it seem like Kathleen had been drunk as a skunk. This theory was undermined by the evidence that Kathleen had been drinking that night. It was also undermined by the testimony of Christina Tomasetti, who witnessed Michael retrieving the wine glasses from the cabinets at approximately 10 p.m.

But if there was blood on these cabinets, it was suspicious nonetheless. Michael must have gone to the cabinets after his hands were bloody. Why?

To answer this, we first need to take a look at where these alleged bloodstains actually were. What did the crime scene photographs show? At trial, it was impossible to tell. In the photographs of the cabinets presented at trial, the images were so overexposed as to prohibit any meaningful identification. They were also discolored with a pervasive sepia tone, which made the entire scene appear a strange shade of burnt orange. The photos that were supposed to represent bloodstains on the cabinets showed nothing at all. In fact, not a single photograph of the kitchen cabinets showed any blood there.

Peter Duane Deaver presents a discoloured photograph to the jury at trial. Trial video.

This was a fact that the authorities openly admitted. At trial, Deaver was asked whether the blood on the cabinets could be observed in one of the shoddy photographs depicting the area. "No" was his simple answer. Deaver was not alone. Dan George was also presented with the discolored photographs of the cabinets. Where, exactly, was the blood to be found?

"The smudge of blood was on the bottom right-hand door of the cabinet molding and on the outside door," George told Rudolf.

"The part you can't see?" Rudolf asked with obvious irritation. The photograph did not depict these areas.

"That's correct, sir."

"Did anyone take a photograph of the part that you could see?"

"Angie Powell was taking the photographs and I don't understand why that photograph is as discolored as it is."

"But even if it was a good color, putting aside the quality, you couldn't see the areas with smudging."

There were other photographs of the alleged bloodstains in the kitchen that were even more problematic. During later questioning, Rudolf presented two crime scene photographs of a kitchen cabinet to George. The two photographs were taken on the very same day. In one of these photographs, there did appear to be a distinct black or crimson mark on the face of the cabinet. In the other photograph of the very same area, there is no mark to see. We know the two photographs were both taken on December 9, but there is no way to tell which was taken first.

What could possibly have happened in the interim of each photograph? Bloodstains on cabinets don't appear from nowhere. And neither do they vanish at will. What was the explanation?

"I was told that this was a photo glitch," George told Rudolf.

"Photo glitch?" Rudolf repeated incredulously.

George nodded. "Something happening in the processing."

"So that's not actually a bloodstain there?"

"No, it isn't."

"And how would someone looking at that photograph know that?"

"They wouldn't."

"Did you note down these glitches anywhere?"

"No, sir."

"Who explained to you that this was a glitch?"

"I don't recall right now."

"Do you know how many glitches there are in the photos?"

"No, sir."

It was a devastating episode of questioning that made a mockery of the claim that the photographs constituted a reliable representation of the scene as it appeared in the hours following Kathleen's death. The police had claimed there was blood all around the kitchen, yet there was no evidence of this at all. Apart from the testimony of the officers, there is nothing to suggest there was any blood in the kitchen.

The North Wall Shadow

The real problem for both the defense and prosecution alike was not the blood; it was the *lack* of blood. There was virtually no blood on the upper portion of the north wall of the staircase. Instead, there was a clean area of wall space that measured about a foot in diameter. It was the first area Deaver noticed as strange, and he wrote in his notes that this was a "shadow."

Despite having first identified the area as a blood spatter shadow, Deaver eventually testified at trial that Michael must have wiped the wall clean. That was the State's explanation. The defense rejected this claim and contended that Deaver's change of heart had been disingenuous. The area really was a shadow after all. But this would mean that some object had gotten between Kathleen and the blood spraying from her head. And what could have been in the stairwell with Kathleen? Wasn't she alone when she fell?

Neither theory is satisfactory. Neither the defense nor the prosecution could explain what had happened. Let's look at the prosecution's explanation first.

There are two reasons that the prosecution's argument fails:

> 1. There was no evidence of any wiped blood on this patch of wall. And so, there was no evidence of a clean-up.
> 2. There was blood spray extending over the clean area, which indicated that Michael had not cleaned the wall after killing Kathleen.

Proving that blood had been wiped away would have been easy. The State could have performed a luminol test or a phenolphthalein test, which would have uncovered any residual serum. Why did they not test this area when positive evidence of a clean-up would have been the nail in the coffin for Michael's defense?

The prosecution tried to account for why there was blood spray extending over the cleaned patch. But they were forced to invoke a totally implausible scenario in which Michael bludgeoned Kathleen in the stairwell across two separate episodes. First, he beat Kathleen across the head until she was unconscious. He then collected cleaning products and started wiping up the blood on the north wall. But Kathleen regained consciousness, and so Michael had to stop cleaning the wall to beat her again until she died. In this final beating, her blood sprayed across the area he had just cleared of blood. After she was finally dead, he discontinued the clean-up.

The prosecution's explanation of the clean patch on the north wall is very problematic. But the explanation from the defense was also implausible. Their best explanation for the spatter shadow was that Kathleen had sputtered and coughed up blood over the walls. Holding her arm or her clenched fist against her mouth, the blood sprayed across the wall, leaving a shadow where the spray had been blocked. This explanation is also implausible for two reasons.

1. At autopsy, Kathleen was found to have a negligible amount of blood in her airway, hardly enough to cough up great sprays across the wall.
2. The force required to cough up blood from the ground to the wall over such a wide area would have been immense—most likely beyond Kathleen's abilities.

So neither the defense nor the prosecution had a good explanation for the anomalous clean patch on the north wall.

The blood on the walls had obviously come from Kathleen's head. She had no other severe cuts on her body. Some object had to be between the wall and the blood spraying from her head. Something must have been in the stairwell with Kathleen which prevented her blood from reaching this area of the wall. What was the object? In crime scene photographs, the spatter shadow has a clear outline. And it is the outline of an object that seems to have been floating in mid-air or attached to Kathleen's head.

The outline of the object is clear and distinct. Like the negative of a photograph, the spray of blood exited Kathleen's head and left the distinct impression of her killer on the wall. This impression—the outline of a bird of prey—is immediately recognizable by simply increasing the contrast of some available crime scene photographs. Two open wings and a pair of feet can be seen reaching down into a waterfall of blood.

Crime scene photo of the north wall with enhancement.

CHAPTER NINE: FEATHERS

MISSING FEATHERS

If an owl latched onto Kathleen, more feathers should have been found. Sure, Larry found two microscopic feather fragments. But if an owl was truly responsible for Kathleen's death, there should have been innumerable whole feathers at the Peterson house that night. There should have been feathers strewn about on the outside path. And there should have been even more found inside the stairwell. But if the police are to be believed, none were found.

In the face of this objection, there seem to be only a few possible answers available:

1. The owl's attack was controlled and quick, and so the bird subsequently lost few feathers. (This was Larry's solution.)
2. There were no feathers out on the path or inside the house. And so, there was no bird. (This was the State's solution.)
3. There were many feathers on the path and inside the house, all of which were destroyed, obscured, or mislabeled by authorities.

The last of these options, outlandish as it sounds, is the true story of the Michael Peterson case. He was not the victim of a homophobic jury but of a corrupt police force. Like the talon shard that conveniently vanished, the feathers were eliminated or hidden before they could come to trial. We will never know what became of them.

Twenty hours after arriving on the scene and operating without any external oversight, the house was finally vacated by the police around midnight on December 10. By that time, a handful of officers who controlled the taped-off areas had removed hundreds of feathers from around the house.

THE DAN GEORGE VIDEO

Some of the best evidence for the existence of feathers in the house is found in the crime scene video itself, although the feathers themselves are difficult to identify with the untrained eye. They are obscured by what seems to be poor-quality film. The footage was recorded by Dan George shortly before dawn on December 9. His video begins outside the house, quite a distance down the front path. The footage was presented to the jury with no audio, and the silence only makes the grisly scene appear all the more sinister.

As the camera is switched on, George films an eerie view of the open front door to 1810 Cedar Street. The yellow light from the inside of the house casts sickly rays across the bushes lining the path. The quality of the footage seems incredibly poor. It is discolored with the same sepia-like tones that had infected all the still photographs Angie Powell had taken.

From his position at the end of the path, George zooms in. He focuses closely on a heavy litter of debris along the right side of the front path. George seems to be filming a pile of dead leaves. He lingers on these "leaves" for a moment, before tracing a line up the path from the debris to the front door. He remains on the front door for several seconds before zooming out. The camera is then switched off.

Why on Earth was the path littered with that stuff?

This is the very first moving image of the crime scene, the first piece of film presented to the jury. And yet it appears to show nothing of much importance. We are shown the front path. We are shown, in detail, a pile of what seems to be old leaves. The camera then pans from the debris to the door. And all of this is shot from a great distance away. So just what visual storytelling is happening here? What exactly is George trying to convey?

Indeed, we should pause to think more carefully. If Kathleen was truly beaten to death in a stairwell, why would George begin his footage outside on the front path, filming a pile of debris that appears to be nothing more than old leaves? Why does he then trace a line that runs from these leaves, along the path, and into the open front door? Wasn't it Larry who first said that the prosecution's narrative had the events of that night back to front? Kathleen's attack began outside.

The debris on the path, taken from the crime scene video.

George lingers on the debris on the path precisely because it is not a pile of leaves. And it is the very first thing he films just because it is so very important. He is telling a story in pictures. The murky light that illuminates the scene makes visual identification difficult, but there are features of the "leaves" that are difficult to make heads or tails of. Notably, the debris is highly reflective. Some of it is drenched in shadow but appears bright white, powerfully reflecting whatever dim light spilled out the front door. The same effect can be seen within the hedges themselves, where sharply defined bright white flecks poke out from the greenery. If these leaves are the remnants of an autumn death, they are not brown and without luster. Instead, they have a strong sheen that glows out of the darkness.

Looking at the debris more closely, some of it appears to have striped markings and odd patterns, consistent with feathers. And remarkably, the distribution of the debris is not random. There is far more of this debris strewn along the right side of the path, directly over the area where the first blood drop was discovered. This fact is anomalous if they were just leaves. But if they were feathers resulting from an owl attack, their location is no surprise.

After filming from beyond the front path, George switches on the camera again. This time, he is walking up it. He comes to the first blood drop, which was found tucked between two pavers several feet from the front door. The stain is surrounded by stripy debris.

After zooming in on this bloodstain, George moves towards the second blood drop, found on the front landing. He stands a few feet away and zooms in on the little red mark which lay in front of a large concrete planter. But there is something strange about this particular drop of blood. It has a vivid white border, as though a chalk outline had been drawn around it. It is not a simple circle of red; it doesn't really look like a plain drop of blood at all.

When George was testifying at Michael's trial, it was the district attorney who first drew attention to the strange white outline.

"Now there seems to be a white circle around the object in this frame. What is that about?" Hardin queried.

"From the time I initially observed this object," George replied, "the paper was placed down. The planter was put there. This was maybe fifteen to thirty minutes afterwards. And this is because of the weather." He then continued, "This has started grabbing a circle around the drop of blood."

"Did you do a lift of this drop of blood?"

"No. That was overlooked."

It is somewhat baffling that the alleged stain of blood is described as an "object" by both Hardin and George. But there are two other oddities to note about George's testimony here.

First, we are given no proper explanation about what caused the white outline. He says it was due to "the weather" but does not clarify what he means. The weather made the blood drop "grab a circle" of white. Perhaps he means to say that the paper was placed on top of the blood drop and was removed sometime after the blood had dried, leaving a circle of white paper that had adhered to the perimeter of the stain. But then, what did the weather have to do with this? It was not raining that morning, so that is not part of the explanation. There was, however, a light breeze that morning. Does he mean that the piece of paper was arranged to stop the drop of blood from blowing away? But blood drops do not blow away with the wind. So what was going on? How did a spot of red blood magically grow a vivid white border?

Second, and perhaps more suspicious, we are told that no lift of the blood was taken. In other words, the blood was never tested. The process of "lifting" a bloodstain is a bit like the lifting of fingerprints, in which a sticky tape is applied to the blood and the transfer is kept as evidence. With no lift having been performed, we have no forensic evidence that what George was filming on the front step was blood at all. All we have are the testimonies of the responding officers, and all they say is that it appeared to be blood.

As with the earlier footage of the front path, the color of the film appears to be entirely washed out. It is extremely difficult to make out much detail. Every object filmed is masked by a warm yellow glow. It is as though the color temperature has been manipulated, obscuring the true differences between white, red, blue, and green. Indeed, when crime scene photographs of the front step are compared with the film, it is clear there are many feather-like objects scattered beneath the door which are not visible in the video.

The crime scene video, then, is failing to tell the whole story. When the footage is submitted for analysis using tools of digital image forensics, a clearer view develops as to the real objects shown in any particular frame. A process of pattern recognition called Principal Component Analysis (PCA) is especially useful here. Using PCA, meaningful patterns can be found hiding in the footage not detectable by the naked eye. These patterns represent significant differences in the distribution of red, blue, and green. PCA can be used to enhance the image of the "blood spot" on the front step. The PCA enhancement indicates that the "blood drop" and its white border is just one large object among many smaller ones.

The "blood drop" on the front step, with enhancement. Crime scene video

The PCA shows us that there are probably several objects on the ground. Despite being difficult to make out in clear detail, they resemble feathers in their size, striped coloration, and shape. Some of the patterned objects extend from the concrete over the paper. This indicates that they are a real feature of what was filmed and not a mere artifact of the PCA enhancement. If these patterns do represent feathers, then they were on the ground when Dan George filmed them. And if George did indeed film them, then the video footage has been tampered with in order to hide them. What seems to be poor-quality film is in fact a consequence of high-tech video manipulation. The video, just like the still photographs, has been altered.

George then turned his attention from the blood spot and proceeded to film the open front door. At the moment he filmed this, a bald police officer can be seen inside the house, standing in the hallway. This unnamed officer lifts a foot to check the sole of his shoe. He then lifts the other foot and does the same thing. What did the officer think had gotten stuck to his shoes? It may pay to note that owl feathers are incredibly fluffy and adhesive, much like cobwebs, because of the down along the base of their quills.

After George filmed the frame of the front door, he lingered to show the audience the doorbell, filming the bell closely for several seconds. Suddenly, there is a break in the film. When the footage starts up again, the doorbell is still the focus of the frame. On first viewing, it appears as though George switches the camera off, then switches it on again mid-frame. The edit is very strange. There seems to be no reason for the sudden stop in the video and it is likely that the middle portion of the film has actually been removed. Given George's fondness for the zoom feature on the camera, it is likely that he had zoomed in on the doorbell. For some reason, the close-up of the doorbell is missing.

The strangeness of this cut was apparent to anyone watching the video. At trial, Hardin questioned George about this suspicious edit in the video footage. "Now, it looks like you're videotaping for a little bit, and then there is a break in the footage, and then more videotaping. Can you explain what is happening there?"

"I was stepping up on the step and trying to step over the blood, so if it looks like it has been... I mean, if it looks like I have been moving around quite a bit, that's exactly what I was doing. Making sure I didn't step in that droplet of blood."

"Is this videotape a continuous stream or are there breaks?"

"There are breaks because of my movement through the house."

This explanation is mystifying. George was standing several feet away from the drop of blood when filming the doorbell. He was nowhere near it, and so he was not stepping over it, and so his explanation must be false—a deliberate cover story.

Indeed, whatever the truth ultimately is for this edit in the tape, the best practice in crime scene videography is to take only one continuous shot. "You should record only one scene on a video tape and the original video tape *should not be edited*,"[28] writes Steven Staggs in his authoritative forensic handbook, *Crime Scene and Evidence Photography*. For this reason, any cuts or edits in the crime scene video should be taken as suspicious.

With that in mind, consider the following: Dan George's video contains twenty-one scene cuts in just over twelve minutes of footage—almost one every thirty seconds. The footage has not only been manipulated, it has been heavily redacted.

So, why edit out a close-up of the doorbell? In no testimony did any investigator state there was anything interesting about the doorbell. There was no blood noted there. And no officer ever mentioned the doorbell as an

28. Staggs, S. 2014. Crime Scene and Video Photography, Second Edition. https://www.crime-scene-investigator.net/video.html

object of interest. Yet George filmed it closely, as though there was something important to see. Again, the quality of the footage is poor, so it is difficult to identify anything on the doorbell with the naked eye. But when image enhancement is applied, it is apparent that an object resembling a short, downy feather is sitting directly over the doorbell.

The doorbell with an enhancement of a probable feather. Crime scene video

After filming the doorbell, George proceeded inside the house and walked down the hallway towards Kathleen's body. Her legs stretched out wide across the hallway. Her head was resting on the bundle of towels on the bottom step. The scene of her death was difficult to make out because it was all so dark. Only the dim bulbs of the adjoining kitchen illuminated her corpse. So, George switched on the hallway light. This was the very first time anyone saw Kathleen's body under proper lighting.

George stepped forward and scanned the body up and down. He documented the items that surrounded Kathleen: tennis shoes, flip-flops, paper towels, a shirt, and Michael's reading glasses. As he panned the camera, a feather can clearly be seen sitting across Kathleen's right ear, tan in color. This particular feather can be seen with the naked eye. Indeed, there were several more that could be seen on her face and hands. But the video manipulation obscures that numerous others cover her hair and face.

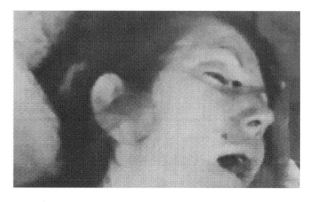

Feather across Kathleen's ear, enhancement of the crime scene video.

When George descended the staircase a few minutes later, the camera caught sight of a feather sitting over Michael's reading glasses and the paper towels. Michael's glasses can no longer be seen. They were obscured beneath the quill. And strangely, the orientation of one of the paper towels has shifted. Having previously pointed up the steps, it now points out towards the exit. It had been moved. Who moved it and why?

Feather across a paper napkin (indicated). Crime scene video.

If there were feathers inside the stairwell—recorded in the crime scene video—an obvious question comes up: why had nobody noticed any feathers in the video before? Part of the problem has to do with their color. The feathers are a sort of reddish-tan. The steps themselves are a brownish-tan oak. There was blood on the faces of the steps. So it is exceedingly difficult to discern any difference between the reddish-tan of the feathers, the red of the blood, and the wood tone of the oak steps. The sepia tone that discolors the video makes it even harder to tell the difference between yellow, red, and brown objects.

Feathers, if they were there, would be difficult to see. Indeed, the police photographer, Angie Powell, would later state in an interview that if any feathers had been lying on the steps around Kathleen, they would have been difficult to discern against the honey-colored wood. This comment is an incredible concession, given the thorough forensic analysis the stairwell was later subjected to. Rather than outright rejecting the claim that feathers might have been in the stairwell, Powell instead provided a strange excuse as to why they might have been hard to see.

George continued with his film. He stood over Kathleen and zoomed in for a detailed view of her right eye. When he zoomed in, a white object (looking something like the reflection of a teardrop) was clearly visible, poking out from the corner of her eye. But of course, this couldn't have been a teardrop. Kathleen had been dead for many hours by the time the film was taken. Any tears would have dried long ago in the ambient temperature of the house. So what was the distinct white fleck sitting in the corner of her eye? It was clearly some kind of object. Why was it not mentioned by the police at the scene or by the medical examiner at the autopsy? Why was George not questioned about it? Again, when PCA is applied, it is clear that the white fleck is only part of a larger object which lay over Kathleen's right eye and across the bridge of her nose. Another one of the feathers. After enhancement, even the most subtle details of the feather's striped pattern can be seen.

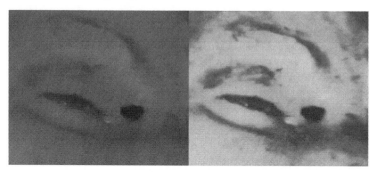

Kathleen's eye in the crime scene video with enhancement.

Coming down from the top of the staircase, George zoomed in on Kathleen's hair, which was supposedly drenched only with her blood. And yet, after forensic enhancement, more white flecks and striped objects can be found behind her ear. The police never testified to finding anything in her hair apart from a single piece of what was regarded as woody vegetation. Could there have been numerous feathers in Kathleen's hair as well? When interviewed, Angie Powell did not deny this possibility. But she again gave an excuse about why they'd be hard to see. If any feathers had been in Kathleen's hair, they would have been difficult to identify after having been drenched with blood. Since owl feathers are not waterproof, they would indeed be soaked with blood.

George carried on with his film. He went to the top of the spiral staircase. He filmed a bookcase at length, for some unclear reason. He entered an upstairs bedroom and zoomed in on a wooden beam clumsily tossed on the floor. He then documented the two sinks in the kitchen. He filmed the couch in the open-plan kitchen-lounge area. And finally, he returned to the body and concluded the video with a morbid scene of the blood pooling under Kathleen's back.

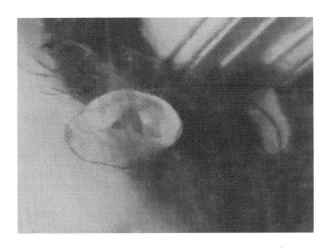

Downy white material in Kathleen's hair,
enhancement of crime scene video.

And that is the video. That is the full extent of it. Surprisingly, many relevant areas of the house were—we are supposed to believe—never filmed.

To name just a few, the "blood spots" on the kitchen cabinets were not filmed. The laundry room was not filmed. The dining room was not filmed. The study was not filmed. The spilled kettle and soft toy on the outside patio were not filmed. The pool area was not filmed. The downstairs garage was not filmed. Out of the fourteen rooms in the Petersons' mansion, only five areas were documented with the camera: the stairwell, the landing, the open-plan kitchen, the main entrance area, and a single bedroom. Some of the items in these rooms were documented in mere snippets of film, some as brief as five seconds. The upstairs bedroom, which was suspected to harbor a "murder weapon" garnered seventeen seconds of film. The couch—smeared with bloodstains when Michael sat on it—was less lucky, receiving only thirteen seconds of coverage.

In truth, it is safe to assume that the rest of the video documenting the scene has been destroyed. Whatever footage remains has been deliberately manipulated. And it has been manipulated for a very specific reason: to obscure the hundreds of brown or reddish-tan feathers that covered Kathleen's body and that were littered around the house.

FEATHERS IN A STRAINER

The quality of the crime scene video was suspiciously substandard. This should have immediately alerted Michael's lawyers to the possibility of tampering. But the poor quality of the video was not a unique problem. Almost all of the crime scene photographs were, for want of a better word, *abysmal*. They were washed out, sepia-toned, blurry, and overexposed. When asked about one severely brownish photo of the kitchen cabinets, George answered with feigned perplexity, "I don't understand why that photograph is as discolored as it is."

"Material" in the strainer. Crime scene photograph.

A particularly poor photograph was taken of a cooking pot, containing a strainer, sitting in the kitchen sink. Some kind of striped material, yellow and black in color, can be seen littered over the strainer. But apart from the yellow, the photograph is almost entirely colorless. It may as well be black and white. It is of such appalling quality that almost no detail can be made out. Are we really to believe that this was a simple mistake made by a professional crime scene photographer? Or is there another explanation?

The strainer was discussed at trial. According to the testimony of Sergeant Terry Wilkins, it was full of a brownish or reddish-tan material, which he claimed he could not identify. Freda Black was the first to question him about it.

"Is this a closer view of the pot in the sink?" she asked.

"Yes, it is," Wilkins answered.

"Are you able to say what was in the strainer?"

"There does appear to be some kind of material in the strainer."

"What color is it?"

"I'd describe it as dark tan, brownish yellow."

Material in the strainer? Dark tan, brownish yellow? What was all this about? Michael's attorney was confused by the line of questioning and quickly zeroed in on the matter during cross-examination. "Let's clear up one thing right away. You told Miss Black that there was something in the pot that was yellow, reddish-tan, or something?"

"Yellow reddish-tan, yes."

"Does that appear to you to be pasta?" Rudolf pressed.

There was a short pause.

"I have no idea what it is."

"Did you draw any significance from the fact that there was a bowl and a strainer and some pasta in the sink?"

"No, sir, I didn't."

"In any event, that wasn't seized as evidence, was it?"

"I don't know. I wasn't there when the evidence was being taken."

Rudolf waited a moment before asking the question that really mattered. "Do you have any idea why you were asked about that particular photo?"

"I-I-I don't," replied Wilkins, stuttering and glancing at the lead detective, Art Holland, who sat watchfully behind the prosecution bench.

At first, it seems obvious that the strainer must have contained leftover food, like bits of pasta. But it is strange that Wilkins chose to call the contents of the pot "material" rather than "food" or "leftovers." And why had he found the material, whatever it was, so hard to identify? Angie Powell, the investigator who took the very photo in question, could likewise give no verdict about the contents of the strainer but offered the explanation that it may have been cork or bits of cork. These are all cover stories. The police knew what they were looking at. There were feathers in the strainer.

Enhancement of material in the
strainer. Crime scene video.

Luckily, the overexposed photo is not the only image of the strainer available. Dan George briefly documented the area in his crime scene video. Comparing the poor-quality photograph with a still frame from the video, one thing becomes clear: the striped, reddish-tan material in the strainer is not pasta or bits of cork.

How did feathers get in the strainer? Were these left here when Michael washed his hands? Or were they deposited at another time, perhaps by a bird flapping inside the house? In some frames of the video, it appears as though there are feathers all over the countertop. Tan debris can be seen lying over other items on the kitchen counter. To give just one example, there are translucent tan objects scattered over a wine bottle stopper that lay beside the sink.

If these are also feathers, then feathers were not only in the strainer in the sink. Instead, they were littered all over the kitchen counter. How they got there is difficult to explain.

Photo Glitches

Obviously, the crime scene video was substandard. And obviously, the crime scene photographs were terrible. But worse than this, the crime scene photographs were contradictory. There are several examples of photographs, taken at different times, in which the locations of supposed "blood stains" move position or disappear entirely. How could this be possible? As we have already seen, Dan George gave the excuse that this was due to "photo glitches" but there were no further details given.

Who told him these were glitches? We don't know.

What sort of glitch? No answer.

If George's explanation is true, then not only were the crime scene photographs blurry, discolored, and overexposed, they were also littered with misleading errors and artifacts from the developing process. What sort of investigation was this?

One alleged example of a "photo glitch" is extremely informative. Two photos were taken of the kitchen cupboards. The photos were taken on the same day. One photo shows a large black or red mark on the cupboard door, while the other photo shows no mark there at all. If George is right, then this is a photo glitch. But if it is not a glitch, then there was some kind of material on the kitchen cabinet which disappeared (or appeared) between the time of the two photographs. And bloodstains do not appear or disappear out of nowhere.

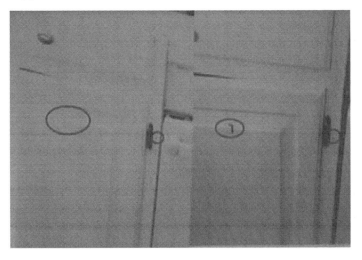

An example of a "photo glitch", as presented
by David Rudolf at Michael's trial.

As with every other crime scene photograph, the quality of both photos is appalling and very little detail can be seen. However, when the "glitch" is enhanced, it is clear that it is larger than just a thin dark line. Whatever was on the cupboard door, it was an object with a striped pattern. And the pattern resembles a pattern that is sometimes found on the smaller contour feathers of some owls: a thick black stripe, L-shaped, often at the base or tip of the feather.

*Crime scene photograph with enhancement
of "photo glitch" at inset.*

Bloodstains don't appear or vanish at will. What we are witnessing between the two photos is the movement of a light and downy feather. That is the reason for the differences between the photographs. This "photo glitch" can be explained if some object was on the cupboard door, which fell away from its original position.

The various other examples of "photo glitches" presented at trial can also be explained as having the same cause. Feathers are light and easily moved from place to place, often by nothing more than a gentle current of air. Bloodstains, on the other hand, stay exactly where they land.

Whether or not you accept that the glitches are actually feathers, it is obvious that something is amiss in the photographic evidence—the color temperature of the photos and video is extremely inaccurate; mysterious blood spots appear and disappear; objects around Kathleen's head change position; overexposure couldn't be controlled.

Two-thirds of the house went unfilmed, and the video itself contains twice as many scene cuts as minutes of film.

Luckily, not every photograph was corrupted. Some clearer photographic evidence of feathers remains. A photograph was taken of Dan George as he stood by the front door. At the base of the door, there is red debris. Its color is just like the material described in the strainer. These objects do not resemble dead leaves—their color is too vibrant. Angie Powell was tasked with photographing this strange debris. It was as though the objects were strange and worthy of documentation. Of course, the close-up photo she took is overexposed. But even in this photo, stripes and patterns can be seen. Why were these reddish-tan striped objects taken to be worthy of documenting? If these were just boring old leaves, it is hard to explain. If these were feathers, the reason is obvious.

Crime scene photograph of Dan George and the red, featherlike debris across the front step.

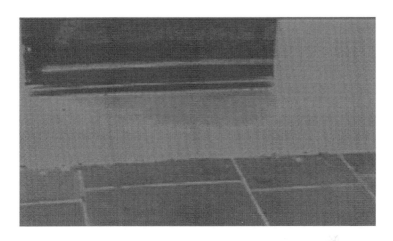

Crime scene photograph of the featherlike debris.

CHAPTER TEN: STAGING THE SCENE

LUMINOL TESTING

Michael staged the scene to look like an accident. That's what the prosecution said. And Michael did all of this staging, they contended, in the hours between Kathleen's death and the arrival of paramedics. According to the State, Michael had been lying when he told the 911 operator that Kathleen was still breathing. Red neurons discovered in Kathleen's brain were suggestive of the fact that she had died long before Michael telephoned. However, red neurons develop in any brain which has been subject to a prolonged period of blood loss. Kathleen's slow exsanguination could also explain these neurons.

The claim that Michael staged the scene made up an important pillar of the case against him. The State argued that Kathleen's death had probably occurred around midnight or 1 a.m., leaving Michael plenty of time to arrange things how he wanted. So what did the prosecution actually think he had done? That all began with the luminol.

We have already encountered luminol. It is a yellowish-white crystalline compound that gives off a brilliant blue luminescence that, when applied to blood, can be seen in a darkened room. It was what everyone thought had caused the white splats on the bottom step.

When used at a crime scene, it is applied as a thin, three-part solution consisting of sodium carbonate, sodium perborate, and the luminol itself, all diluted in distilled water. It is applied by forensic investigators to test for the presence of blood in areas where blood is suspected, while none is visible to the naked eye. It is sprayed carefully—thinly and evenly—over the surface to be tested. A bright blue reaction will occur where any blood is found. The glow may last for around ten to twenty seconds.

Luminol testing was largely restricted to the floor of the house. It was mostly applied to check for the presence of bloody footprints. The aim was to see where Michael had traveled and what he had done. But there were many problems to contend with.

> 1. With bloody feet, hands, and clothes, we know that Michael moved around the house before and after paramedics arrived.
> 2. Todd, with blood transfer stains on him, also moved around the house.
> 3. Heather Whitson and Ben Maynor (who was visibly drunk, by all accounts) moved around the house.
> 4. Dozens of investigators, paramedics, and fire officers also moved around the house while wet blood was still on the scene, long before any luminol test was performed.

With so much activity in the house prior to testing, there was little doubt that some of the blood detected with luminol would be a result of contamination of the scene.

Contamination was the defense counsel's favorite word when it came to the luminol evidence. But the defense also had another ace up their sleeve: the police had made no proper documentation of the results of the tests performed. At trial, the testimony of the forensics team about their observations was the only evidence offered to the jury. No photographs of the glow of luminol were taken. No contemporaneous diagrams were drawn. And the memory of each officer on the scene contradicted the others. The testimony itself, when it wasn't contradictory, was baffling. In sum, the luminol evidence was confusing. The testimony of the officers was a grab bag of bizarre and incoherent clues about Michael's movements around the house.

So, taking very careful steps and without jumping to conclusions, let us look more deeply at what was actually proven by the State's luminol tests.

THE FIRST TESTS

The very first luminol test occurred on the evening of December 9, around twelve hours after the discovery of the body. Dan George's right-hand man, Eric Campen, conducted the test under the direction of Duane Deaver. It was Deaver's suggestion. He directed Campen and made all decisions relating to what to test. The first test Deaver suggested was a rather sensible one. He asked Campen to spray luminol at the top of the staircase. Testing for the presence of blood at the top of the staircase was essential to deciding whether Kathleen had first been attacked at the top of the stairs or the bottom.

Campen confined himself to the top six steps. He began at step six, proceeding up to the top of the stairwell. Behind him, the agent Angie Powell followed with a chemical called phenolphthalein in order to conduct corroborative tests of anything that might glow. Phenolphthalein tests are almost always conducted in order to exclude any false positives. This is because luminol can sometimes glow in the presence of substances other than blood.

Step six had no reaction. Step five had no reaction. Step four had no reaction. But on step three, the luminol suddenly glowed like a firefly. On the right side of the step, a small pattern lit up. It appeared to be blood that had been smeared or scuffed. On the first step, in front of the kickplate, Campen discovered another solitary glow. Two more areas of blood on the landing were identified. And finally, the door beside the staircase was tested, where a small reaction happened on one panel.

Did these areas of blood prove that part of Kathleen's attack had occurred at the top of the stairwell? Nobody thought so. Each impression was consistent with contamination of the scene. No cast-off patterns or drips were found. Blood had most likely been trodden on by Michael or an investigator well after Kathleen's death and then been deposited in the upper portion of the staircase by the scuff of shoes and the push of a hand. The marks seemed unrelated to Kathleen's death, a fact Agent Deaver himself testified to at trial. Of course, the blood in these areas might have been deposited by Kathleen herself, but no one was conjecturing that this was the case. And since Michael retrieved towels from the upstairs bathroom, it is no surprise that some small specks of blood were found in this area.

On the same day, another test was performed. The location of this test was somewhat surprising. Luminol was sprayed on the door and walls and steps of a separate internal staircase which led to a downstairs garage. This internal staircase went under the site of Kathleen's body. Exactly why the investigators felt that this area was of particular interest is quite unclear. Perhaps they believed Michael had taken the blow poke to the basement. But whatever the reason was for testing this area, Campen reported finding nothing.

Ultimately, the first day's luminol tests were without reward. They uncovered nothing incriminating about Michael's movements. But that would all change on the second day of tests.

The Footprints

On the morning of December 10, a briefing occurred at police headquarters to discuss what further searches needed to be conducted and what further tests needed to be done. At the meeting, it was decided that the kitchen needed to be tested with luminol, as did the hallway which led from Kathleen's body to the front door.

Arriving at 1810 Cedar around 10 a.m., Campen arranged crime scene tape around the property line and spent most of the morning outside, collecting any evidence submitted by crime scene technicians from within. During this time, an empty soda can was collected as it had blood and hair on it. An unused condom and its wrapper were also collected from an upstairs bedroom. Strangest of all, a biopsy container was collected from an outdoor trash can.

By now, Kathleen's body had been removed and the autopsy was being performed. All that remained was a dried crater of blood beneath where her back had been lying. The floor between the bottom of the steps and the inside of the kitchen could now be checked for footprints. Alongside Campen and George, there were two others; lead Detective Art Holland and Detective Vince Bynum would observe the luminol test. After carefully mixing the chemicals, George began to spray the floor in a fan-like pattern, on hands and knees, crawling backwards. The thin film was evenly spread over the floorboards. The glow immediately started to appear.

The detectives followed the tracks that lit up for a few seconds at a time. It became clear that they exhibited directionality. One set of tracks led from the body, rightwards around the kitchen bar towards the fridge. Abruptly, the steps stopped in the kitchen. They just stopped.

Another set of tracks, apparently trodden over the first, went from the body, leftwards around the couch, and into the utility room. Again, the steps came to an abrupt halt in the laundry.

Neither set of tracks exhibited a return route. They simply terminated with no onward course. Despite the strangeness of this feature of the prints, the State now had something interesting to work with. It seemed that Michael had been rummaging about in the kitchen and utility room just after Kathleen's death. Curious.

The test of the hallway then began. This test was particularly important for the prosecution's case. After all, it was their contention that Michael had taken the murder weapon out the front door to dispose of it. George and Campen sprayed the entire length of the hallway, from the front door to the dark red circle of dried blood beneath where Kathleen had been lying. Holland watched in the company of Bynum as George went about—again on his hands and knees—waiting for those incriminating footprints to turn a guilty iridescent blue. But despite the spray of luminol, nothing glowed. There was nothing at all. The luminol failed to reveal any footprints. There were no tracks—none. This severely undermined the claim that Michael had fled the house carrying the murder weapon. And it also undermined the claim that Michael had been responsible for the blood smears on the back of the front door.

Despite this setback, investigators felt confident that the luminol tests of day two still provided evidence of staging. Sure, they had no evidence of Michael's alleged disposal of the murder weapon. But they had something else. So far as they could tell, Michael had walked from the body to the utility closet directly after murdering Kathleen. Why? Well, to get cleaning products, of course. What else was in the utility room that he could have been looking for? Furthermore, they could see that he had entered the kitchen after murdering Kathleen. Why? The prosecution said it was so he could collect and set down the wine glasses.

The lack of any footprints in the hallway was nothing but a minor hiccup. At least, that's what police believed. The agents had found different evidence altogether, which suggested crafty staging by the murderer. Why, after all, would Michael visit the utility room? Why, after all, would he visit the kitchen? It all looked like Michael had cleaned up and then planted evidence to suggest Kathleen was inebriated. And even if none of this directly proved that Michael murdered his wife, it showed, at the very least, that his priorities in the wake of discovering his wife's dead body were very strange indeed.

MAGIC FEET

At first, this all sounded like bad news for Michael. The jury was probably confused by Michael's alleged movements that night. Why had he gone into the utility room? What had he been doing there? And why the kitchen? Hadn't he remained with his wife after finding her body? If not, why not?

Of course, there was no debate that Michael had moved around the house after finding Kathleen dead. And the items surrounding Kathleen's body give us a clue as to some of his movements. For example, we know that he must have collected towels to place beneath her head. The paper towels are also suggestive of a trip to the kitchen. And we know that he must have collected the telephone to call 911. The portable phone usually resided on its receiver, just beside the kitchen counter. But even so, none of this would see Michael venturing into the utility room or deep into the kitchen. So, the tracks were a problem for the defense to explain. If Michael did leave the tracks behind, we need to understand why he went into these areas. After all, the luminol evidence clearly proved this was where he went. Or did it?

As a matter of fact, the prints that were found on the floorboards defied comprehension. Campen, George, and Bynum all agreed that one set of bloody marks traveled through to the utility room and that another set went through to the kitchen. And yet, magically, neither set of prints returned. It was as though whoever went into the utility room had hopped up on a shelf and stayed ever after. And it was as though whoever went into the kitchen opened the fridge and stepped inside, leaving no trace of a forward path. The bloody prints did not simply fade until they could no longer be seen. The footprints, if that's what they were, simply stopped. It was as if the maker of the bloody tracks had been suddenly plucked out of the universe by an interdimensional wormhole. All in an instant, the walker was zapped out of existence. And unfortunately for the prosecution, they could not appeal to wormholes.

To a layman, an immediate solution presents itself: the prints were made by both Michael and Todd. Despite seeming to have arrived at the same time as the paramedics, Todd had been there all night and was somehow involved in Kathleen's murder. One man went to the utility room and the other to the kitchen. Using a sink each, they meticulously cleaned their feet so that no more bloody tracks would be left. But this solution is a non-starter. No evidence of foot cleaning was found. And even if such a clean-up had occurred, luminol is powerful enough to detect even the most minute traces of blood. Heavily diluted blood, if it had been there, would have glowed.

Their sudden termination was not the only strange property of the footprints. The blood which had been trodden on the floor was eked out in a way that made no sense. Rather than finding the bloodiest footprints closest to the source of blood—the area around Kathleen's body—investigators said that the bloodiest footprints with the clearest outlines were at the sites of their termination. The two clearest sets of prints were found directly in front of the fridge and directly in front of the sink in the utility room. The bloodiest prints were found at the sites where the magical wormholes had opened. None of it made sense.

To understand how strange this situation is, consider how footprints are left after getting out of a swimming pool. The wettest and clearest footprints are found at the start of the stroll, and with each footstep, the clarity fades. Eventually, as the foot becomes dry, there is nothing to see. All the water has been removed.

But these feet were magic feet. They left tracks that got wetter the more they walked. And they left tracks that terminated suddenly, as though the walker had suddenly vanished into nothing. The tracks were not consistent with common sense. And seemingly, they could not even be made consistent with *un*common sense. They exhibited properties that were incongruent with a regular stroll made by bloody feet.

THE CONTRADICTIONS

The State's witnesses disagreed about what they had witnessed during the luminol testing. The disagreement crossed a spectrum, with Bynum at one end saying that only one or two whole footprints were observed, Campen in the middle saying that a clearly trodden path was seen and that every print observed was a complete footprint, and George claiming that there were so many footprints and scuffs observed that the effect was something like an expressionist painting.

"There were just so many. It had just been tracked so much," he said. To George's eyes, the sheer number of overlapping footprints made a clear observation of even a single one challenging.

Given the three men disagreed about the number of whole footprints observed, our best course of action is to only count the whole footprints all three of the investigators agreed about. Bynum observed two complete footprints facing the kitchen sink; George agreed there were footprints here, as did Campen. On this single point, they stood in unison. They disagreed about everything else. The investigators were sure that blood had been tracked on the floor, but the only two footprints they all saw clearly were down in front of the kitchen sink.

This may sound like nitpicking. They all saw prints... and prints are prints, aren't they? Even if the prints were strange in their shapes and distribution, they all suggested that Michael staged the scene. Didn't they? What else could have left the bloody marks running between the kitchen and the utility room?

Contamination.

Michael was the only person on the scene in bare feet. He had removed his shoes upon finding Kathleen's body. He said that the floor was too slippery. So if there were any bare footprints found on the floor, these must have come from Michael. But the only identifiable bare footprints were two that were found in front of the kitchen sink. So, it is possible that the rest were the result of contamination. It is possible that the "rabbit tracking" George witnessed had been caused not by Michael but by the more than forty individuals who had been through the scene that night. Michael himself might not have left *any* of the other prints. Of course, he most probably was responsible for some of the marks, but not necessarily those that entered the utility room or the interior of the kitchen. There is no reason to believe that any of the other marks were related to Michael's movement through the house.

Certainly, the bare footprints in front of the kitchen sink must have come from Michael. He was the only person moving about without shoes on. But these marks are hardly incriminating. We know he washed his hands in the sink that night. Investigators watched him do it. And if he stood in front of the sink while he did this, with his feet still bloody, then it is little wonder that his bloody footprints could be clearly seen on the floor in precisely that area. Indeed, it would be strange if no prints had been found here.

The movements of Todd Peterson may also explain why tracks were found in the utility room. Todd had brought a can of soda to his father shortly after the arrival of Heather Whitson and Ben Maynor. Soda was kept in the utility room. Todd had been close to Kathleen's body at least twice that night: he was the first person to pull his father away from the body and he also asked the investigators if he could approach to take a closer look. In fact, he had also retrieved the phone from beside Kathleen's head when Officer Juanetta McDowell had requested it. There is little doubt that the soles of his shoes would have collected blood. And since no other complete bare footprints can be independently corroborated by the investigators, it is reasonable to think that Todd's movements around the house would have caused at least some of the blood tracking.

Ultimately, the luminol evidence fell very far short of its intended purpose. No records of the test results were given to the jury. The glow of the luminol was not photographed. And the memories of the investigators were mutually inconsistent. The jury never had the opportunity to view the results of the tests and the testimony they heard during trial was contradictory.

Campen's decision not to keep a record of the luminol tests was based, he said, on the fact that all the investigators would be seeing the same thing he saw. In other words, he trusted that each officer's testimony would corroborate the others'. Yet, very clearly, this failed to happen. The result was a hodgepodge of distorted memories which—two years after the fact—were about as reliable as a flat tire.

Bloody footprints do not suddenly disappear mid-walk. And bloody feet do not leave behind clearer and more distinct impressions the longer they walk. The investigators had clearly gone wrong somewhere in their analysis, but how they got it so wrong remains a mystery to this day. In any case, what the police claimed to have observed was almost certainly not what was seen. And if the blood on the floor truly did exhibit the out-of-this-world properties the prosecution maintained, then it was not Michael's innocence that the State denied; they were denying the very laws of nature.

THE CHAMPAGNE FLUTES

A key aspect of the State's argument was that Michael had removed champagne flutes from the kitchen cabinet and arranged them on the edge of the breakfast bar. He did this, they argued, to give the impression that Kathleen had been drinking the night she died. As we know all too well by now, she had been drinking on the night she died. Not much, we can agree. But she presumably wasn't taking great big swigs directly from the wine bottle either.

Even so, Michael's fingerprints were the only ones found on the glasses. SBI Agent Joyce Petzka testified that she lifted Michael's prints from one of the glasses. His fingerprints were also found on the wine bottle beside the two glasses. The prosecution was eager to remind the jury that none of Kathleen's prints had been recovered from either the bottle or the two glasses.

And yet, Kathleen obviously had been drinking that night. She must have drunk from one of the glasses on the kitchen counter. So why were none of her prints found? There is an explanation available: if she held the wine glass around its narrow stem, then her fingerprints would have been extremely difficult to collect.

Photographs of Kathleen at social events showed this was a way that she often held her wine glasses. She daintily clutched her wine glasses by the stem. If Michael had taken charge of pouring the drinks, then perhaps it is no surprise that none of Kathleen's prints were found.

Was there blood found on the glasses? If Michael had moved them into position with blood-soaked hands, then surely some blood was found. But none was. A molecular geneticist, Suzi Barker, swabbed both wine glasses in an effort to identify traces of blood. Nothing was found. And on a simple visual inspection, no red residue remained to be seen on either glass.

So, according to the State's theory, Michael collected wine glasses from the kitchen cabinet, leaving bloody stains all over their surfaces, yet he left no bloodied marks on the glasses themselves!

A STAGING OF WHAT?

Michael did not need to stage the scene as though Kathleen had been drinking. The toxicology exam showed that she had alcohol in her system. She was not blotto. She was far from soused. But the fact that she'd had anything to drink that night undercuts the claim that Michael staged the scene to appear as though she had been drinking. Michael didn't need to stage anything.

And what a bad job of staging he must have done! If Michael had wanted investigators to connect the dots between Kathleen and alcohol, he could have smashed a glass of wine beside her body or left a glass in her hands. Had he truly wanted Kathleen to look like a drunkard, he could have left an empty wine bottle in her lap. Why arrange two empty wine glasses neatly on the kitchen counter beside some expensive bubbly? Far from making Kathleen look like a sloshed mess, the arrangement leaves the impression of a relatively sedate night of entertainment, including a glass or two of wine. The fact is, the way that the glasses were arranged on the counter is in perfect accord with the way things actually stood. Michael and Kathleen watched a movie together, had dinner, and throughout the night, she had two or three glasses of wine.

The idea that Michael staged the scene also overlooks the various ways in which the scene was clearly poorly staged: The front door was wide open and wiped with blood;

Michael had bloody hands and his shorts were smeared with wet red stains; Kathleen's body was surrounded with towels and paper towels; Michael washed the blood from his hands in full view of the police—he may as well have been holding a smoking gun in his hand.

If Michael had hours to stage the scene, would he really focus on leaving such subtle clues? Why bring out two respectable wine glasses and empty a bottle of expensive wine down the sink? Why had he not cleaned the blood off the front door? Why had he not even shut the door? Why had he not changed out of his bloody clothes before officers arrived? Why had he not showered? Why didn't he wash his hands in the sink before the police could witness him doing it? Why had he not disposed of the paper towels that were so suggestive of a clean-up? And why—just why—would he invoke an unconvincing fall-down-the-stairs story rather than the more obvious intruder scenario?

The answer to all of these questions is one and the same: Michael did not stage the scene. He was not creeping around the house meticulously arranging things in the hours before investigators arrived. Michael, it is readily apparent, was a highly intelligent man. He was a university-educated man—a loquacious and acerbic social critic—and well-traveled to boot. He had reached a high status in the military and had certainly killed people in Vietnam. He was the sort of man who most probably could get away with a devious murder plot if he put his mind to it.

The truth is that Michael found Kathleen, he nursed Kathleen, wiping her face with paper towels and placing towels under her head before calling 911. He did not worry about how drunk the police might think the woman had been. He did not worry that her level of sobriety would be a key detail in a future criminal case. He worried only about one thing: that his wife might not survive to the morning.

Had Kathleen been drinking that night? The answer is yes. Had she been drinking from one of those glasses? The answer is almost certainly. Was blood found around the kitchen cabinets? If you trust the testimony of the officers of the Durham police department, then you'd probably say the answer is yes. But if you have absorbed the corruption that imbued so much of their testimony at trial, you will, at the very least, have serious doubts.

If Michael staged the scene, he focused all his energy on doing four irrational things.

1. Wiping two tiny areas on the bottom steps.
2. Emptying a bottle of wine down the drain.
3. Putting two champagne flutes on the kitchen counter.
4. Hiding the murder weapon, all the while floating out the front door like a ghost.

We must suppose that he spent all his time wondering how to make Kathleen appear drunk rather than changing his clothes or cleaning the blood from his hands and body. And we must suppose further that in the course of his deceptive staging, he had magic feet that could also become bloodier with each step, or he could float. The owl theory may sound improbable to an intelligent person, but at least it is not impossible.

CHAPTER ELEVEN: A TRAGIC COINCIDENCE

MICHAEL IN GERMANY

The Petersons settled in West Germany in 1974. They had moved to a little hamlet called Grafenhausen, a thirty-minute drive from Frankfurt. This was a different pair of Petersons: Michael and Patricia, his first wife. Patricia, known by the nickname Patty, was the mother of Clayton and Todd, Michael's only biological children, born in 1974 and 1976, respectively. The pair had married in 1966. Patty was a grade-school teacher with the Department of Defense. She was the only one employed. Officially, Michael had no income at all. Patty brought in the only salary to the household while Michael was engaged in a carefree life of writing and frequenting the gym. That was the story they told their friends and family.

Those who knew the Petersons found the situation difficult to understand. They lived a lifestyle that seemed beyond the capacity of a one-income household. Expensive cars, refined decor, regular holidays, and two spoiled children: it all looked too good to be true. Everyone thought that Michael must have been providing, somehow. But how? There were rumors, bubbling away, that spoke to some involvement with the intelligence community—the CIA, to be precise. Frequent overseas trips to East Germany, Yugoslavia, Japan, and Ethiopia were hinted at, which lent further credence to the idea Michael's life was far from ordinary. His prior involvement with the military was no secret. He was a Vietnam veteran and a distinguished one. But whether he was involved with the US defense apparatus at higher levels, no one was really sure. In a 1990 media interview promoting his war novels, Michael stated he had been acting as a "security consultant for the government" for fifteen years. And one can only guess that *security consultant* may have been a euphemism for something much more sensitive.

But beyond the speculations of friends, and perfectly acting out the role of househusband, Michael seemed content with his empty days, writing screeds of fiction and editorials through the night and visiting the gym during the day. The life he wished to portray was simply ordinary. This was how things appeared to Michael's sister, Ann, when she spent more than a year in Europe visiting her brother in 1981. She saw Patty working while Michael was working out. She found that the pair had developed a tight-knit group of friends—mostly expats—who lived in the same neighborhood. They all looked out for each other. They took care of each other. Even the care of the children was divided amongst the collective, who seemed to live their lives in the style of a hippie commune rather than as military adjuncts. "It was like one big family," said one observer. It was during this trip to West Germany that Ann met a particularly endearing friend of Michael and Patty's. The woman's name was Elizabeth Ratliff (née McKee). She worked in the same school as Patty—the Rhein-Main Air Base School.

Ann could never predict that just four years after her visit, Elizabeth would die a terrible death. The uncanny demise of Elizabeth would eventually cast a long shadow over Michael's trial. At the time, Michael had never been a person of interest in Elizabeth's death. But after the death of Kathleen in 2001, attention was turned back to the events that unfolded on that awful day in West Germany in 1985. Elizabeth, you see, was found at the bottom of a staircase.

This coincidence strikes most people as beyond troubling. For many, it is taken as conclusive proof that Michael was a killer. Not only had Michael killed twice, but he had done so using the very same modus operandi. Michael was not just a murderer, but a serial killer: the Staircase Killer.

By the time of Michael's trial, eighteen years had passed since Elizabeth had been found at the bottom of the steps inside her home. At the time of her death, the coroner had judged that she had died from a stroke. Patty Peterson was alongside the medical examiner as he viewed the body. "He took the spinal tap and held the contents up so that he could view it," said Patty. "I could see that it did not look clear, and that's when he made the statement, right there by her body in my presence, that she had died of a cerebral hemorrhage."

This cause of death would later be disputed by the medical examiner, Dr. Deborah Radisch, who argued in court that Elizabeth's death, like Kathleen's, was the result of blunt force trauma to the head. The finger, of course, was again pointed at Michael.

THE DISCOVERY

On November 24, 1985, a terrorist attack in Frankfurt was carried out by an Iranian national. The target had been US military employees and their families working at the Rhein-Main Air Base. A BMW carrying explosives was detonated in the parking lot of the Post Exchange. Thirty-five people in the vicinity, mostly Americans, were injured by the immense blast, which blew out numerous windows and left the car itself in shredded pieces. A six-foot crater was left in its wake. This was the second terrorist attack on Rhein-Main's personnel in four months. In August, three

Americans had been killed and more than twenty injured when the base was bombed by the West German Red Army Faction.

No doubt the Petersons and their tight-knit group of friends were extremely disturbed by these ongoing attacks. They were the targets of this fresh wave of terrorism. They were employees of the Department of Defense at Rhein-Main. Only as teachers, to be sure, but they still felt like walking targets. The air base had been taking measures to beef up security, but these new protocols were clearly not working. Personnel had been increasingly targeted. Everyone was living in a state of high alert.

It was the very morning after the Rhein-Main car bomb tore a hole in Frankfurt. A young woman named Barbara O'Hara turned up to work as usual. The weather was cold and snowy, so she opted for a taxi instead of her usual bike. She was employed as a nanny to assist with Elizabeth Ratliff's two young children, Margaret and Martha. Margaret, or Gigi, was nearly four years old. The younger sibling, Martha baby, was only two. Elizabeth needed the extra help. The father of the children had died in 1983— George had vanished during a secret military operation, which was rumored to have been the United States' invasion of Grenada in 1983. The circumstances of his death were withheld, giving Elizabeth little room to grieve. In the years following George's death, she struggled with depression. Both the cause and location of death were officially stated as "unknown."

The taxi pulled up. O'Hara hopped and trod through a little snow to the front door, only to see all the lights inside the house were on. This immediately struck her as unusual. She opened the door to find all the dishes laid out for breakfast. There wasn't a sound. No footsteps or clanging of pots or noisy children were heard. As she turned her head left, she saw a body in a heap at the bottom of the stairs. A spray of blood was along the wall beside the body. The face was so covered in blood as to be unidentifiable. Attached to the feet was a pair of yellow snow boots. They were Elizabeth's boots.

O'Hara began to hyperventilate. She launched over the body and up the stairs towards the telephone. She lifted the phone to her ear, but there was no dial tone. The line was inexplicably dead. She turned the numbers of the old-fashioned phone clockwise on their wheel. They whirred back into place. Still nothing. Racing out the front door, she found the taxi driver lingering outside. "Call an ambulance," she cried, "and call the police!"

She ran past the idling car and fled to the Petersons' house, which was only a few doors away. She thudded at the door for what felt like forever. It opened. "Hurry, quick, come with me!" she shouted at Patty, draped in a robe. "It's Liz!"

Michael emerged from the bedroom with tired eyes, woken by the sounds of panic downstairs. "What's this about Liz?"

With the situation explained, the trio ran to the Ratliff house. "She's still warm," the nanny panted as she ran, "but bleeding."

As they came to the door, they found Elizabeth's body on its side, almost in a fetal position. Michael crouched down and placed a hand on Liz. He sighed. "She's not warm, Barb," Michael said. "That was just the underfloor heating. She's dead, Barb."

Patty went to the kitchen and steadied herself on a stool, vacantly staring out at the snow. Everyone remained silent, including the two children who were asleep upstairs.

The children! O'Hara remembered the little girls, still in their beds upstairs. *They can't see this*, she thought. She ran upstairs, bundling up Margaret and Martha across two separate trips, taking them to be watched by the Petersons' boys, Todd and Clayton. She carried the girls down a back exit—a fire escape—to avoid them getting a glance at their mother's body. With the children now safely removed, O'Hara ran to the nearby house of Amybeth and Bruce Berner, two more close family friends. She was crying when she told the pair of the gruesome discovery.

Throwing on some clothes, Amybeth and Bruce followed O'Hara out the door toward Elizabeth's house. They ran as fast as they could. *Not Liz… Not Liz*, Amybeth's thoughts looped in a mantra of panic. *Please not Liz…*

But it *was* Liz. Or at least, it had been Liz. Now it was simply a body, a human corpse, bereft of life. The two new arrivals stood in the company of Michael and Patty, staring at the body of a deeply loved friend. Both women felt unsteady on their legs and sick in their stomachs. Amybeth did not stay long. She ran from the house almost as soon as she arrived. Reaching home, she called through the mail slot to her dog, who wagged her tail with excitement and bounded to the front door. Jumping up, as she had been trained to do, the dog expertly turned the lock mechanism with her bite and let her master enter. "Good girl," said Amybeth, a force of habit. She raced to the kitchen while the dog barked at the ongoing excitement, blissfully unaware of the human woe in its midst.

Amybeth grabbed a cookie tin filled with the phone numbers of important contacts. She opened it and found the number of Tom Appel-Schumacher, another close friend of Elizabeth. "Tom, you need to sit down," she said over the line. He followed her directions. "Liz has had an accident." The Appel-Schumachers soon rushed to the scene.

When Amybeth arrived back to the body, Patty was still sitting there in the kitchen, gazing at nothing, fixed in place by a deep emptiness. Michael was on the phone, arranging things that needed arranging. As Amybeth looked up and down the stairs, she saw a bloody footprint on the step. "Has anyone seen this?" she asked.

The others came over to look. Barbara O'Hara spoke first. "That was me," she said. "I went up the stairs to get the children."

Amybeth shook her head with irritation. "This is a crime scene. It needs to be investigated. Please don't walk on the stairs."

Amybeth remembered this exchange vividly as she testified at Michael's trial eighteen years after the traumatic event. Indeed, she claimed to have been having "flashbacks" of the events from nearly two decades ago—flashbacks which, strangely, went far beyond the content of her original written statement to the prosecution (a statement which never even mentioned Michael). "I have come here to testify to finally put this fire out," she stated with intensity, staring at Michael. She had come to believe he was responsible.

Amybeth's flashbacks included the troubling detail that Michael had been the first person on the scene to claim that Elizabeth had died from a brain hemorrhage, even before the medical verdict. Outside the presence of the jury, she also related that Michael had once told her directly that he was with the CIA, that he could arrange for a person to "disappear" and that he had done exactly that during the Vietnam War. And yet, incredibly, she testified that she had never suspected Michael, an admitted killer, was involved in Elizabeth's death. That is, not until she heard about Kathleen's death (which occurred nearly twenty years after Elizabeth's). Indeed, Amybeth's testimony was strange in its scope and detail, which was seriously at odds with her first written statement. The passage of time, far from corrupting her memory, seemed only to enhance it.

Back in the Ratliff home, the German medical officers had arrived and were drawing fluid with a spinal tap. Michael was communicating with them in broken German. Despite speaking fluent German, Amybeth stood back silently. The pathologist held up the vial of fluid and gave the verdict: a stroke.

Elizabeth had been afflicted throughout her life with von Willebrand disease, an inherited ailment shared by her father and siblings. Her father had also died of a stroke ten years beforehand. And in the weeks leading up to her death, Elizabeth had been complaining of increasingly frequent headaches. On the previous Thursday, she had a headache of such severity that she arranged a doctor's appointment for the following week.

Michael went away and called Elizabeth's employer, the Department of Defense. Shortly after the call, a US military policeman arrived. He was Steve Lyons, an exceptionally tall man who needed to duck under the frame of the door to make his way inside. The first thing he noticed was the pool of blood around Elizabeth's head. But he saw little else of interest. He had come to the scene to decide whether the death was suspicious and whether it would fall within the jurisdiction of the Americans. He took brief statements from all of Elizabeth's friends. Michael was the most animated among those at the house, given the troubling circumstances, and he led Lyons from person to person, proffering introductions.

The questions Lyons asked were straightforward: How did you know the deceased? Who found the body? When did you arrive? Had she been drinking? To this last question, one of the men (possibly Michael) stated that she had drunk one glass of champagne the previous evening.

Lyons asked the German medics about what had happened. The Germans were satisfied that a stroke and a fall had occurred. And all those interviewed echoed what the Germans had told them. Elizabeth had succumbed to the same fate as her father and then fallen down a flight of stairs. In sum, the scene did not appear to fall within the interest of the military police. Nothing looked particularly sinister to Lyons. So he left.

By the early afternoon, Elizabeth's body had been removed from the house by mortuary services. The blood from the cuts on her head had pooled onto the rug on which her body lay. Despite the immediate cause of death being a spontaneous brain hemorrhage, the scene was bloody and took many hours for the Appel-Schumachers to clean. Elizabeth's friends all had an inkling that her death was quite suspicious.

Barbara O'Hara was the most doubtful of all. Why had Elizabeth failed to remove her yellow snow boots at the front door, as was her usual practice? Had she skipped a step in her routine? Or had she been distracted by someone? Why was the phone line dead? Had it been cut? Or had Elizabeth simply failed to plug it in when she moved it to her bedroom for the night? What had actually happened here?

These were difficult questions that would never be answered. There were no other signs of foul play. Nothing was missing from the home. There were no signs of forced entry. The injuries to Elizabeth's head, although extensive, were arguably consistent with a fall. And at the time, nobody found Michael's behavior at all suspicious. Despite the fact that one witness claimed Michael had dropped her home the previous night—walking back to his house at a quick pace afterwards—nobody at the time doubted his love for Elizabeth and the two small girls. Nobody imagined for a moment that Michael would have killed his friend.

As things stood, Elizabeth Ratliff fell down the stairs after suffering a brain hemorrhage. Her head had been lacerated as she fell. That would remain the official cause of death until Michael's trial nearly twenty years later.

THE CHILDREN

In the aftermath of Elizabeth's death, Michael and Patty assumed custody of Margaret and Martha. The two girls now belonged to a much larger family of six. It was not a radical change for them as they had so often been cared for by Michael and Patty in the past. Elizabeth changed her will shortly after the death of her husband. The two events were directly related. An earlier version of her will granted custodianship to George's parents. Elizabeth, now having a closer relationship with the Petersons than her one-time in-laws, felt that they could provide a more natural and familiar home environment. The Petersons often took care of the girls. The girls knew the Petersons. To the youngsters, they were not just Michael and Patty; they were Aunt Patty and Uncle Mike. These eminently capable parents seemed to share the same values as Elizabeth herself. The terms of the will were clear:

> I hereby nominate, constitute and appoint Michael I. and Patricia S. Peterson as Guardians, acting jointly or separately, of each of my minor children until he or she reaches majority or is otherwise legally emancipated.

It was the sort of agreement that made perfect sense for a solo mother living far from her native Texas. However, after the staircase death of Kathleen Peterson, doubts arose as to the unusual terms of Elizabeth's will.

In North Carolina, suspicions about the real relationship between Michael and Elizabeth were growing. "Don't those girls look just like him though?" Durham's housewives whispered to each other after church. These rumors came to be taken seriously by the lead detective on the case, Art Holland. Indeed, the girls did look like Michael. It was indisputable. In particular, Margaret's distinctive Roman nose, which was met at the bridge by high, inquisitive eyebrows, perfectly mimicked the characteristic features of the man she knew as her father. And why else would Michael have assumed custody of the girls after Elizabeth's death? He must be the father. The State took measures to establish that the rumors were true.

In June 2003, Margaret wrote a letter to Jim Hardin. Surprisingly, the letter concerned an overdue video rental. Blockbuster was seeking late fees for the DVD copy of *America's Sweethearts*, which had remained in the evidence room for two years. Detective Art Holland requested that the letter be sent to LabCorp. The stamp on the front of the envelope was carefully peeled off and swabbed for DNA. The saliva, presumed to be Margaret's, was then compared with Michael's. The result of the test? "Michael Peterson was excluded as being the biological father of Margaret Ratliff," Holland wrote in his notes.

The negative test result left Holland at a loose end. After all, if the girls had been Michael's by blood, then he had discovered an obvious motive behind the murder of Elizabeth. Michael wanted to take his children away. But if the test is to be believed, then the girls had been fathered by George Ratliff, not Michael. And so, this wild conjecture was dead on arrival. Despite the uncanny resemblance between Michael and Margaret, the two were apparently unrelated.

But even if the rumors had been confirmed, it is unclear exactly what Michael stood to gain by taking the children. Upon returning to the United States shortly after Elizabeth's death, Michael now found himself in the difficult position of caring for four children—two biological boys and two adopted girls. When Patty and Michael divorced in 1987, the girls stayed with him in Durham. The strain of caring for such a large family as a solo father, soon became untenable. Around this time, Michael proposed that Martha be sent to live with her aunt and uncle, who lived in Rhode Island. Martha was increasingly prone to tantrums and Michael found the charge too demanding. If he had killed Elizabeth to steal the children, he had obviously soon regretted it. Ultimately, the decision was made that separating Martha and Margaret would only traumatize both girls further. They needed each other now more than ever. Martha would not be fostered in Rhode Island.

By this time, the girls had lost a biological mother, been transported across the Atlantic, moved between states, and witnessed the divorce of Michael and Patty. Life was unpredictable and precarious. When they were little, the little girls used to run about saying, "My mommy's dead. My daddy's dead," and then asking, "When are you going to die too?"

Life remained this way until the family structure was stabilized by the introduction of Kathleen into Michael's life. Living only a block away, the two little girls would go to play with Kathleen's daughter Caitlin. One thing led to another and the two parents quickly became lovers. They moved in together around 1992.

By 1997, they had married. Kathleen—the intelligent and charming socialite—brought her own Caitlin into the large family. Moreover, she brought along a large income, sufficient for the care of all five children while Michael's hefty income came in more sporadically (his book earnings secured the Cedar Street mansion). With the much larger family unit established (a family of seven), the Ratliff girls discovered a degree of solidity and reliability that had largely been absent in their younger years. The trauma of their mother's death had finally been superseded by a new reality: a stable and supportive household. The girls had finally found someone to whom the word "mom" could apply. Indeed, all the children referred to Kathleen this way.

This peace lasted seven years. It was a time during which love, empathy, and discipline prevailed—the sorts of virtues kept by healthy families. The girls finally felt safe in a home built with consistency and care.

All of this lasted until Kathleen died. In an act of cosmic injustice, the girls lost yet another mother. Margaret was told of Kathleen's death just one day before she would turn twenty years old. Martha was on campus at the University of San Francisco when Michael called to tell her the news. It was the most unnatural cruelty. The grief that descended on the girls was mixed with a reopening of ancient wounds. The tombs in which they had set aside their childhood despair had been pried open, releasing a thousand ghosts. And the coffin in which their birth mother had slept for two decades was also about to be pried open.

In April 2003, Elizabeth Ratliff was torn out from the ground by a mechanical digger.

THE EXHUMATION

In the beginning of 2003, the two daughters reluctantly agreed for Elizabeth's body to be exhumed and reexamined. They expressed their distress in the strongest terms. "How will you be able to sleep at night," the daughters questioned Jim Hardin, "knowing that you are the cause of our family's grief and pain?"

Hardin was approached for comment when the letter made it to the newspapers. "No comment," he answered.

Elizabeth's coffin was brought to Dr. Radisch on April 16. It was in excellent condition, without rot or mold or breakage. The lid was sealed hard, and it took considerable effort to force it open. Autopsies on the exhumed were always a challenge for Radisch as she was never sure what condition the body would arrive in. But Elizabeth's body had kept well. The tight seal of the coffin, combined with the efforts of the embalmers, had delivered Radisch a body that appeared more or less like a woman asleep.

Elizabeth wore a lacey two-piece dress with stockings. Alongside her body were tucked meaningful grave goods: a children's book, a seashell, a soft toy lamb, and a bundle of flowers, now black and withered. Her skin was leathery and mottled in places, but that was the extent of her deterioration.

Before the autopsy began, Radisch had already reviewed the original examiner's report. She was struck with wonder by the stated cause of death. It had been described as an "intracranial hemorrhage (cerebellar brainstem) secondary to von Willebrand's coagulation abnormality." In twenty years of experience, she had never encountered such a cause of death.

The stated cause of death was all the more surprising given the existence of multiple lacerations on the back of Elizabeth's head. These deep cuts had been poorly described in the first autopsy report. Radisch already had doubts before the casket was opened.

During the embalming process, the cuts on Elizabeth's head had all been glued and sewn shut to prevent leakage. After removing the body from the casket, and after removing Elizabeth's clothes, the wounds were carefully reopened. Some of the cuts had gone down to the skull. Radisch was surprised to find seven cuts: precisely the same number as she had identified on Kathleen. It was a coincidence that would fire many imaginations… Michael, the sinister and calculating staircase killer, had a very particular method indeed. Or, more likely, this was just a coincidence.

Compared to Kathleen's lacerations, the head wounds on Elizabeth were relatively simple. They were linear and measured a couple of inches apiece. They were arranged in a disorganized grouping on the back of her head, with one of the cuts suspiciously placed on the top of her head. On the base of the skull, directly beneath one of the lacerations, the bone had fractured. At Elizabeth's first autopsy, all of the contents of the skull had been removed. Her brain and the dura mater were gone. This made it easy for Radisch to observe the skull fracture. A hemorrhage around this fracture spoke to an injury sustained before death. Inexplicably, no skull fracture had been mentioned in the original autopsy report.

Radisch observed the wounds and set them out on a diagram. She noted small bruises on the left hand and wrist, which were consistent with defensive injuries. But then, the presence of von Willebrand disease would complicate any conclusions about the cause of any bruises. There was also a minor tear inside her mouth on the top gums. This was the full extent of Elizabeth's external injuries.

Radisch then shifted attention inwards to the original cause of death: a brain hemorrhage complicated by von Willebrand disease—a stroke, to be brief. It was an unusual verdict to begin with. Von Willebrand disease typically presents as a minor abnormality in the blood clotting process. This manifests, in most cases, as something like a mild version of hemophilia. Bleeding noses are common and bruising occurs more easily, but seldom do fatal strokes occur.

So what evidence was there that such an event had caused Elizabeth's death? Radisch analyzed a microscope slide of a segment of brain tissue. Observed microscopically, the material on the slide was found to have lesions. But the pathologists of the day disagreed amongst themselves as to what the lesions represented. Some said it was evidence of a brain hemorrhage. Others said it was merely an artifact of the collection process. Whatever the truth may be, Radisch sided with the latter.

But Radisch was not the only expert brought forward. A neuropathologist, Dr. Aaron Gleckman, was presented with preserved sections of Elizabeth's brain removed during the initial autopsy. Gleckman, it should be noted, did not have access to the entire brain. During his analysis, he discovered areas of hemorrhage consistent with blunt force trauma. He did not find any hemorrhaging consistent with a stroke. For these reasons, he also sided with Radisch: Elizabeth's death was a homicide.

But Gleckman's opinions about the cause of death must be understood in the light of the evidence he had available. Elizabeth's brain had already been dissected in 1985 by the original medical examiner, Dr. Larry Barnes, who carved up the brain into smaller pieces. Barnes had had the opportunity to study the entire brain. His conclusion was a stroke had been the cause of Elizabeth's death, since he observed hemorrhaging consistent with the fact. In contrast, Gleckman had only half of Elizabeth's brain to study in total: half of the brainstem, half of the cerebellum, and half of all midbrain structures.

Some contradictions between Barnes and Gleckman were baffling: In 1985, Barnes stated that blood filled all the brain ventricles; in 2003, Gleckman observed no blood in the ventricles. In 1985, Barnes attested to blood in the spinal fluid; Gleckman disagreed. On one point, however, Barnes and Gleckman stood in unison: there was herniation of the brain consistent with a stroke.

So then, what was the cause of death? It was difficult to say. Evidence that may have supported a spontaneous hemorrhage was no longer available, and all the evidence which remained indicated trauma to the head. Of course, neither the defense nor the prosecution disputed that Elizabeth would have suffered blunt force trauma. The question was only whether this trauma was the ultimate cause of her death. Drs. Radisch and Gleckman were crystal clear in answering this question: Elizabeth Ratliff did not have a stroke; she died from blunt force trauma to the head. The manner of death? Homicide. The person responsible? Take a wild guess.

COINCIDENCES

So what do we really know? In 1985, Michael's close friend died and was found at the bottom of a staircase. Sixteen years later, Michael's wife died and was found at the bottom of a staircase. In both cases, there was blood at the scene. In both cases, there were serious head wounds. Is it a coincidence? It certainly is. But is it only a coincidence? That question is harder to answer.

To attempt to answer that question, consider a different coincidence altogether. In May 2021, a seventeen-year-old Californian teenager was found dead. He had drowned in fast-moving water. Melino Liu's bloated corpse was pulled from a twenty-foot-deep channel in the American River in Rancho Cordova. His family was distraught when the authorities came to the door with the news.

"He's too young," his mother Sosefina Liu told the media. "But he is in a better place."[29]

His death was just like any other accidental death in California that year except for one thing: his older brother Paul had drowned in the upstream Lake Natoma six years beforehand. In fact, they had both succumbed in the very same month. Melino had been one of four drowning deaths in Northern California across that fateful week in May 2021. In the years that followed Paul's death, Sosefina had forbidden Melino from going in the water. He had not listened. The loss of Melino after Paul made this family tragedy all that much worse.

What are the odds that two brothers from the same family, six years apart, would both drown to death? What are the odds that the two deaths would happen in the very same month? Whatever the odds are, they are obviously minuscule. Few mothers could be more unfortunate than Sosefina Liu: two sons, in the same month, six years apart, drowned to death, in the same stretch of water.

What relevance do these drownings have to Elizabeth's death? Well, it's all about coincidences and evidence. What does it mean when we speak about a coincidence as evidence? What do coincidences like these mean? Do they ultimately mean anything?

---

29. Hahn, J. "Family in Mourning After Son Drowns 6 Years After His Brother Drowned in the Same River." People. May 19, 2021. https://people.com/human-interest/family-in-mourning-after-son-drowns-6-years-after-his-brother-drowned-in-the-same-river/

Coincidences can be meaningful, and their meaning is hidden in the world of mathematical probability. In layman's terms, coincidences like these are said to "go against the odds." A betting man would not put any money on the unlikely event occurring. We know that it is extremely rare for some particular person to drown to death. And we also know that if two members of the same family both drown to death in separate incidents, years apart, this is even more rare. A gambling man would not bother taking such a punt. Such a one-two punch is so exceedingly rare that it suggests to any normal-thinking person that both deaths may have a common cause. It is not proof that there is a common explanation for both deaths, but since the two deaths have such an unlikely feature in common, we naturally seek a single explanation that might be able to account for the strangeness of the coincidence. We are, as human beings, desperate to bring order to our chaotic world.

So now we must ask, just how rare is it to drown to death? Exactly how unfortunate was the suffering mother to have two sons perish like this? Luckily, we do not have to guess. We have some numbers to work with. In the United States, four thousand people per year die in accidental drownings.[30] This is quite a small number relative to other leading causes of accidental death, such as motor accidents. It would not be as unlikely, for example, to have two members from the same family die in separate car crashes since there are around forty thousand motoring deaths each and every year.[31] Some causes of death are more likely than

---

30. "Accidental Drownings" Centers for Disease Control and Prevention. https://www.cdc.gov/drowning/facts/index. html#:~:text=While%20children%20are%20at%20highest,11%20 drowning%20deaths%20per%20day

31. "Newly Released Estimates Show Traffic Fatalities Reached a 16-year High in 2021." National Highway Traffic Safety Administration. https://www.nhtsa.gov/press-releases/early-estimate-2021-traffic-fatalities

others, and if they are more likely, the probability of finding coincidences like these increases.

That is what it means to take coincidences as evidence. The less likely the coincidence, the more likely there is to be a non-random explanation. To illustrate the idea, consider a more obvious example: If someone wins the lottery twice in a row, we suspect a rigged system rather than dumb luck.

And here is the moral of the story for Michael's case: the average American is about three times more likely to die from a fall than from an accidental drowning.[32] All else being equal, Kathleen's death from a fall was three times more likely than Melino's death from drowning. But that is just one person. We can now ask what the probability is that two particular people chosen at random (call them Kathleen and Elizabeth) would both die from falls. We can then compare this probability against the probability that two randomly chosen people (call them Melino and Paul) would both die from accidental drowning.

The numbers are confronting: Michael's situation was nine times more likely than Sosefina's. In other words, the average American is nine times more likely to be personally acquainted with two deaths by a fall than two drowning deaths. For a gambling man, choosing between Michael and Sosefina is easy: Michael was nine times more likely to be in his situation than Sosefina was to find herself with two drowned sons. Of course, one could give a more nuanced analysis of the probabilities involved (we could adjust the table of probabilities to include age, location, or time of death), but this basic analysis is informative all the same.

Are the two drowning incidents evidence that Sosefina may have been involved in her sons' deaths? Few would think so. The very thought that she may have been involved is a cruel conjecture. Yet in Sosefina's case, the coincidence

---

32. Federal Transit Administration. 1985. "Pedestrian Falling Accidents in Transit Terminals" https://ntlrepository.blob.core. windows.net/lib/34000/34200/34281/DOT-TSC-UMTA-84-36.pdf

is far more stark than in Michael's case. If Michael's two staircase deaths are evidence that he was somehow involved, then Sosefina's two drowning deaths are even greater evidence that she was involved. That is a simple matter of relative probabilities.

But the fact of the matter is that, sometimes, unlikely events occur. Coincidences can be just that. Indeed, we should remember that Michael's two alleged "staircase murders" were in fact two separate deaths, from totally different causes, which occurred sixteen years apart on different continents. The wounds in each case were very different. And the relationship between Michael and the victims was different again. If Michael had a penchant for disposing of unwanted women by faking staircase accidents, he made use of this unusual tactic only twice in his life. He was not the "staircase killer" that the prosecution painted. He was the victim of unfortunate—and highly improbable—circumstances.

Was Michael responsible for Elizabeth's death? Ultimately there is little evidence to suggest so. The strongest evidence available is that he had dropped her home the previous evening. That is suggestive of his involvement, but if Elizabeth's death was due to foul play, there may be a thousand other possible suspects with a thousand differing motives.

Who else might we suspect? Elizabeth's role at the Rhein-Main Air Base School would have made her a potential target for terror groups. Employees at Rhein-Main had twice been targeted in the month of November alone. Targeted assassinations by the Red Army Faction, in particular, were numerous. And there is some evidence that Elizabeth may not simply have been a teacher for the Department of Defense, but an employee or intelligence contact at the American Consulate in Frankfurt.

Recently released US consulate telegrams out of Frankfurt (made available via Wikileaks) note a woman named Elizabeth McKee working to move a Polish woman from out of the Iron Curtain into West Germany in the late 1970s. Was Elizabeth's role as a teacher only part of her assignment at the Rhein-Main Air Base? She had the right sorts of intelligence connections. Her husband had died in a classified military operation. And her close friend Michael was rumored to be with the CIA. What do we really know about the members of this tight-knit community of Department of Defense employees working in Frankfurt?

Indeed, at the same time that Elizabeth was apparently working with the American Consulate in Frankfurt, another character from our story was involved in a highly publicized exfiltration attempt between East and West Germany. Alan van Norman (the raptor expert and neurosurgeon who wrote an affidavit for Pollard's MAR) had attempted to smuggle a Soviet doctor and his family to West Germany in a modified VW Beetle that had a secret compartment in its bottom. Van Norman was imprisoned by the East Germans before becoming part of a high-profile US-Soviet prisoner exchange in 1978. Upon his release, he was warned by the US Embassy to consider "the fates of others involved" in the operation before talking to the press.

In the very same year that van Norman was released, Larry Pollard himself was detained by Soviet military police in a hotel room in St. Petersburg. Larry and a handful of US legislators had been visiting Russia and Estonia. Authorities on both sides of the Iron Curtain were concerned that the group may have been in contact with Soviet dissidents or that they may have been photographing sensitive military installations. The Soviet military man had broken into Larry's room and was waiting for him after he returned from dinner. Suspecting espionage, the officer demanded answers to questions about the activities of Larry's group, including what photos had been taken and who had been consulted with. When interviewed by the American Consulate, however, Pollard was adamant that he had not been in contact with dissidents and nor had he photographed military sites. So what really happened here? The details of this episode are few and far between.

Did Elizabeth have a stroke and simply collapse, cutting her head on the steps on the way down? It seems a difficult explanation to believe, and unfortunately, any evidence for it has been lost to the abyss of history. Elizabeth's death will forever remain fairly mysterious.

Is Elizabeth's strange death evidence against Michael? In some sense, it certainly is. It is simply far weaker than most people take it to be. There is no material evidence implicating Michael in her murder. This is no small quibble. It is one thing to suspect a convicted murderer of having committed a second murder. It is altogether a different thing to point to a suspicious death in West Germany nearly twenty years prior, and to conclude that because Michael was a very close friend of that deceased woman, he must have killed her as well as his wife. Elizabeth's death was suspicious, without a doubt. But given her situation in West Germany at the time, all sorts of scenarios might explain her death. She was associated with the Rhein-Main Air Base and was therefore a walking target.

Not every lottery is rigged. Some lucky people win twice in a row. And some unlucky people lose friends in very similar ways. There are, in this world, some true coincidences. That's all there is to it. There is no pattern. There is no explanation. There are only unfortunate, disconnected events. The staircase deaths of Kathleen and Elizabeth, like the drowning deaths of Melino and Paul, dwell in that world where patterns are mirages, where only chaos reigns.

CHAPTER TWELVE: MONEY, LIES, AND SEX

MONEY

There was a reason the Petersons' attic was full of bats. They were in debt—a lot of debt. Money to make essential repairs to the house was increasingly unavailable. The situation was paradoxical. After all, Michael was a *New York Times* bestselling novelist. The manuscript for his first book, *A Time of War*, was acquired by Simon and Schuster for the tidy sum of six hundred thousand dollars. A later unfinished manuscript gained a four hundred and fifty thousand dollar advance from the same publishing house. However, since the peak of his fame, royalties from his books had been waning for years. His main source of income was a veteran's disability allowance. Michael had brought in no taxable income for three years.

And then there was Kathleen. She was an upwardly mobile executive at a telecommunications giant but one which would soon be a victim of the dotcom bubble of the early 2000s. Nortel had already rapidly fallen downhill before her death and many teams had already had their numbers severely cut back. Shockingly, by the end of 2001, the Canadian company had actually more than halved its workforce from 94,500 staff to 45,000. And Nortel declared bankruptcy less than eight years after her death after a long period of attrition and decline. There were rumors—

well-substantiated—that industrial espionage from China, and aggressive tactics from Huawei in particular, played a part in its demise. When Nortel's offices in Toronto were eventually vacated, they were found to be bugged. But fraudulent bookkeeping, which started when Frank Dunn took the helm as CEO just weeks before Kathleen's death, would be the final straw that broke the company's back.

The Petersons' financial ship appeared to be in rough seas. Money was coming in, but plenty more was going out. Michael's royalties were drying up. Kathleen's company was dying. All of this looked like good news for the prosecution. Like vultures following a limping beast, the prosecutors spent three full days of the trial prodding at the finances of the family.

The defense objected at length that the family's financial assets were both inadmissible and irrelevant. In fact, there was good legal precedent for this objection. In prior North Carolina cases where financial records have been brought forward to provide evidence of motive, there has usually been a direct link that could be drawn between the state of the finances and the commission of a crime. In a later appeal document, Michael's attorney, Maher, gave the following examples:

> In *State v. Bishop*, 346 N.C. 365, 488 S.E.2d 769 (1997), the victim confronted the defendant about outstanding debts, and there was testimony that the defendant promised a portion of the proceeds of a life insurance policy on the victim to a co-defendant who assisted in the murder.
> In *State v. White*, 340 N.C. 264, 457 S.E.2d 841 (1995), defendant was charged with the murder of her stepson. ... Defendant's husband, with her knowledge, amended a life insurance policy days before the stepson's death ...

In *State v. Stager*, 329 N.C. 278, 295 (1991) defendant was charged with shooting her husband. … Defendant had secretly borrowed large sums of money, had forged her husband's signature on loan applications and checks, and was in danger of having a bank contact her husband due to missed loan payments.

In each of these cases, the jury did not need to speculate about whether there was any link between the defendant's financial circumstances and the crime.

So when this kind of financial evidence is presented at a trial, it is supposed to illustrate the direct link between money and murder. Yet in Michael's trial, there was nothing to link the death of Kathleen with the couple's finances. No will had been recently amended. No statements by Michael hinted at a windfall from the death of his wife. And nothing suggested that Kathleen had been coerced into renegotiating the terms of her estate. Thus, any supposed link was pure conjecture by the prosecution. The prosecution could only show that the Petersons were in a somewhat precarious financial position. And poor finances are a poor argument for motive.

For such an argument to succeed, far more evidence would be needed.

It is true that for a brief time, Kathleen had been considered for redundancy by Nortel. Indeed, "a brief time" is something of an understatement. She had spent just three days on a list compiled by Nortel execs who were considering which candidates' necks should be next on the guillotine. For whatever reason, she was promptly removed from this list. And Kathleen herself had no knowledge she was ever on such a list. By extension, Michael didn't know either. This was all insider knowledge—secrets held between a select few at the top of the company hierarchy. Kathleen never knew she faced the chopping block. Michael was entirely oblivious. It could not have played a role in her death.

Having said that, nearly everybody working at Nortel through its darkest days felt that their employment was under threat. Having already cut a remarkable fifty thousand jobs by the end of the financial year, and having declared some of the largest quarterly losses in the history of any listed company, everyone working at Nortel knew they were crewing a sinking ship. Helen Prislinger, Kathleen's colleague, testified to this fact on the stand. Nortel staff was anxious. Many families had been made destitute.

Yet Michael seemed wholly unperturbed. "She's a survivor and in no trouble," he wrote to a friend in one email on the topic (the only email discovered to even address Kathleen's employment status). The idea that Michael was anticipating Kathleen's redundancy was a figment of the State's imagination. But it was this leap of the imagination that would invite every juror to speculate about sinister financial motives for murder.

The prosecution argued that the family had been spending far more than it was receiving in income. The way of life to which Michael had become accustomed had become unsustainable. Indeed, in many of the years examined by certified accountant and NCSBI Agent Raymond Young, Michael received no taxable income at all, with Kathleen's income being the only real cash flow into the household. Shockingly (to the average person), the family's total credit card debt was $143,000, distributed between several accounts (that's equivalent to nearly $230,000 in today's money). Moreover, Kathleen had a life insurance policy for $1.4 million, ten times the amount of debt. If Kathleen died, the insurance would more than cover the debt they were in. It is obvious there were clear and attractive inducements to murder, whether or not they had ever crossed Michael's mind.

But even if the evidence showed that the couple was reckless with credit cards, there was no evidence that Michael was particularly concerned by this. The State made much of the fact that Michael had emailed Martha's uncle to ask for assistance in paying her college tuition. His email was replied to in fast time: "That sounds great, I am now committing to $5,000 per semester." It seems doubtful that a few thousand in school fees turned Michael towards murder.

During Raymond Young's testimony about the family's finances, David Rudolf challenged the methodology of this section of the investigation. Young had only analyzed income and outgoings across the three years leading up to Kathleen's death. Young didn't go back further in time because, he claimed, "you start getting difficulties in getting any bank records from further back." This fact alone limited the conclusions that could be drawn. However, there was clear evidence of mismanagement of the household finances.

In the three years before the tragic death, Michael and Kathleen sold off more than $278,000 in Nortel stocks and real estate. By the end of 2001, the family held a total of $1.6 million in assets, including North Carolina properties, bank accounts, and various retirement funds. Most importantly for the prosecution, each year surveyed saw a net deficit in income: in 1999, the family spent $184,000 more than was earned in the same year; in 2000, the deficit was $98,000; and in 2001, the family spent $188,000 more than was earned.

It seemed that their pockets were full of holes and that their financial situation was truly perilous. That's the way it seemed to outsiders, but was their situation so dire? Or was Young's analysis flawed?

The analysis was far from ideal. The full details of the Petersons' financial situation were not provided. The period investigated—just three years—is far too short to develop a meaningful picture of their accounts. It was not clear whether the financial deficits incurred each year were due to fixed costs the family was struggling to keep up with. And it was not clear whether any of the cash flow went towards the acquisition of stable assets that were merely hard to track, such as jewelry, cars, antiques, artwork, renovations, etc. With three children in prestigious colleges (the University of San Francisco, Tulane, and Cornell), the Petersons were undoubtedly investing heavily in the education of their children. And this is typically a short-term cost, which can put many families into debt for a few years.

There was no mention of Michael's parents, their ages, or the inheritance he stood to collect upon their deaths. If Michael was likely to receive his inheritance in the coming years, it seems even more unlikely he would kill Kathleen for the insurance payout. Rudolf grilled the agent as he sat on the stand.

"Wouldn't knowing what elderly parents were planning to leave someone be relevant in determining a financial motive for murder?" Rudolf asked.

"I didn't see a need to investigate it," replied Agent Young.

Rudolf continued on, uncovering further flaws in Young's methodology. "With regard to your cash flow analysis, would you agree that in analyzing expenses, it's relevant to distinguish between fixed expenses, such as a mortgage; non-recurring expenses, such as buying a car; and discretionary expenses, such as trips abroad?"

"There are expenses like that, yes, sir, and it would have been nice to have all that information."

"My question, sir, was, are those three different kinds of expenses useful in a cash flow analysis?"

"Yes."

"And the reason they're useful is because, obviously, fixed expenses tell you what the person has to make every year without getting behind, right?"

"That's right," Young agreed. "Expenses they have to pay."

"In looking at the analysis that you did yesterday. Let's go to the numbers here. Let's take 2001. I think you said that they spent $288,000. Is that right? How much of that was fixed expenses?"

"I don't know."

"Want to take a guess?"

"I'm not going to make a guess."

"How much of it was non-recurring expenses?

"I don't know."

"How much of it was discretionary expenses?"

"I don't know."

Demonstrably, the analysis of the financial situation was too simplistic. The fact of the matter is that the family was absurdly wealthy and were hardly in what one would call financial straits. The sale of the palatial property at 1810 Cedar Street would have garnered well in excess of half a million dollars (after paying off the remainder of the mortgage), which easily dwarfs the $143,000 credit card debt the family had accrued and would still leave room for another mansion to boot. In the week before Kathleen's death, Michael had received notice that a recently published book about a Chinese political dissident was in the sights of a Hollywood producer. His hopes were high.

Kathleen was well aware of the troubles that Nortel faced. She had even mentioned her concerns about the direction of the company to her sister, Candace Zamperini. And yet there is no evidence that she felt she was soon to be kicked out of her role. Given her wide experience in telecommunications and her postgraduate education at one of the most prestigious universities in the United States, Kathleen would hardly have landed on the trash heap if she had been expelled from her executive role at Nortel. This was something that Candace often reminded her about.

"Even if Nortel goes belly up, you'll land on your feet," she would reassure Kathleen.

And Rudolf's remarks about Michael's inheritance were not plucked from thin air. They were extremely salient to the overall financial picture. Indeed, on June 27, 2002—just six months after Kathleen died—Michael's elderly mother passed away. She had fallen, broken a hip, and subsequently entered into a coma from which she never recovered. Eleanor Peterson died just weeks before she would have celebrated her sixtieth wedding anniversary and just months after Michael had been arrested and charged with murder.

Money is a major point of stress in nearly every relationship under the sun. And yet it is clear the pair were relatively confident that their way of life was not immediately under threat. Perhaps they even suspected that things were about to get better. Even if the future of Nortel looked bleak, Michael's news from Hollywood was promising. And so we might ask: why, if Michael's financial luck was about to change for the better, would he jeopardize it all by murdering his wife?

In the midst of this period of supposedly dwindling finances, the Petersons had deposited more than eighty thousand dollars into Caitlin's account to help with college. Had things been so deeply desperate, such a hefty deposit for a young daughter begs belief. And even if this is not the case—even if Kathleen was worried and Michael pessimistic—there was still no evidential link whatsoever to be drawn between the family's bank accounts and the death of Kathleen. At best, this was circumstantial evidence of the weakest sort. At worst, the State only further demonstrated to the jury how enviably wealthy this family from Durham was. They did not agitate any of their creditors and they continued to keep up with all essential costs. "No checks bounced and nobody sued them," as one of Michael's lawyers put it. The Petersons may have been bad with money, but money had been good with them.

He called himself Brad but his real name was Brent—Brent Wolgamott. He was a young gay man living in Fayetteville, North Carolina, and he was an active-duty soldier. He was clean-shaven, had a blond crew cut, and had the sort of physique that most men would envy. He was planning a chemistry degree at college after military service and he badly needed money. In March 2001, he placed his profile on a gay escort website, in which users could place reviews for Brad. At the same site, others could find his email address and phone number. New clients were coming in rapidly for his sexual services, which included, as he stated at trial, "just about anything under the sun; safely, I might add." A line which caused the jury to giggle like coy schoolgirls.

In August 2001, Michael found Brent's details and contacted him via email. Michael's email address began with the initials MP. When Brent opened his inbox, this made him startle. In military jargon, MP stands for Military Police. Brent thought he was under investigation but he soon realized that this was a prospective client. The email exchange went back and forth for a few weeks, through the course of twenty messages or so. Brent courted the prospective client MP: not the Military Police, but Michael Peterson. The majority of the email communication occurred during a five-day period between August 30 and September 5. There was nothing too unusual about the communication: a bit of flirting, a bit of a jab here and there, and simply getting acquainted. Brent sent several topless photos, showing off his impressive pectoral muscles. Michael liked what he saw. Brent quoted Michael one hundred and fifty dollars an hour for anal sex.

In the course of the emails, Brent was taken aback by Michael mentioning his "great marriage" in which he seemed to have "a lot of warmth and affection for his wife." Why, then, was Michael seeking out gay sex? The explanation was forthcoming. "I'm very bi, and that's all there is to it," he wrote to Brent. In the course of the email exchange, a rendezvous was set up for September 5. The plan was that Brent would travel to Durham and hook up with Michael, either at his home or at one of the Petersons' rental properties.

When the day of the liaison finally arrived, Brent was packed and ready to go. He had brought along his military uniform as requested by Michael. But as the morning made its way to evening, Brent began to have second thoughts. Michael had seemed like a genuine guy—a nice chap—but a long night of sex with yet another client just didn't sound appealing. Brent was all set for a vacation the following day and wanted to be well rested. He had booked a flight to Palm Springs the morning after the rendezvous. He was heading to a "clothing optional" resort with one of his best friends for a holiday filled to the brim with all the sorts of things that young people like to indulge in. Did he really have the energy to kick off the trip in style after a night with a client?

After a moment's reflection, Brent decided that Michael would just have to wait. He did not call Michael to cancel— he simply never showed up. Michael called Brent on the night of the booking, checking in, but he got no response. And that was that.

On September 30, more than three weeks after the botched rendezvous, Brent emailed Michael to apologize for the no-show. Michael did not reply to this message and never contacted Brent again. The meeting never occurred and communication ceased. That was the end of it. Apart from this expression of interest, there is no other direct evidence that Michael ever had sex outside of the marriage with Kathleen.

As a matter of fact, the defense contended that Michael's messages to Brent had been mere "research" for an upcoming book. At the time, Wolgamott took this to be a transparent fabrication on the part of the defense, but looking back, he now wonders whether the lengthy

242 | TIDDY SMITH

email correspondence was more than a simple expression of interest. No other clients had asked as many questions as Michael during the run-up to a rendezvous. Wolgamott, now in his forties, sometimes reflects on his role in the trial. "I don't know whether Michael is guilty or not. But I hope," he lamented, "that my testimony wasn't anything that determined the outcome."

What can we infer from the email exchange between Michael and a gay escort? At most, we can infer that Michael was most probably willing to engage in extramarital sex, possibly—or even likely—without Kathleen's knowledge. And perhaps we can also infer, with a little more certainty, that Michael's sexuality was a strange beast. "I used to pay to fuck a super-macho guy who played lacrosse," he wrote to Brent in one of the emails. Whether or not he was fucking the lacrosse player while he was with Kathleen, we don't know. Michael was certainly bisexual—this fact is well known—and he once referenced the porn director Dirk Yates in another email to Brent. It is worth noting that the movies of Yates specialize in hardcore gay and bisexual sex within military settings. If Michael had a fetish, this seems to have been it: military-themed gay sex.

The escort's testimony was supposed to make up the most compelling part of the prosecution's argument for a motive. Their story went that Kathleen had discovered Brent's emails on the night of her death. A fight ensued, during which Kathleen was killed. The discovery of the email exchange was the catalyst for murder. Kathleen had previously divorced a cheating husband and why should Michael be any different?

Whether or not Kathleen discovered the email exchange, we need to assess two different questions about Kathleen's knowledge of Michael's sexuality:

1. Did she know that Michael was bisexual?

2. Did she know that Michael was having (or planning to have) extramarital sex with men?

There is virtually no reliable evidence available on which we can base an answer to either of these questions. At the time, Brent took Michael's openness about his wife as unusual, and he assumed that she must have been aware of his sexuality. But this was just an assumption. Let us look at some of the other evidence.

First, what supports the idea that Kathleen knew Michael had a thing for men and women alike? Some statements from members of Michael's family indicate that it may have been something of an open secret—at least among the grown-ups. The children, it is clear, knew nothing.

Bill Peterson, Michael's brother, informed the children about Michael's sexuality before the explosive details would emerge at trial. Caitlin remembered vividly the moment she was told:

> Bill said, very straightforward, that Mike was bisexual. Bill told me that my mother knew and was okay with it. I accepted it because I assumed that my mother had. But I *will* say that my mother divorced my father for cheating on her with other women, so I cannot imagine that she would possibly be okay with her current husband having sex with other men.

Caitlin was certainly skeptical. And she would later bring Michael to civil trial for the wrongful death of Kathleen. But if Bill is to be believed, then Kathleen knew that Michael was into both men and women. Michael's parents knew it too, according to Bill. For Bill's own part, he claimed to have known of Michael's sexual preferences, even as a young teenager. If all of this is true, it would be odd if Kathleen was unaware, but there is very little evidence other than snippets of testimony such as these.

In *The Staircase* docuseries, Todd Peterson shared a story of eavesdropping on his parents as they argued about pornographic photos on Michael's computer:

My father had received a computer virus several months earlier. The virus took all the files from the desktop and emailed them to everyone on his email list, including these pictures.

> I was over at the house one weekend, watching a football game, and on my way into the TV room, I heard a discussion inside the kitchen that sounded pretty interesting. I crept up to the kitchen, listening in. It was Kathleen talking to my father about the photos on his computer. She was saying: "I want you to get them off. These possibly could have been sent to our friends or to our neighbors, and I want you to get them off. If you ever get this virus again, I don't want to have to worry about this!" So it was a full conversation acknowledging the fact.

Together, the testimony of Bill and Todd indicates that Michael's sexuality was a known fact. But strangely, Michael himself, during the filming of *The Staircase* docuseries, contradicted what Bill and Todd said was common knowledge:

> I've never talked to a soul about it, and this is the first time I've even remotely touched on it, and that's okay ... This is who I am and it takes a long time to get to that point. ... To make that leap is very difficult, and I didn't make that leap with Kathleen ... I couldn't have been that comfortable with it because I was hiding it.

It's a pretty damning quote, which virtually negates the idea that Kathleen knew anything at all. It all but excludes the possibility that Kathleen knew about any extramarital liaisons. Indeed, nothing supports the idea that Kathleen knew about gay sex possibly happening outside the marriage.

If Michael was hiding his sexuality from Kathleen, he must have thought Kathleen would disapprove. He may have suspected that this revelation would cost him the marriage. It was, it seems, a secret he was willing to keep to hold the relationship together. And if Kathleen had never unearthed the facts about this side of Michael, perhaps it would have remained an ongoing deceit throughout a much longer marriage. Interestingly, Wolgamott testified that many of his clients were like this: married men who were secretly looking for a bit of spice on the side.

What value does any of this have as evidence? Not much at all. Unfortunate as it may be, millions of married couples persist in the midst of deep secrets and lies that are never brought to the fore. If the hidden truths are ever disclosed, the usual remedy is an uncomfortable series of counseling sessions with a would-be specialist, not homicide. And there is no evidence at all that Kathleen uncovered the secret of Michael's sexuality on the night of her death. The email from her coworker was never opened, which suggests that Kathleen didn't open Michael's inbox. Just as was the case with the alleged financial motive, there is no direct link to be drawn between Michael's sexuality and the commission of murder. All that remained was speculation.

And this unbridled speculation was at the heart of the prosecution's case. In her closing argument for the prosecution, Freda Black rejected the defense's claim that the Petersons' relationship was a deep connection between soulmates.

> Soulmates say these types of words to each other: "I, Michael, do take thee, Kathleen, to be my lawfully wedded wife. To live together in

marriage. I promise to love you, comfort you, honor you, keep you for better or worse, for richer or poorer, in sickness and in health and forsaking all others."

The implication was that Michael had hardly forsaken all others. She pressed harder at the idea of infidelity.

The only reason that meeting didn't take place was because of Brad. It wasn't because of Mr. Peterson. He was fired up and ready to go. Even got the price right.

And you honestly believe Kathleen Peterson knew about that? Would have approved of that? Can you imagine? How in the world would she hold her head up high at her arts council meetings? Do you honestly think that she would have approved of that type of activity? And it wasn't just Brad.

You saw the rest of the things on his computer. Once again, these things are so filthy we can't even show them on TV. Filth. Pure filth… Do you think she approved of this type of activity while she's off at work or sleeping? I argue to you that doesn't make sense. And that's not the way that soulmates conduct themselves.

Michael was, according to Black, nothing more than a filthy, cheating gay man. His activities were not just outside the norm, they were almost criminally deceitful. They were an abuse of Kathleen's trust. And moreover, they were—she hoped the jury would agree—simply disgusting.

Did these biases about Michael's sexuality contribute to the guilty verdict? Since the time of the trial, several of the jurors have come forward to reject this accusation. Ultimately, Michael's sexuality played very little role in their verdict. It had all been a question of the evidence, they said. And, on balance, the evidence was insufficient to support the fall theory. Everything looked as though Kathleen had been attacked. And indeed, on this point, the jurors can hardly be faulted. She looked like she had been attacked because she had been.

LIES

During his time fighting in Vietnam, Michael was awarded both the Silver Star and the Bronze Star. These medals are intended to reward gallantry and valor, respectively, in the line of duty. Both the Silver and Bronze Stars are listed in Michael's service record. Yet Michael insisted that, in addition to these two noble awards, he had also received two Purple Hearts, awards which are given to all combat soldiers injured in the line of duty by hostile forces. He claimed that these awards were received during his deployment in Vietnam. And yet there is no mention of any Purple Hearts on Michael's military service record.

Michael had made much of his Purple Hearts while campaigning for the Durham mayoralty. It was all part of a ploy to win over the vote of veterans. Yet journalists covering the election soon discovered that his military record said nothing of Purple Hearts. In response, several influential ex-servicemen who had once committed themselves to Michael's campaign publicly withdrew their support.

When pressed to provide more details about the apparent inconsistency, Michael provided a confession in an editorial with Durham's *Herald-Sun*. His injuries had not been incurred during his time in Vietnam, he admitted. The whole affair had been so troubling, he wrote, that he had never wanted to revisit the events.

He stated that the injuries had actually happened in Japan, not Vietnam, shortly after his redeployment in 1970. Moreover, the injury (a broken leg) was received, he said, in the course of a car accident outside the Atsugi Naval Air Facility. Michael had not been alone in the car. He was driving in the company of Sergeant Kenneth Beverly. The men came to a stop at a flashing railroad crossing when suddenly, a huge truck trundled forward attempting to beat the train. The truck hit their car head-on. Now trapped in the crushed vehicle, Michael was forced to listen for half an hour as Beverly cried and pleaded for help before dying. That was the real story, Michael said. It was a puzzling admission.

Since the broken leg happened in Japan and not Vietnam, the injury would not have qualified for the award of a Purple Heart. Yet Michael continued to insist that he had received the Purple Hearts. It is an odd contradiction. If the injury was sustained on the outskirts of Tokyo in a motoring accident, then it wasn't an event that would qualify for a Purple Heart. And yet Michael repeated what seemed to be a bald-faced lie. He did have two Purple Hearts, he said. Why would he continue to insist that he had received them? There is a good possibility that any Purple Hearts Michael received were not listed on his service record. If the awards had been received in the course of secret operations, for example, such awards might have remained classified. Indeed, given the suspicion held by many of his friends that he was involved with military intelligence, this hypothesis may have something to speak in its favor.

Tellingly, there is a grave at the Enon Cemetery in Georgia for Sgt. Beverly. The date of death is, as Michael stated, 1970. Yet according to both his headstone and data available from the US National Archives, he died in Indochina during the war. His death had not occurred in Japan.

Whatever the true story about Michael's broken leg and the death of Sgt Beverly, he must have lied at some point in the story. And this is not the only example of deceitful behavior in the personal history of Michael Peterson. During a visit to Berlin in May 1983, he allegedly withdrew hundreds of dollars from the bank account of his host, a woman named Pat Finn.

Finn had noticed that her account had had several thousand dollars removed during the visit of Michael and Patty. With no other suspect in mind, she confronted Michael about the transactions that had all occurred during his visit. Incredibly, Michael confessed to having secretly taken off with the card each day for four days to withdraw the maximum amount from a nearby ATM. The story goes that he had rummaged through her study to find the PIN written down somewhere. But it may be more simple to assume that at some point he had overseen Pat herself entering the number on a keypad. It is an outrageous abuse of trust, in either case. Moreover, it is clearly a criminal offense.

Faced with such inexcusable behavior, Michael promptly apologized and agreed to return the full amount.

When we consider these examples of deceitful behavior, a pattern appears to emerge. If Michael also lied about his sexuality to Kathleen, then much of his adult life would appear to have been built out of a strange web of lies. Altogether, these examples suggest that Michael was a compulsive liar—a pathological narcissist. He would deceive whenever it suited him. Given a choice between an unattractive truth and a beneficial falsehood, Michael would pick the falsehood every time. We can call Michael dishonest, sure. We might even call him a terrible person with a severely skewed moral compass.

But can we therefore call him a wife-killer?

MOTIVE
The prosecution's argument from motive, then, can be summed up by the following three claims:

1. Kathleen discovered that Michael was bisexual.
2. The family was heavily in debt.

3. Michael was a compulsive liar.

So which one motivated Michael to kill his wife? It cannot be all three claims together. If Kathleen discovered Michael's sexual secrets on December 9, and if this led to a fight culminating in her death, then the murder was a crime of passion. It occurred in the heat of the moment, without forethought or planning. If, on the other hand, the murder was committed for financial reasons, then it was presumably premeditated over a period of weeks or months. It was murder in the first degree, crafted by Michael as a means to major financial benefits.

For most people who haven't looked at the forensic details closely, these motives all seem like good evidence against Michael. The trouble with these theories of motive, however, is that they are balanced almost equally by the testimony of Michael's friends and family, many of whom describe an idyllic, loving relationship between virtual soulmates. Kathleen was beautiful, fit, intelligent, cultured, wealthy, and had a lust for life that most people lose by their mid-thirties. Michael was visibly adoring of Kathleen and hung on her every word. The pair had immediate plans on the horizon, including a romantic second honeymoon on the Indonesian island of Bali (an island, it might be worth noting, well-known for its abundance of male escorts).

Consider the following comments, taken from the docuseries, on the pair's relationship:

> "She was the only reason I only ever saw my father happy. I never knew my father to be happy before Kathleen came along." Todd Peterson

> "It was beautiful. They were just really happy. They loved each other. They didn't ever fight and they just took so much joy in each other's presence... I never saw any problems." Martha Ratliff

"She was always straightforward with us. If there was ever any problem in the family … we had family dinner every night so it was hard not to bring that kind of thing up in conversation. We were a very open family. I always felt like I could talk about anything and I know that Mom talked about everything with us too." Margaret Ratliff

"I was kind of jealous of [the relationship between Michael and Kathleen], because the relationship he had with my mom had never been romantic or intimate—very platonic—and to see him happy with a woman, with Kathleen, the two of them were really good together. They connected on a different plane." Clayton Peterson

And then, of course, we have Michael's own summary of the relationship:

"Kathleen and I were enormously happy. Always. Always! If we ever argued it would only be for a couple of minutes… We fit together perfectly. She was her own person. And I was my own person. But we fit together perfectly… I know people think that I killed the person I love the most, but that doesn't bother me. I couldn't live with that if it were true." Michael Peterson

Any evidence that suggests that Michael wanted to kill Kathleen is equally well-balanced by testimony like this, which suggests exactly the opposite. In total, there is really very little evidence to sway us one way or the other.

CHAPTER THIRTEEN: LOOSE ENDS

THE LEFTOVERS

The police had a responsibility to collect all the relevant evidence from the crime scene. Yet some of the most crucial pieces of evidence were never collected. The way that the crime scene had been handled by police baffled Michael's lawyers and apparently baffled the agents themselves. When they sat on the stand facing questions about why important pieces of evidence had not been collected. The agents would reply, as if on a pre-recorded loop, "No, I can't explain that."

What had the officers failed to collect?

Let's begin with the cordless telephone. When help first arrived, the phone was directly beside Kathleen's head. It was on the bottom step, as if she may have tried to use it herself. By the time the forensics team began documenting the scene, it had been moved to the kitchen countertop. The phone had, by then, purportedly been handled by Michael, Todd, and the first on the scene, Officer Juanetta McDowell. Moreover, Dan George can be witnessed flipping the phone over while making his crime scene video. He noted that a red substance, which he called probable bloodstaining, was smeared on both sides. So, at least four people handled the phone after Kathleen died.

The phone was covered in something red and there certainly would have been fingerprints. It was an essential piece of evidence. It had been lying inches from Kathleen's nose when her body was discovered. Had she tried to call

911 during the alleged domestic attack? Were there anyone else's prints or DNA on the phone? Was there any substance on it apart from blood? These questions could never be answered—the phone was not taken into evidence. Why?

Rudolf questioned George at trial, passing him a picture of the cordless phone. "Do you see a little bit of red in the very corner of the phone there?" Rudolf asked.

"Sir, there was some staining on the phone but I couldn't determine whether it was blood or another kind of stain," came George's answer.

"You saw some staining on the phone, and in the crime scene video, you actually flipped the phone over because there was even more staining on the back?"

"That's correct."

"And you said you weren't sure if it was blood or something else?"

"That's right."

But what else could it have been? Puzzlingly, George had all the necessary chemical test kits available to him if he wished to carry out a presumptive test on the red marks on the telephone. Deciding whether they were actually blood would have taken only a minute or two. He gave no explanation as to why no test was performed, and he claimed to simply overlook taking the phone into evidence—all of this despite knowing the phone had been inside the stairwell with Kathleen's body when she was first discovered, and despite knowing that something resembling blood was on the phone. Baffling? It was.

What about the paper towels? There were two of them, directly up from Kathleen's head. Both the crime scene video and the photographs taken at the scene clearly show they had blood on them. And if it wasn't blood, then some other red marks coated their creased edges. At trial, George admitted they were bloodied. So how had the paper towels gotten there? Did Michael bring them to Kathleen after she died to nurse her? Did he use them to clean up the blood on the skirting boards? Or had Kathleen grabbed them herself at some point? What secrets did they have to offer? We will never know. They were not taken into evidence. Perplexing? Certainly.

Beside Kathleen's head, lying immediately between the two paper towels, was a pair of reading glasses. They belonged to Michael Peterson. They were a necessary accessory that would have harbored important information. They obviously had something to do with Kathleen's death or the discovery of the body, as they lay inches away from her head. Were they bloodied or not? Whose fingerprints were on the lenses? Had Michael taken them off when he found Kathleen? Had Kathleen borrowed them for the night, having misplaced her own? Or had she grabbed them from Michael's face while he repeatedly thrashed at her skull? What evidence could the glasses have provided? We don't know. And we will never know. They weren't collected into evidence either. Suspicious? Extremely so.

Sitting under Kathleen's head, Michael had placed a number of thick cotton towels. They had been bundled up into something resembling a small parcel. They were soaked with wet blood and made up an essential part of the crime scene. Since they were bundled up, anything could have been hiding inside their folds. The towels (and anything inside them) were crucial to the prosecution's claim that Michael had staged the scene. After all, if Michael killed Kathleen, then he put towels beneath her head only to act out how a worried husband would behave.

So, many questions arise: Were they inserted beneath her head before her death, or were they put there after all the life had left her body? Were the towels wet with blood alone, or were there other substances to be found? Was there anything hidden inside the bundle? Perhaps there were cleaning products, soaked into the fibers. Perhaps DNA could be drawn. Well, you guessed it. They weren't collected as evidence. At trial, George had no explanation.

"Why did you decide that the towels had no relevance if you could have found out whether they were placed there after Kathleen had stopped bleeding?" asked Rudolf.

"That was a decision that I made, sir," answered George.

"Do you have no answer as to why the towels had no relevance?"

"No, I don't."

The towels had been removed from under Kathleen's head even before Kenneth Snell, the arriving medical examiner, had had a chance to view the body.

In the hallway, virtually touching Kathleen's bare feet, two rubber flip-flops had been tossed. They belonged to Kathleen. It seemed as though she had kicked them off during her beating or fall. Despite the fact that all of the clothing of Michael and Todd Peterson was collected as evidence, the footwear that Kathleen wore in the seconds before her death went uncollected. Why? George had an answer here: if any blood had been discovered on the rubber soles, it all would have been Kathleen's anyway. But would it have been? And what if there had been no blood at all? Then what?

It is all simply extraordinary. Here is the situation. A woman is dead in an apparent homicide. There are at least seven important objects scattered around her body: a pair of glasses, several blood-drenched towels folded into a bundle, two bloodied paper towels, a pair of flip-flops, and a cordless phone that Kathleen may have used to beg 911 for help during an attack. And yet every single item on the bottom two steps, within inches of the site of Kathleen's body, was left behind.

There was no reasonable explanation the police could provide. Every item on the stairs and around the body required detailed analysis. They were all crucial to the criminal case mounting against Michael. Could an analysis of these items have helped the prosecution? If Michael had killed Kathleen, then clearly the answer is yes. Perhaps her bloody fingerprints were on the phone. Perhaps more fingerprints were on the reading glasses and paper towels. And who knows what secrets the blood-drenched towels could have disclosed? Yet it is crystal clear that the police were unwilling to take the items. Why weren't they collected? Perhaps investigators knew, from the outset, that the items surrounding Kathleen's body would point in a different direction, at an altogether different culprit.

You could argue it was simply shoddy police work. Police make mistakes all the time. But such a degree of shoddiness is beyond comprehension. It is incongruent with the degree of precision and attention to detail that the detectives applied elsewhere. Forensic investigators felt it necessary to collect individual pine needles from around the body into evidence. They collected empty soda cans and used champagne glasses from the kitchen counter. Dan George tweezered out single hairs and fibers from the ridges of the stairs. Every piece of clothing from Michael and Todd was collected as evidence. Both of the wristwatches of Michael and Kathleen were bundled into paper bags. Yet inexplicably, the State left behind each and every object found directly beside and even touching Kathleen's head. All the items were clearly evidence, even to a layman. It didn't take a genius to realize their central importance to a criminal case. They were impossible to overlook. It cannot be explained by shoddy police work. The decision was deliberate.

This fact needs to be emphasized. The police did not simply forget or overlook taking the items for investigation. As the police photographer Angie Powell stated twenty years after the investigation, the collection of these items was a matter of "forensics 101." The decision "must have been deliberate," she said. And yet, she could not explain what the motivation could possibly have been.

THE MURDER WEAPONS

Apart from these shocking examples of police malpractice, the State's case suffered from an additional shortcoming. There was no murder weapon discovered at the house. No rod-like object was seen or recovered. At trial, the prosecution argued that Michael had hidden the blow poke after killing Kathleen. That was why the police had never found it.

But the truth is rather different. As a matter of fact, two possible murder weapons were identified during the investigation.

In an upstairs bedroom, a wooden stick lay on the floor. It sat on a Turkish rug between a chest of drawers and the wall. The stick was clearly disturbed, lying at a thirty-five-degree angle to the wall, as if clumsily tossed to the floor. It seemed to serve no purpose within the room and it drew the immediate attention of the police.

Wooden stick in the bedroom. Crime scene video

On the stand, Dan George discussed some of his thoughts when he first viewed the object. "It appeared to me that this was some kind of a walking stick or a piece of wood. At one time, we thought that that may have been used as some kind of weapon."

"But you did not seize it?" Jim Hardin asked.

"See anything on it?"

"No, I said, 'you did not seize it,' correct?"

"Oh yes, that is why we did not seize it," George answered. "It was checked for blood and there appeared to be none there."

When it was first spotted, the wooden beam was considered to be a possible murder weapon. It looked like a "rod-like object" of precisely the sort that Snell had advised investigators to be on the lookout for. Kathleen had been struck across the head with something long and blunt, and this heavy stick may have been what killed her. Was it collected into evidence? Of course not.

Just like every other obvious item of interest, the beam was not collected into evidence. It clearly resembled the description of the murder weapon that Kenneth Snell had offered investigators. It seemed disturbed and out of place, and investigators admitted to thinking it may have been involved. Yet the stick was just left there. The police seemed to seriously drop the ball when they had the chance to test this item in more detail. What caused them to change their minds about it? Why were they so certain that the beam could be eliminated as the murder weapon? Was it the lack of visible blood? Why would this matter if Michael had cleaned up the scene? Undoubtedly, if he used the wooden stick to kill his wife, he would have cleaned the blood from it.

So, the State had discovered an object that they believed could have been the murder weapon, and yet they just left it there on the floor, unseized and untested. And troublingly, the long piece of wood was not the only possible murder weapon discovered.

As a matter of fact, the mythical "missing blow poke" had never been missing at all. It had been discovered, photographed, and tucked away by police over a year before the trial began. The blow poke, the crux of the State's case, was hiding in the basement. And the police knew all along that it had nothing to do with the crime.

The story of the notorious blow poke began just months after Kathleen's death. On February 11, 2002, Candace Zamperini, the younger sister of Kathleen, sent a fax to Detective Art Holland. In this fax, a crude drawing of a fireplace blow poke was scrawled. The poker had been a gift from Candace to Kathleen decades before. Candace described it as about forty inches long, brass, and hollow.

Candace's suspicions were heightened because she believed it was missing from the Petersons' home. She was convinced that she had personally used it at the Peterson house on Thanksgiving Day, the year before Kathleen's death. But during her most recent visit to the house (during which she became convinced that Michael had killed her sister), she found that the blow poke was gone.

The officers sat up in their seats when they received Candace's sketch. Not only did the blow poke fit the description of the murder weapon given by Snell, but it had also vanished from the home. If it had vanished like this, then Michael must have hidden it or thrown it away. It had to be found. To that end, a search of the property was undertaken in June 2002. Campen and George were looking for the blow poke. They searched from top to bottom. And within a couple of hours, they had found it. The blow poke was not missing. It was propped up against a concrete wall in the dark of the basement.

The long brass rod was visually inspected for any bloodstains, hairs, or damage. There was nothing like that. It was then photographed, but not collected. And that was that. Its discovery was never made public. Its existence was suppressed. The blow poke was returned to its resting place inside the Petersons' basement. When it was finally recovered by the defense team (after having been found late in 2003 by Michael's son Clayton), it was collecting dust and cobwebs. It had no dents or bends and no encrusted blood spatter or hairs on its frame. It was just a neglected old blow poke sitting alone in the corner of the basement garage.

The defense had the item photographed in place. The poker was then carefully packaged in a clear plastic tube, before being brought to trial on September 21 on one of the final days of witness testimony. It was presented to the court in dramatic style. The media heartily enjoyed the spectacle.

The police, however, were enjoying it less. As he sat in the witness box, Detective Holland was questioned by Rudolf about the blow poke. Had it ever been found? Holland was adamant that the blow poke was missing from the home.

Rudolf approached the stand and placed the long plastic container in Holland's hands. The tension in the room was palpable. "Let me show you," said Rudolf, "what has been marked as Defendant's Exhibit 280." Holland took the encased blow poke from Rudolf and scanned it from tip to tip. After giving the officer a minute to act surprised, Rudolf continued with his questions. "Now, that's a blow poke, isn't it?"

"It appears to be a blow poke."

The jury could hardly believe what they were witnessing.

"Do you know," asked Rudolf, "where Defendant's Exhibit 280 has been for the last twenty months?"

"No, I don't," replied Holland.

"This doesn't appear to you to be mangled, does it?"

"It is not mangled."

"Dented?"

"It doesn't appear to be dented."

"Does this appear to you to be the blow poke which Mr. Hardin has stated was mysteriously missing?"

"Objection!" Hardin bellowed.

"Sustained," Judge Hudson agreed.

The jury was sent to the deliberation room while the status of the new and shocking piece of evidence was assessed. A ten-minute break was allowed while the prosecution could review the court order allowing the poker into evidence. In the courtroom, those sitting beside Michael were glowing with fresh hope. Not only had the State's murder weapon been found, but it had clearly not been used to kill anybody. Those sitting behind the prosecution bench were furious. They simmered with new disdain at what they perceived to be prejudicial lawyerly theatrics. The decision was made then and there by the prosecutors not to submit the poker to any forensic tests. One can only assume that they already knew what the outcome would be.

When the jury returned, Holland told Rudolf that he had searched the basement twice between December 9 and 10. The basement was dark and cluttered, he said, as he tried desperately to provide a plausible reason for his failure to spot the murder weapon. And yet despite the searches conducted in the basement, by both himself and other agents, he remained unshakeable in his testimony. "That poker was not in the basement."

Neither Holland nor Campen nor George ever testified that the missing blow poke had been found, had been photographed, and had been left behind. All three men knew it was the weapon on which the State's case hinged. And they never said a word.

The blow poke had not been used during a murder. And the police knew it. All evidence of its existence had been suppressed. It was a clear betrayal of Lady Justice.

UNTESTED

The police deliberately left behind many important pieces of evidence. Many others were never tested. These included:

1. At least two blood-soaked towels, bundled up beneath Kathleen's head.
2. Two blood-stained paper towels on the steps.
3. Kathleen's rubber flip-flops.
4. Michael's reading glasses, which lay on the bottom step.
5. The portable phone, which was coated with blood.
6. A possible murder weapon, made of wood, discovered in an upstairs bedroom.
7. The blow poke in the basement.

And to this list we can add many more anomalous failures:

8. The white splats—bird feces—on the bottom steps were never tested.
9. State's Exhibit 12—a chip from a talon—disappeared before the jury could view it.
10. Alleged bloodstains on the kitchen cabinets were never photographed or tested.
11. The alleged blood drop on top of the kitchen counter was never photographed or given a presumptive test.
12. The sink drain was never tested for the presence of alcohol.
13. The objects—most likely feathers—on Kathleen's body and face were never collected.
14. The debris on the front path—feathers again—were not collected.
15. The shadow on the north wall of the stairwell was never tested for blood.
16. The results of the luminol tests were not photographed or even documented in a diagram.
17. The spilled kettle of some sort of liquid on the outside patio was not tested.

18. The strainer and pot in the sink, with their unusual contents, were also not collected.

One could go on. But what is surprising about this list is not the sheer number of items on it. What is surprising is that so many of the items listed are obviously central to any criminal case against Michael. If Michael killed Kathleen, then a few simple tests of some of this evidence would have definitively proven his guilt. Yet the investigators carried on as if already aware that such tests would point in the wrong direction. And indeed, perhaps they would have.

Take State's Exhibit 12. It was presented as a chip from a murder weapon which was either wooden or metallic, as if the difference between the two substances was irrelevant. But a simple test could have unlocked the mystery. What if this object had been tested and had been found to be brass? What more evidence would be needed to establish that Michael used the blow poke to murder Kathleen? And if it had been found to be wood rather than metal, then was it the same sort of wood as the wooden beam in the upstairs bedroom? And what if it had been found to be neither wood nor metal, but the talon of a bird? Apparently, the State felt that solving these questions would be more trouble than it would be worth. On the other hand, forensic tests of empty soda cans and champagne glasses, now that was important.

As a matter of fact, State's Exhibit 12 may not have been the only evidence of a talon shard at the scene. Larry Pollard had first suggested the possibility that the alleged "wood splinter" found on Kathleen's head represented a chipped talon. And at trial, Angie Powell gave testimony in conflict with the State's case that it had been a simple sliver of wood.

Powell described the shard entirely differently from the SBI trace evidence team, who eventually called it a piece of "woody vegetation." Powell called it a "wood-metal chip." Again, the description of the item as something like "wood-metal" exactly echoes Campen's testimony about State's Exhibit 12. And this shard had not been found sitting loose in Kathleen's hair, but embedded in the back of her head. Both Powell and Campen described something harder than wood, but not quite like metal. The consistency of the two objects was the same.

Indeed, Powell would later state that the "wood-metal chip" was not just similar in its solidity but generally "very similar" in appearance to State's Exhibit 12. She speculated that wherever the shard came from, its source was the same as what Campen had plucked from the step and what George had described as "like a mini-talon." Whatever the object's composition was, it was not readily identifiable as an ordinary twig or a metal shard. And since this object may have been lodged against Kathleen's skull, we have good reason to think that it may represent another piece of talon recovered from the scene.

Clenching its grip, the owl broke its own weapons. It did so twice. One of these chips conveniently vanished, while the other was mislabeled as a piece of vegetation. The jury would never learn that the two shards were almost identical in appearance.

THE PLANTER

The police did not only fail to collect crucial evidence. They also failed to follow some of the most elementary rules of police protocol. When investigating a crime scene, there is a golden rule that every officer knows: don't disturb the scene!

It's not rocket science. We all know why you shouldn't disturb the scene. Important evidence could be destroyed or moved in ways which might accidentally exculpate a guilty person. On the other hand, evidence could be moved or changed and an innocent person gets put behind bars. If the general layout of a criminal scene is drastically reorganized, the forensic analysis that follows may be deeply flawed.

Yet by 6 a.m. on that fateful day in 2001, the police said that they had already made a major modification to the front of the house. A heavy concrete planter, about two feet tall, had been moved to the middle of the front step, essentially blocking the front door. The planter was moved about six feet, and placed down next to the drop of blood on the front step.

The planter in front of the door. Crime scene video

Why had this large piece of outdoor decor been moved? George tried to explain at trial. "The planter was moved from the side of the doorway to denote the droplet of blood so that no one would be stepping on it."

At first, a ripped and folded piece of white paper had been put down over the blood drop. But George worried that investigators might trample on it. So an officer had picked up and moved the heavy concrete planter. The idea was that this would protect the blood drop.

Is this reasonable behavior at a crime scene? Sure, if you wanted to remember to avoid an area on your own front path, you might put something large in the way. If you break a glass in the kitchen, you might put a vase there to remind yourself to avoid the area. But here we have a trained forensic scene technician moving a heavy concrete planter several feet from its original location in the midst of an active investigation. And this was done, it was argued, in order to "protect the scene."

It simply makes no sense. Angie Powell, who would go on to become the manager of forensics within Durham's police force, later stated that this dramatic change to the front of the house was in clear violation of basic principles of police investigation. "A road cone," she stated, "could easily have been used instead." If the planter had been moved by police, it was a ridiculous decision.

Consider also that by the time the planter was moved, the entire front path had already been cordoned off with crime scene tape. Nobody could enter or exit without police permission. All access to the area was tightly controlled. And yet we are supposed to believe that the drop of blood (the drop which was neither lifted with tape nor given a presumptive forensic test) was so fussed over that the layout of the furniture on the front path needed to be radically changed, even before the crime scene video was taken. No officer worth their salt would do this.

The claim that the planter was moved by investigators is, at best, a bald-faced lie; at worst, it shows that the investigators at 1810 Cedar Street were so inept as to not even understand the most basic principles of containing crime scenes.

It all suggests either that the explanation the police gave for their moving of the planter was false, or the police did not move the planter. Let's look at why the first explanation might be true.

When Dan George was questioned about the blood drop on the front step, he made a very strange comment about the weather. He noted that a piece of paper had been placed over the blood drop. He then adds that the planter was moved towards the blood drop afterwards. And he ends his short story by noting that it all had something to do with the weather that morning. He never elaborates on what the weather had to do with all this.

What weather event would have caused a police officer to move a large piece of outdoor furniture from one place to another, thereby massively distorting the scene? Of course, if it had been raining that morning, the planter might have been moved directly over the blood drop to keep it from washing away. But the planter was not on top of the blood drop and it was not raining that morning. Instead, the planter was several inches away from the spot of blood and there was only a light but persistent breeze.

Perhaps the weight of the planter can give us a clue as to why it was moved. It was heavy enough to hold something in place under its foot, even as the gentle breeze continued to scatter light debris. Did something need to be kept from blowing away? The police would be forced to act like this only if the blood was on an object that might fly in the breeze, like a feather. The planter, then, would be acting like a paperweight, keeping the bloodied feather in place.

That is just one hypothesis. The alternative is that the police did not actually move the planter at all. Perhaps the police arrived at the scene and found the planter already in front of the front door. This may seem wild speculation, but there is no testimony indicating which officer was responsible for moving the planter. If the planter was already there when police arrived, then they needed to develop a story to explain why it was sitting where it was, directly in front of the door.

Why would the police lie about this? One reason might have to do with their theory about what had happened that night. The police believed that Kathleen's attack occurred entirely inside the house. So, if the planter was moved by Kathleen on the night that she died, then this would have indicated that part of her struggle had occurred outside. Perhaps she fell against it or attempted to use it to block the front door.

If Kathleen had moved the planter, then this fact would contradict the picture that the State wanted to present. According to them, Kathleen had found Michael's illicit emails on the computer, causing a fight which led to Michael killing Kathleen. According to the State, all the action had happened inside the house. No part of the scenario indicated any activity outside the house. So if the planter had been moved before police arrived, they just could not explain it. Instead of explaining it, they explained it away.

So what is the truth about the planter? We will probably never know. If it really was moved by the police, then it was a reckless rearrangement of the crime scene. And given everything else we know, it ought to be taken as suspicious.

THE SHOE PRINT

The defense faced an uphill battle that went beyond police corruption. The fact of the matter was that the weight of the evidence supported the view that Kathleen had been attacked. In contrast, the evidence for a death from a couple of falls at the base of a staircase was weak. And indeed, the jury would ultimately be right to judge that Kathleen had been attacked; they would simply identify the wrong killer.

But some evidence did link Michael directly with Kathleen's death. It was not circumstantial evidence, like the evidence of gay relationships and bad finances. It was solid evidence that connected the body of Michael with the body of Kathleen.

On Kathleen's sweatpants, there was a stain. It was not blood spatter or spray; it was a transfer stain. A bloody object had come into contact with Kathleen's white sweatpants and had left a distinct impression. It was the bloody outline of the sole of a shoe. It came from Michael's tennis shoe: one of a pair of shoes that lay scattered in the hallway beside Kathleen's feet. Perhaps unsurprisingly, the police had collected Michael's tennis shoes into evidence despite leaving behind Kathleen's flip-flops that lay beside them.

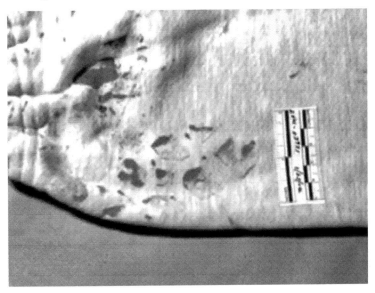

The bloody footprint on the ankle of Kathleen's sweatpants.

Michael had already removed his white sneakers and double-layered socks by the time the paramedics arrived. He was wandering around with bare feet. "The floor was slippery" was his explanation. When Michael was outside on the patio, being assessed for shock by Dr. Heather Whitson, he still had no shoes on and was clothed in nothing more than a t-shirt and shorts. It was certainly odd, especially for a winter's night, even a warm one, in Durham. And it made little sense since even if the floor had been slippery with blood, it would seem that rubber soles would grip better on a wet floor than bare feet. So why did Michael remove his shoes?

One possible explanation is the simple explanation he first gave: the floor was wet and he slipped. Having slipped, he decided to remove his shoes and socks. Perhaps he was mistaken to think that this would afford him a better grip on the hardwood floors, but being wrong about something is not indicative of anything sinister.

The prosecution, however, was not buying this story. They took Michael's shoe-removal as evidence that he was attempting to, quite literally, cover his tracks. He had stepped on Kathleen as he bludgeoned her, then realized the shoe print on her sweatpants would incriminate him. He removed his shoes so that it would be harder to link him to Kathleen's death.

Without doubt, it is very strange that Michael removed his shoes. But it hardly seems that he removed them to avoid incrimination. After all, he left them right beside Kathleen's body. He told police he had been wearing them the moment he found her. So what would he gain by removing them? If the State's explanation was right, then it seems impossible to understand Michael's motives and actions that night. If he wanted to hide the shoes, why didn't he?

The print on the sweatpants was not smudged or scuffed. This indicated that the print was left in a way that was limited in movement. Kathleen was not writhing underneath Michael as he stepped on her ankle. And the print was not the result of a violent kick or a stomp. Even the direction of the print is inconsistent with having been inflicted during a beating, as the toe of the shoeprint faces down the ankle towards Kathleen's foot. If Michael had been standing upon Kathleen as he beat her over the head, then his shoe print should have been facing her head, not her toes. And so, the print is ultimately consistent with an accidental footstep on a motionless body. It is less consistent with having been made during a beating. When Michael left the print, Kathleen was most likely already unconscious and motionless, and he simply misplaced his footing as he found the body in the dark.

THE CONDOM

Other evidence that was discovered defied any explanation by either the defense or the prosecution. In an upstairs bedroom, an unused condom lay unfurled on the floor beside an empty wrapper. It was totally unclear whom these had belonged to. But Campen had taken them into evidence on the chance that they might have secrets to tell. Who had had sex (or tried to have sex) that night? Unfortunately, the tests were without reward. No traces of DNA were found on the inside or the outside of the latex. It was almost as though no penis had been inserted into it, and that it had not been used to penetrate anyone.

Some believed that the condom had something to do with Todd. Freda Black, the more aggressive of the two prosecutors, mentioned that she had been told of Todd's plan to sleep with Mrs. Tomasetti, a married woman, at the Peterson home that night after returning from the Christmas party. But apart from this claim, nothing linked the condom to anyone or anything. There are clues that the condom remnants may have been quite old. Rudolf noted that when collected, the condom and its wrapper were said to be covered in something resembling cobwebs. Was it an old condom that had been left in a corner and forgotten. This sounds unlikely to be true, given Kathleen's well-known fastidiousness about cleaning.

Was the condom relevant to the events that transpired that night? It is difficult to say. In any case, neither the defense nor the prosecution offered a compelling explanation.

THE TOOL MARK

There were thousands of bloody marks in the stairwell. Most of them were spray and spatter. But one of the marks was supposed to show that a tool had been used in Kathleen's beating. The bloodstain came to be known as the "tool mark" since it was shaped like some kind of man-made artifact. It had sharp edges that could not be explained by clothing or random blood spatter. It was the only bloodstain on the stairs that suggested that a transfer of blood had come directly from a weapon.

The "tool mark". Crime scene photograph.

It was just a few inches in height and breadth. Duane Deaver tried to prove that the mark had been caused by the tip of a blow poke. He did some experiments. Dipping a blow poke in red liquid, Deaver pressed the implement against parchment paper from various angles. His attempts to convince the jury were failures. There was no resemblance between the tool mark on the step and the marks that Deaver had made in his experiments.

Early in the investigation, it had been postulated that the mark resembled something that a tire iron might cause. But this supposition was quickly abandoned when it became clear that it had been based on an incorrect understanding of the dimensions of the transfer stain, which was far smaller than anything a tire iron could leave behind.

So what caused the tool mark? A plausible hypothesis not explored at trial is that the mark may represent the inside edges of the tread of a shoe. The mark, therefore, could have been yet another example of crime scene contamination. Another explanation is it was somehow related to a bird that moved around the stairwell with Kathleen. The mark may have been caused by the bird's toes or by the capillary action of blood within the feathers. In fact, Angie Powell suggested the tool mark may have been compatible with some part of the body of a bird of prey.

But ultimately, no party at Michael's trial had a good explanation for the so-called tool mark. Only guesses and hunches remain about what caused it.

CHAPTER FOURTEEN: KILLED BY AN OWL

THE EIGHTH OF DECEMBER

Michael brought out a bottle of Moet & Chandon.

"What are we celebrating?" Kathleen asked as Michael popped the bubbly.

Michael winked at his wife and smiled brightly. "Here's to *Charlie Two Shoes*!" he said, pouring out a couple of glasses.

Charlie Two Shoes—his most recent book about a Chinese dissident and political prisoner—had a Hollywood producer chasing an option. He had received a call a few days prior. Stratton Leopold, a major name in the industry, thought the tale would make a great film. The bubbles were downed, dinner was eaten, and Michael popped on a film he had rented: a comedy called *America's Sweethearts*. Michael had collected it from a Blockbuster franchise around 7 p.m.

It was around 9:45 p.m. when Todd and Christina Tomasetti stopped by the house. They witnessed the celebration. Michael was in the kitchen, collecting the bubbly and some champagne flutes for himself and Kathleen. The young couple left for a Christmas party shortly after. They went together in Todd's car.

Was the expensive bubbly all to do with the news from Hollywood? It seems there may have been more to the story. The champagne and the film were probably something of a peace offering. Michael's tail was between his legs. To the irritation of Kathleen, just minutes before she would arrive home for the night, Michael had darted out to the local YMCA. He had called Kathleen at six to inform her of his plans, but instead received an earful of Kathleen's frustration with his frequent trips to the gym. It may be the case that "the gym" had already become a euphemism they both used. This particular gym was well known as a cruising location for gay men. "Fair enough." Michael sighed. "How about we spend the night in with a movie?" The plan was made.

Presumably, after watching the film, the pair shared their critiques of the plot, the acting, the jokes, and everything else. They then made their way to the study. At precisely 11:08 p.m., the phone rang. It was Helen Prislinger. She asked for an email address so she could send through some files. Kathleen was sober and calm as she attended to the call. "What's the address?" Kathleen asked someone in the room with her. A man's voice answered. "MPWriter at RR dot NC dot com." Prislinger sent the files before midnight, but the email was never opened.

According to Michael, Kathleen followed him outside. The pair had gone to the poolside with glasses of white wine. The bottle of bubbly had already been finished. They chatted for a while, enjoying each other's company. Kathleen then left Michael alone. He puffed on his pipe, in solitude, and imagined how Hollywood might butcher the book.

Of course, they were bound to ruin it. But did it really matter?

Fuck it, he thought. The whole thing was a serious coup. It had felt like eons since any new artistic successes had come his way. And this was a big one. Hollywood would tell the story of *Charlie Two Shoes*. It was a story close to his heart, with several of his friends (including Nick Galifianakis) having been personally involved in the campaign to grant American citizenship to the Chinese political dissident.

Michael lay back and reflected on the year he had lived through. It had been no ordinary year—2001. It was

America's year of infamy. It was a turning point for the United States, replete with terrorist attacks, anthrax letters, and invasions of foreign lands. A country that had for so long felt immune from the chaos of international politics had now gained its diploma in the school of hard knocks. Michael thought about the renewed rhetoric around al-Qaeda and the Bin Ladens. He remembered Vietnam. And naturally, as both a war veteran and a Democrat, he feared for the futures of the thousands of young men who were being deployed under the Orwellian guise of Enduring Freedom.

Freedom. Did that word have any meaning these days? The towers fell for geopolitics, the troops were sent off for "national defense," the police were emboldened by the dystopian Patriot Act, and on the streets, whole neighborhoods were enacting modern-day Jim Crow policies, resegregating communities with Blacks increasingly marginalized. Everything was a mess and the American Dream had been exposed as a fantasy. The land of the free, not at all; but certainly the home of anyone brave enough to stay.

Through clouds of tobacco smoke, Michael exhaled a breath of disappointment. The nicotine met the alcohol and Michael's eyelids drooped a little. A hint of melancholy descended. Hope for any serious change was dwindling. Michael had failed to change the political course of his community in Durham. Was he a failure? *Most probably,* he thought.

The numbers had been released just over a month ago: sixty-one percent against him, thirty-nine for him. It hadn't been a whitewash, but it wasn't a great result either. Still, he had put up a good fight. In some sense, it was encouraging, right?

No, it wasn't; it was a loss. The incumbent of nineteen years, Howard Clement III, would keep his seat. And Michael would have to wait years before trying for a council seat again. He had vowed to audit the city, to get a total financial breakdown of loans and programs. It was not only in an effort to secure fiscal soundness for the city of Durham, but also to investigate and eliminate growing corruption within the entire state of North Carolina. "This city…" He sighed.

It was a worry that had been growing for Michael, especially over the previous few years. Corruption, and police corruption in particular, was all through the papers. "Durham can drive you schizoid," he had editorialized earlier that year at his personal website *Hizzoner*. "Some days I'm filled with hope and enthusiasm about Durham's future. Other days I'm worried to the point of despair."

Tonight was no different. It occurred to him that chasing votes was virtually impossible in a country quickly losing respect for the very concept of democracy. Chasing money as a writer, though, was even harder. And hell, in that respect, at least he had something to show for his efforts. *Charlie Two Shoes* would get to the box office. A big check would arrive in the mailbox. At least, that's what he believed. *There was a path forward*, he thought as he lay there on a deck chair in the dark. Better times lay ahead. Although the road ahead was full of obstacles, he knew that with each obstacle overcome, one step was put ahead of the other. There was only one direction: onwards!

He closed his eyes and rested. Did he doze? Maybe.

THE OWL STRIKES

The owl stretched its wings and flapped them a couple of times. It had been difficult chasing bats between the branches of the trees. Every now and then, one could be snatched up. It made a good meal. But catching those airborne rodents was harder than getting the dumb mice that slowly scuttled between the hedges. There was plenty of good food around this nest, for sure. It just took a bit of effort to collect.

The time was around 1 a.m. It was early afternoon for an owl. Looking down on the path from high above, the owl's eyes tracked Kathleen's movements. She was a small woman and she was carrying some wooden thing shaped like a reindeer. To the bird, she was just movement. She was a target. The eyes locked onto the circle of bobbing hair. As Kathleen came down the path, she unknowingly encroached on territory already claimed as the domain of the nest. As Kathleen walked, she was entirely unaware that every step was being closely watched. She was unaware of the hostile invasion she had launched. The owl twisted its neck, fixing its eyeballs on the movement below. Kathleen set down the wooden reindeer by the front gate. She turned and returned up the path.

With every step towards the front door, the trajectory between the tree limb and Kathleen's head was being calculated with mathematical precision somewhere inside the owl's tiny brain. It opened its wings. The apex predator cruised like a missile towards the back of her head.

Did Kathleen hear a sound? Probably not. The owl's soft feathers muffled the sound of the attack. Her own footsteps were deafening by comparison. Without warning, she was instantly struck to the ground, like a baseball bat had been belted against her head. She collapsed and cried out. Was she bleeding? Most likely. Already, deep linear cuts had scored through her scalp.

Lying there on the paving stones, she knew she had been struck. By whom, she didn't know. Her head throbbed with pain and blood dribbled down her forehead. She staggered to her feet, turning to see her assailant. But there was no one there. No footsteps. Nothing. The path was empty. *Who had done this?* She felt a dribble of blood fall down her temple. She was bewildered and terrified.

The owl was back on a branch, watching as she turned to run. She raced towards the front of the house, with her hair bobbing against her shoulders, enticing the owl like the bushy tail of a squirrel. She felt that powerful strike again. Like a lightning bolt to the skull. This time, feathered wings covered her face. She felt talons digging into her head. It was an owl. *Good god!* It was an owl trying to kill her!

She tumbled into the bushes that lined the path, trying to pull the owl from her head as it pecked at her face. She rolled with the owl through the neatly trimmed hedgerows. She crawled to the path, covering herself in pine needles. The pair rolled, wrestling, pulling, and kicking. She reached at her scalp to grab a fistful of wings or a foot of the bird. Her hands collected a film of tiny feathers caked in her own blood. She screamed.

As she reached the front step, she pushed open the front door. She got inside and crouched behind the door. She tried to wedge the owl into the slam of the door. She finally got the owl in between the doorjamb. She pulled at the door, attempting to crush the owl's body. She slammed the door hard, again and again, flattening the body of the bird. It screeched and flapped. But the grasp of talons was stronger than she could fight. The more she slammed the door, the more she pulled the talons through her head. Her fight was futile. The more she yanked at the door, the more she spread her own blood across the back of the door and its frame. The owl was unrelenting. She screamed out for Michael. She heaved at the door. It was useless.

With the owl still attached to her scalp, she flung the door open and ran down the hallway past the giant nutcracker dolls. They stood there in silence as the strangest sight fled past. Drops of her blood fell on the wooden floorboards beneath her feet, leaving a trail of evidence. She came to the bottom of the stairs when the owl released its grip.

For a few seconds, it hopped around her and she kicked at it in a pathetic attempt to shoo it away. This only antagonized the owl, which hissed and rattled its throat. There was nowhere to hide.

From a few feet away, it spread out its wings to prepare to jump at her head. Covering her face with her arms, Kathleen saved her eyes from the forward lunge of the owl's claws. Its talons connected with her elbows, leaving six unique puncture wounds, and the force of the attack threw her down back into the stairwell. She hit her head on one of the stairs and her head wounds now splattered blood profusely on the walls. The owl, now bloody itself, battered its wings against her arms and sprayed fan-shaped blood sprays from the tips of its wings in a series of sideways cast-off patterns that would later perplex investigators.

The bird again released its grip and perched in the hallway. It watched the human bleeding, writhing, and screaming in terror. The death blow was only moments away. Kathleen got up. She felt weak from blood loss. Her only escape, her only place to hide, was up the stairs, behind the wall of the stairwell. The owl clattered its voice box. Its eyes were wide and black, and they stared deeply into Kathleen's. Kathleen turned and presented her back to the animal, preparing to sprint up the stairs away from the horror.

If she had been just a moment faster, she might have avoided its fatal lunge. But she wasn't. The owl leapt at her skull and pierced her scalp in eight places. A great spray of blood hit the north wall, leaving behind the shadow of the bird above her head. It battered its wings between the narrow walls of the stairwell, kicking erratically, and chipping a talon, which embedded in a step. The attack floored Kathleen. She was knocked down to the bottom of the stairwell. The owl's wings, now drenched in blood, beat and flap, spraying copious blood spots, over ten thousand spatters, across the walls in repeated horizontal cast-off patterns. Its wings repeatedly flapped blood against the walls, against the skirting boards, against the metal chairlift, and against the frame of the stairwell.

Kathleen fell, wedging the owl beneath her head and the bottom step. The owl heaved at her body. Another shard of talon was broken on her skull. It flapped its wings repeatedly, and the tips of each wing wiped away the blood from opposite sides of a step. It deposited heavy white droppings over the blood and under Kathleen's head. Kathleen was now unconscious, lying across the three bottom stairs. Her blood began to pool around her. The bird, still attached to her scalp, pulled its talons tight in an effort to lift the body. It beat its wings relentlessly. But the small bird could never carry her away. She weighed one hundred and twenty pounds. The bird, at best, was just over two pounds. In its attempt to lift the body, it shredded its claws through the skin on her scalp, leaving two distinctive trident-shaped wounds. It shed dozens of feathers in its attack, which are strewn over her body, mostly in her hair.

The woman was still breathing, but could no longer fight. Kathleen was not in the room. Her body was there, but her brain was shutting down. The blood oozed from her cuts and the life slowly left her body. Kathleen's last experience, dimly perceived, was of those feathers repeatedly stroking her face. The owl pecked at her unresponsive head. There was no fight. Kathleen was limp. A blood-soaked owl hopped around the body, guarding its kill.

Time stretched out. Kathleen continued to sleep. After an hour or so, the owl lost interest. With Kathleen no longer moving or making any noise (apart from infrequent gulps of air), the bird was satisfied that it neutralized the threat. It emerged from the stairwell victorious, shook itself off, and took flight inside the house.

For an hour or more, the owl was stuck inside the Petersons' home. It fluttered to the closest room and left a scattering of bloody feathers on the kitchen counters and around other areas of the house. It tried several times to make its way out the windows, scratching with its feet at what seemed to be an exit. The owl finds no escape.

Around 2 a.m., the bird finally found its way across the hallway and through the open front door. It was back in its familiar forest surroundings. Now the house was quiet, the sounds of wings flapping and claws scratching were gone. Kathleen's shallow breaths were all that remain. She has been unconscious and losing blood for at least two hours. Over time, the breaths got shallower and shallower. Within a few minutes, she will have died.

THE DISCOVERY

"Kathleen!" cried Michael, "stay with me!" He slipped as he ran to her body. A blood-soaked shoe landed on her sweatpants. The blood made the floor slippery like ice. But it is not the only thing making the floor wet. Kathleen has urinated while in her death throes. Michael kicked off his shoes and removed his socks. He raced to the linen closet to collect towels and, returning, lifts her head to shove them in the gap, hopelessly trying to hold back the blood like a dam. He runs to the kitchen to collect the phone and he dials 911. Kathleen was still breathing, but only tiny gulps.

"1810 Cedar Street. Please!" He ended the call. Help is on its way.

Michael went to the kitchen to gather a roll of paper towels. Back with Kathleen, he tore a few away and nursed her head and face. He lifted her body, moving her into a prone position so she might breathe. He cradled her body in the dark, weeping. The urine from Kathleen's sweatpants wet Michael's shorts, diluting a patch of blood on the front.

What's taking them so long? Michael fretted. It had been eons. It had *felt* like eons: six minutes of clutching his dying wife. At last, a rattle came from Kathleen lungs. She took a final breath. Her body was silent. Kathleen died in his arms.

He rapidly called emergency services again. "Where are they?! This is 1810 Cedar. She's *not* breathing! Please! Please! Would you hurry up!"

"Breathe… Breathe," whispered a voice.

A couple of minutes passed before the paramedics arrive, led by Todd, through the open front door. At the base of the stairwell, they saw a man holding a lifeless corpse. They approached.

"Dad, step away. Mom's dead. The paramedics are here."

Michael stepped away. Monitors were placed on the body. They delivered the verdict: Kathleen is gone.

The paramedics saw a huge amount of blood around Kathleen. They saw wipe marks on the door as they entered. They saw a man talking about a fall, when it was obvious no fall had occurred. It all began then and there. The call was made to the police and the cogs of the machine that would imprison Michael were set in motion.

THE ALIBI

That is the story of Michael's grisly discovery. Or at least, that is half the story. I wish it were as simple as that. But it just can't be.

There is a major discrepancy in Michael's account of that night. The paramedics on the scene were adamant that Michael's first words to them were, "I was just going outside to turn off the lights. I came back in and found her." Yet in all subsequent accounts, Michael states that he had been outside all along. He had been dozing by the pool. Later, at around 2:40 a.m., he says, he came inside and found the body of his wife.

These are two contradictory stories. Both stories can't be true. So which is it? Was Michael going out or coming in?

The drastic change to Michael's alibi is a troubling fact. It seriously undermines any attempt to defend his innocence. If his alibi changed over time, then Michael had something to hide. If Michael is actually innocent, then there are, it seems, only a few options to explain the differences between the accounts:

1. The paramedics misheard Michael when he stated how he discovered the body.
2. Michael was confused and said the wrong thing while in a state of shock.
3. Michael lied about being outside by the pool, possibly dozing, in his subsequent accounts.
4. Michael lied about going outside to turn off the lights in his initial account.

The first three of these explanations are difficult to swallow. And there is much to suggest that the last option may be true. If so, Michael was not by the pool—whether dozing or otherwise—before he found Kathleen. He fabricated this alibi for all subsequent testimony. The paramedics did not mishear him, he was not confused, and when he said he was going outside to turn off the lights, that's exactly what he was doing. Indeed, being closer in time to Kathleen's death, we should take his initial account as more likely to be truthful. There are other reasons to think that Michael had never been out by the pool.

It was December when Kathleen died: winter in North Carolina. On the night of her death, it was not cold. But equally, it was not a comfortable temperature. The outside temperature on the night she died was between 51-55 degrees Fahrenheit. Yet Michael maintained that when Kathleen had fallen to her death, he was lying by the poolside in shorts and a t-shirt, possibly asleep. And if his story is to be believed, he would have been out there for two or three hours. The temperature may have been far from freezing that night, but it would certainly have felt icy after an hour, especially with the breeze.

This temperature was not the only reason to doubt Michael's story of a poolside nap. When Candace Zamperini arrived at the house in the days following Kathleen's death, she happened to notice, looking out an upstairs window, no furniture was set up beside the pool. There were no deckchairs set up on which to doze.

For these reasons, Michael's alibi strains credulity. It is almost certainly false. No normal person would find this temperature tolerable, in minimal clothing, for up to three hours. And no one would find the weather so comfortable as to wind down and possibly take a nap.

But if Michael lied about his whereabouts, then this suggests that he was trying to hide something. So what was he trying to hide? The answer may be more obvious than it seems. He was trying to hide an unfortunate truth which would not have been believed by any jury.

If Kathleen's death was a prolonged ordeal, and if she spent an hour or more writhing in the stairwell slowly bleeding to death, Michael should have been able to hear her cries and shrieks so long as he was inside the house. The idea that he was in the house but failed to hear the shrieks would be a terrible alibi. For this reason, Michael decided to change his story. Place yourself, he was most likely told, as far from the site of Kathleen's death as possible. So long as he was far from the staircase, he could argue that he never heard her wailing. And so, the safest policy was adopted: Michael maintained that he was not even inside the house when Kathleen died.

If Michael was inside the house that night, why did he not hear his wife's cries for help? Here's a guess. Michael was blind drunk. There were two empty bottles on the kitchen sink, with Kathleen having only had a couple of glasses. He probably went upstairs shortly after midnight, staggering into bed. "Night, darling," he most likely slurred as he left Kathleen. But Kathleen had held back. She was planning to work for an hour or so that evening, arranging Christmas decorations and preparing notes for her upcoming trip to Canada. As her blood alcohol showed, she had imbibed, at most, a couple of glasses of wine. The rest of the alcohol, nearly two bottles, was in Michael. He flopped into bed, and everything went black. When Kathleen died, he was sleeping like a baby. Well, he was blackout drunk. And this is why the sounds were never heard.

The timing of his discovery of the body fits this hypothesis well. On this account, Michael passed out around midnight. Kathleen was attacked and mortally wounded in the stairwell, between midnight and 1 a.m. Michael was not roused. He awoke close to 3 a.m. with a case of the dry horrors. He descended the main staircase to pour a big glass of water and to switch off the outside lights. He doesn't understand why Kathleen hasn't done it herself. And he wonders, *where is she anyway?* On his way back inside, he discovers her dying body sprawled across the hallway, taking shallow, desperate breaths. Still drunk, Michael stumbles over her body as he tries to help.

This theory has plenty to recommend it. Michael's hazy and confused state as well as his inability to answer the paramedics' simple questions can be explained if we assume that he was still drunk when the police arrived. Indeed, Michael could barely remember the events of the preceding night. There were big gaps in his memory.

Michael had passed out drunk that night. But if the real story had been presented at trial, it would have done him no favors. On the night of his wife's death, he would be forced to confess that he had been asleep in bed. Indeed, he would be forced to admit that he could barely remember the hour or so inside the house before he fell into bed. No jury would buy it. The prosecution would make mincemeat of it. "I cannot remember what happened throughout most of the night of my wife's death" is perhaps the worst alibi imaginable. So a different story, a more palatable one, was concocted. He claimed he had been out by the pool.

Alas, that is the politics of a criminal investigation. The truth, when it rears its head, is a rare beast to find. Michael lied in an attempt to place himself as far from Kathleen's death as possible. And, most likely, he simply slept through the horrific death of his wife as she screamed and clattered in the stairwell. A sober man may have been able to come to the rescue, but drunk as he was, Michael was utterly powerless. He was not even conscious while his wife screamed for an ambulance. And ever after, Michael lied in a desperate attempt to save his skin. No more, no less.

Is it so unbelievable that someone as pragmatic and deceptive as Michael would trade an undesirable truth for a better falsehood? Diane Fanning made this point best in the afterword of her own book on the Peterson case:

> Despite public opinion to the contrary, the legal system is no longer designed to find the truth–it is constructed to decide a winner. Although life and death lay on the line, many players in the courtroom see it all as a game where cleverness and ruse win the day. A place where a desperate desire to deceive means truth is to be avoided at all costs.

As Michael's Alford plea proves, and as his sexual behavior might indicate, Michael has always preferred to buy a degree of freedom in exchange for lies. And if the better alibi placed him far from the site of Kathleen's death, he knew it was a tale he would have to run with. So he did.

THE CONSPIRACY SIMMERS

Dan George was utterly exhausted. He had been at the Peterson house right through the early hours and into the late morning. He had made a video recording of the front path, the bedroom, the kitchen, and the stairwell. At length, he had filmed the bloodied body of a woman who had no reason to be dead. He had taken some perfunctory notes while the witnesses were confined to the downstairs study.

He knew one thing with confidence: this wasn't a fall. But there were a few things he couldn't make sense of.

- Why was her body covered in pine needles?
- Why was the front path littered with feathers?
- And why were there even more of these feathers all over Kathleen's body?

Now in the police mobile command center, George sat back and narrowed his brows. He remembered the moment that he turned on the hallway lights. He had been the very first person to view Kathleen under good lighting. And there they were: feathers on her face, feathers in her hands, and feathers entangled in her hair. What the hell had happened here?

While Michael and Todd were remanded to their improvised cell, George turned the question over and over again in his mind. Just what could the feathers possibly mean? No bird could have killed this woman. That much was obvious. And no feather duster was used to inflict the fatal blows. She was not killed during a vicious pillow fight. Nor was she smothered with a ragged or torn duvet. She had been beaten across the head—the head wounds proved it—and that had nothing to do with feathers. It was a puzzle without any real answer, he ultimately decided. The meaning of the feathers was nothing at all. They were a distraction.

And what a distraction to boot! What would the defense claim if they got their hands on this so-called evidence? A bird got into the house, perhaps they would say. It gave Kathleen a fright at the top of the stairs. She fell down and died, but the real culprit was a sinister sparrow! Or perhaps Michael's hotshot lawyers would claim that a killer bird, a hawk or falcon, had nested inside the house and fought a bloody battle to the death with Kathleen.

But all these scenarios were clearly false and preposterous. She had been beaten over the head! There was blood everywhere! It was just obvious that Michael had killed Kathleen. The feather evidence, if collected, would throw a cat among the pigeons. Or rather, it would throw a pigeon among a crime scene. The existence of the feathers would make it impossible for the State to carry out its duty. Clearly, Kathleen had been murdered. She did not fall. And she wasn't pecked to death by a crow. The State needed to prove this beyond a reasonable doubt. None of this debris, none of these feathers, mattered. And if Michael's defense team got their hands on them, there was no telling what crazy scenario they would invent.

"Get rid of them," said someone at some point.

And just like that, the feathers were picked from her hair, clothes, feet, and face, and those that were littered across the path were essentially kicked under the bushes. It wasn't hard to do. It was quite easy. The few other fragments that were found around the house, in the kitchen, and on the walls were removed one by one, and disposed of.

It was admitted at trial that George and Campen had together spent many hours tweezing out "fibers" and "hairs" from the bottom steps. The towels under her head, the telephone, the flip-flops, the paper towels, and the glasses were too likely to harbor more feathers. Even if these were carefully removed one at a time, they may have left distinct impressions of their shapes. So all these crucial pieces of evidence went uncollected. Nearly forty officers were on the scene for twenty hours during the first search of the house. What had they been doing? They were not only looking for a murder weapon. They were painstakingly clearing the scene of reddish-tan feather quills, one at a time.

The feathers were the key to securing Michael's freedom and the State simply swallowed that key. There was no real malice, as such, behind the decision. The feathers were simply considered irrelevant to the question of how Kathleen died. The police weren't hiding evidence, they reasoned. Rather, they were clearing away meaningless fluff which might lead a jury down the wrong path.

After several weeks, however, investigators soon realized that Kathleen's death was an enigma. After the bird droppings were noted under Kathleen's head, after the tip of a talon was unearthed, and after they saw the uncanny shape of the wounds on Kathleen's head, they had a hunch that a bird of prey may have been involved in her death. The pieces of the puzzle all came to fit, eventually, and the picture it created was beyond incredible.

But by then, it was all too late. The ball had already started rolling in the criminal case against Michael. The blood spatter was being analyzed by the SBI. The emails soliciting gay sex were found. Michael's bloody clothes were collected and tested. The shoe print on Kathleen's sweatpants was identified. By the end, there was enough evidence to secure a guilty verdict. And that would make for an easier trial.

By the time the trial commenced, there were already people in the know. Some officers had enough of the picture in view to see what a bird of prey had done. Precisely who knew is a question that needs answering. But so long as nobody ventured this theory—so long as no one mentioned that feared three-letter word—there would be enough evidence to land a conviction. All the evidence that was presented to the jury showed that Kathleen was killed in the stairwell. It showed that Kathleen had been attacked. There was enough evidence to prove it beyond a reasonable doubt. But the jury would never realize that the killer had not been Michael.

In December 2003, Larry Pollard began to use the three-letter word that the police had feared would emerge. Luckily for the authorities in Durham, his conjecture was met with abject ridicule. With every legal effort Larry undertook, he was blasted in the papers as a kook and a nutcase. Despite the miraculous discovery of the feathers on Kathleen's hair,

Larry was seen to be grasping at straws to free his much beloved neighbor. Of course, this was very far from the truth. Larry had simply followed the evidence where it led, and it had led to an owl.

What Larry had not known was that the police had already considered the owl scenario. They knew such a hypothesis could have succeeded at trial. And the evidence that pointed to an owl was accordingly hidden or mischaracterized. The district attorney failed to report the existence of the miniscule fragments of feathers because of this larger conspiracy. The droppings were not tested. The talon was destroyed. The blow poke was hidden. And hundreds of feathers were cleared away. All that remained was the body of a woman, covered in blood, at the bottom of a staircase. What remained was a slightly unusual murder scene.

A Difficult Conclusion

On October 10, 2003, Michael Peterson was convicted of murder. His children bawled wet tears as he was led to prison. The morning papers would deliver the news to the citizens of North Carolina on the 11th. The *Herald-Sun* carried a single word headline: **Guilty**. *The News and Observer* had two words on its front page: **Verdict: Guilty**. Everyone knew what it meant. The *Herald-Sun*'s front page was a photograph of the guilty man being placed in handcuffs. *The News and Observer* had a stranger photograph, one in which Michael almost seemed to smile. This historic piece of newsprint was soon framed and mounted on the wall in the foyer of the *News and Observer*'s head office. Like one of Larry's deer, it was as though the media had collected a trophy head. In a sense, they had gained a scalp. The extensive coverage of the trial had been markedly slanted against Michael.

The assistant district attorney, Freda Black, expressed her sadness for Michael's daughters, who had adamantly denied their father's guilt. "I feel so bad for those young women," she stated. "I feel bad because I don't think they're ever going to be able to acknowledge the truth." For his own part, Jim Hardin confessed that he was looking forward to life returning to normal, a luxury he had snuffed out from the Petersons' lives.

The people of Durham were, by and large, satisfied that justice had been served. Within a year, the docuseries was released, and the whole world was soon familiar with the case. But public opinion largely sided with the State. Michael, a liar and multiple murderer, had killed Kathleen and Elizabeth. Michael's appeals and subsequent release from prison were all little more than a postscript. The details of the investigation and the true extent of the State's corruption were never presented in full.

What remained was little more than what had been known since the beginning: A woman was dead. A husband was pleading innocence. Blood was everywhere. He simply must have done it. But despite appearances, no man killed Kathleen.

When the evidence is seen for what it is, the hypothesis that Kathleen was killed by a bird of prey outcompetes any other theory. Moreover, the idea that a conspiracy transpired is not an inference drawn from a hyperactive imagination. It is justified extensively by the evidence. There were various examples of the State hiding or disposing of evidence that are well documented, e.g., the untested bird droppings on the bottom step, the disappearance of State's Exhibit 12, the district attorney's denial of the existence of any feathers at the scene, and the forensic team's discovery and subsequent silence with regard to the blow poke. The behavior of the police was reprehensible. There is no question that a conspiracy occurred. The only question is exactly how large this conspiracy was. It is a question that may never find an answer.

Michael was railroaded. The decision to hide crucial evidence was ultimately made either by the Durham police, the SBI, or the district attorney's office. It was a decision that transgressed all the codes of ethical judicial conduct.

But was this kind of behavior unusual for Durham? Perhaps not.

THE DUKE LACROSSE CASE

Three years after Michael's trial, Durham would again come to worldwide notoriety for another example of unethical judicial malpractice. In 2006, three Duke University student lacrosse players—young white men—were accused of the violent, racially-motivated gang rape of a Black woman named Crystal Mangum. The men were having a party and had hired two exotic dancers to entertain them that night. When it was first reported in the local papers, the case generated protests from North Carolina's Black community, who demanded swift justice. The political consequences of the trial would be hefty. Failure to right the wrong would be perceived as yet another example of entrenched racism within the legal system. If the white students were exonerated, this would be perceived as yet another example of white privilege trumping Black lives. The gang rape was seen as a horrific manifestation of long-standing racial injustice.

But as the world would soon learn, no rape had occurred. Exculpatory evidence had been discovered when Mangum had been tested with a rape kit. Although she had DNA traces from multiple other men in her anal and pubic regions, none of these were traced to any of the lacrosse players. The results of the test were immediately suppressed by the district attorney and hidden from the defense attorneys. The district attorney was Mike Nifong, who took the helm after

Jim Hardin took up a new position in the superior court in 2005.

The exculpatory DNA test was not the only evidence Mangum's allegations had been fabricated. She had previously made false claims of rape and she had provided more than five conflicting versions of the events that night to police. The other dancer who had been with Mangum at the party that night contradicted her story, calling it a "crock." Nevertheless, for clear political reasons, Nifong pushed investigators forward to pursue the rape charges. He went to the media more than fifty times, making statements to the effect that this was a racially-targeted attack and the perpetrators would be punished. He would, he believed, be lauded in Durham as an anti-racist hero.

When Nifong's lead role in the conspiracy was finally exposed in 2007, he was disbarred, removed from office, and put to criminal trial for contempt of court. He was found guilty, but served just one day in prison. All charges were dropped against the three men and they were declared innocent. Mangum herself would go on to murder her own boyfriend in 2013, stabbing him multiple times. She was sentenced to a minimum of fourteen years.

During the mid-2000s, actors within Durham's judiciary and police force were demonstrably corrupt. Is it so unbelievable, then, that Michael Peterson was facing similar unethical tactics? Is it so unbelievable that he was playing at a crooked table? Corruption appears to have been endemic in the city during the first decade of the twenty-first century. Far from being an unimaginable taboo, this kind of illicit and conspiratorial behavior appears to have been the norm for the authorities in Durham.

MICHAEL'S INNOCENCE

Are there other questions about this case that remain? Undoubtedly. Why did neither Michael nor Todd describe any feathers on Kathleen or around the house that night? Why did Michael remove his shoes, despite these affording a better grip on a slippery floor? What left the "tool mark" stain? What role did the unfurled condom play in all this? How was it that Todd arrived at exactly the same moment as the paramedics? Why were the floodlights lighting up the house that night for the first time in living memory? And what, precisely, was the State's real motive for undertaking such a risky cover-up?

And did a bird really manage to find its own way out of the house that night? This is a troubling question. Birds trapped in houses are notorious for failing to find any exit. But if a bird attacked Kathleen that night and if that bird made its way inside the house, there seem to be only two possibilities: either it flew out from the house on its own, an hour or so after Kathleen's death, or the bird never left the house at all. It remained in the house, alive or dead, eventually being discovered by investigators.

If the bird never escaped the house, then the most likely place it would have been found is under Kathleen's head, wrapped up in the towels. Remember, owls have digital tendon-locking devices—ratchets—in their feet. So even if the bird had died during the struggle with Kathleen, its toes would remain clamped in place. It would have been nearly impossible to remove it from her scalp.

It would be a very bizarre situation indeed. If the owl was bundled up in the towels under Kathleen's head, then Michael knew that a bird of prey had killed his wife and he had wrapped it up to hide it. Not only would Michael have been trying to hide this fact, but the arriving investigators would be hiding the fact too. It pays to remember, however, that the towels and their contents were removed very early in the investigation, never to be taken into evidence. The whole situation would amount to a strange double-sided conspiracy, seeing both Michael and the authorities covering up what they knew. Could something so strange have occurred? If a bird attacked Kathleen that night and never made its way outside the house, then this seems to be the only option.

All these questions and all these hypotheses are worth investigating. Not every question will find a satisfying answer. The best we can do is appraise the evidence and attempt to develop a solution. I don't claim to know the true and complete story as it unfolded that night. This book has only been an attempt to explain, as concisely as possible, the unusual facts surrounding Kathleen's death.

Far from solving every problem this strange case presents, there remain many loose ends within the theory presented in this book. But the loose ends that remain are comparatively trivial. The fact remains that a bird of prey is a better explanation than a fall or a murder. The major hurdles that face both the fall theory and the murder theory can be overcome. There is sufficient evidence to believe that Kathleen was killed by a bird of prey, that the raptor found its way inside the house with Kathleen, and that the police actively conspired to hide this fact.

The truth takes a long time to surface from a sea of lies. And it is already more than twenty years after Kathleen's death. Many of the investigators who were involved in the case have moved on, retired, or died. Michael himself is nearly eighty years old. His children seek a life away from the drama and media attention that have infected it for so long. Almost nobody who was involved in those terrible events wishes for the old wounds to be reopened. For many, silence has remained the best policy.

Nowadays, Kathleen lies in a grave at the Maplewood Cemetery in Durham. She is remembered by all who knew her as bubbly, intelligent, vivacious, and kind. The story of her death is tragic, awful, and entirely unusual. But the story of her husband's trial—and the conspiracy which it embodied—is at the heart of the tragedy.

The philosopher Hegel once wrote that the owl of Minerva takes flight only when dusk is starting to fall. The meaning behind this poetic idiom is that the truth emerges only long after all is said and done. The facts are never directly apparent to us, but only become clear once the fog of ignorance has lifted. In this exceedingly strange case, the owl of Minerva has only just opened her wings. The awful truth is only beginning to be uncovered.

Dusk, for Kathleen, has finally started to fall.

To view the color versions of the black and white images in this book, please visit **wbp.bz/DBTgallery**

*For More News About Tiddy Smith,
Signup For Our Newsletter:*

http://wbp.bz/newsletter

Word-of-mouth is critical to an author's long-term success. If you appreciated this book please leave a review on the Amazon sales page:

http://wbp.bz/deathbytalons

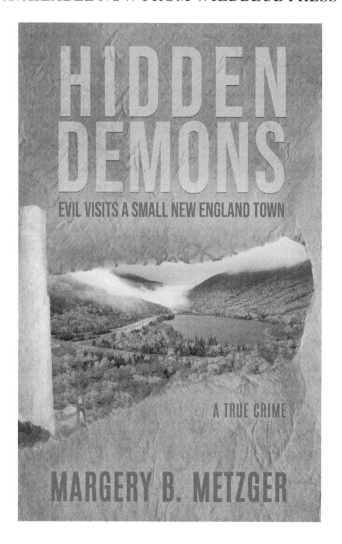

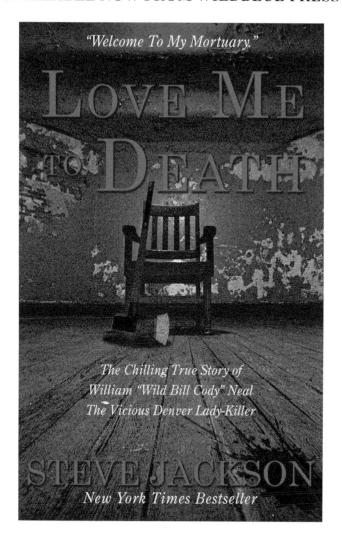

http://wbp.bz/loveme

Originally released in 2011, New York Times
bestselling author Steve Jackson has revised and
updated this classic true crime about one of the most
monstrous serial killers in American history.

Made in the USA
Monee, IL
11 June 2023

ec40ef69-fd5a-4eb7-b0de-d2baea22448bR01